Library of
Davidson College

AFRICA IN THE MODERN WORLD

Edited by GWENDOLEN M. CARTER
Indiana University, Bloomington

The Cameroon Federal Republic
by Victor T. Le Vine

Dahomey: Between Tradition and Modernity
by Dov Ronen

Ethiopia: The Modernization of Autocracy
by Robert L. Hess

Guinea: The Mobilization of a People
*by Claude Rivière; translated by
Virginia Thompson and Richard Adloff*

Liberia: The Evolution of Privilege
by J. Gus Liebenow

Rhodesia: Racial Conflict or Coexistence?
by Patrick O'Meara

West Africa's Council of the Entente
by Virginia Thompson

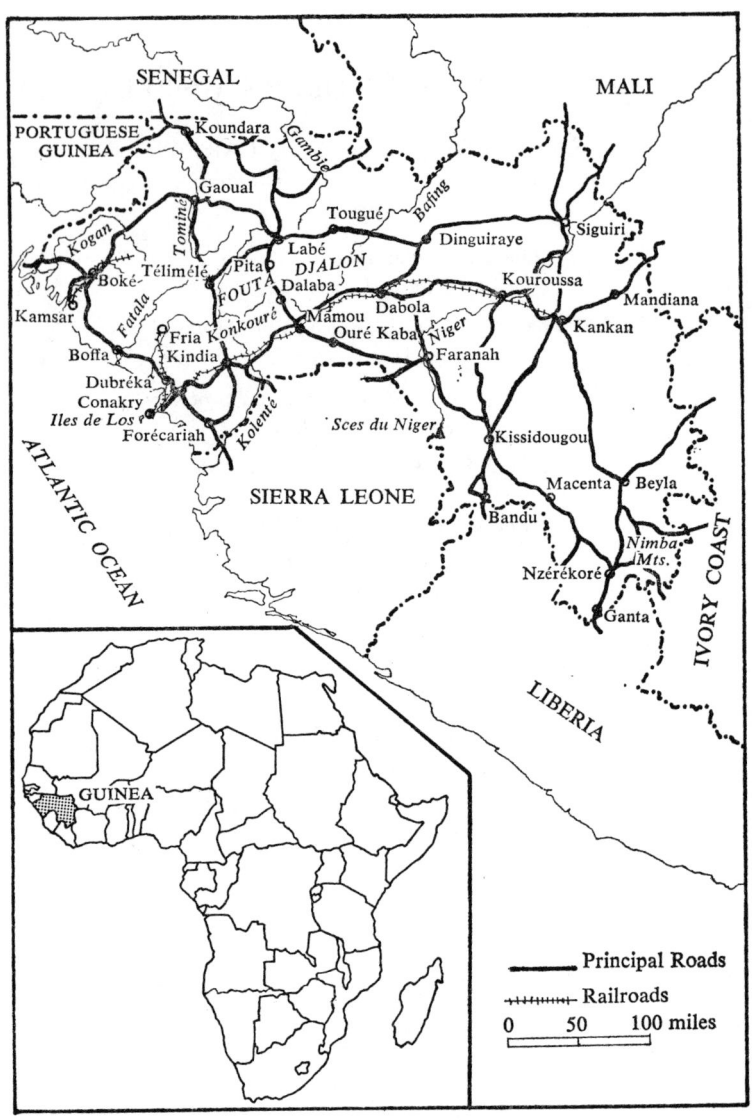

GUINEA

GUINEA

The Mobilization of a People

CLAUDE RIVIÈRE
UNIVERSITY OF PARIS V—SORBONNE

Translated from the French by
VIRGINIA THOMPSON
and RICHARD ADLOFF

Cornell University Press
ITHACA AND LONDON

Copyright © 1977 by Cornell University

All rights reserved. Except for brief quotations in a review, this book, or parts thereof, must not be reproduced in any form without permission in writing from the publisher. For information address Cornell University Press, 124 Roberts Place, Ithaca, New York 14850.

First published 1977 by Cornell University Press.
Published in the United Kingdom by Cornell University Press Ltd., 2–4 Brook Street, London W1Y 1AA.

International Standard Book Number 0-8014-0904-7
Library of Congress Catalog Card Number 76-50262
Printed in the United States of America by York Composition Co., Inc.
Librarians: Library of Congress cataloging information appears on the last page of the book.

To Georges Balandier

Foreword

Since the West African countries became independent some fifteen years ago, it has been more difficult to obtain reliable information about Guinea than about any of the others. Its president, Ahmed Sékou Touré, has been particularly suspicious of outside contacts, especially while the Portuguese controlled adjacent Guinea-Bissau, whose liberation movement, the Partido Africano da Independencia da Guiné e Cabo Verde (PAIGC), he supported, and from which, allegedly, Guinea was invaded in November 1970. After the PAIGC was recognized as the legitimate government of Guinea-Bissau, following the coup of April 1974 in Portugal, Sékou Touré has shown less apprehension of possible external threats to his country. Guinea is still less accessible to most outsiders, however, than are its larger neighbors. Claude Rivière's study is therefore especially valuable, for it not only reflects his firsthand observations in Guinea but also embodies the results of long-term and recent research by this eminent French scholar, who is internationally recognized as an outstanding authority on the country.

The center of power in Guinea is its president, a striking but controversial figure because of his unpredictable and, in some instances, brutal actions. An outstanding champion of Pan-Africanism, he led his country in 1958 to a formal break with France by opting for independence at a time when all other Francophone states remained associated with the former colonial power. Growing tension between Guinea and France culminated in November 1965 in the rupture of diplomatic relations, which were not reestablished for nearly ten years. Touré has quarreled with his Francophone neighbors except Mali, whose political ideology approximates his own. In particular, he has frequently accused President Léopold Senghor of Senegal and President Félix Houphouët-Boigny of Ivory Coast of plotting to overthrow his government, and in November 1971 he withdrew from the OERS (the organization for development of the Senegal River valley), of which, along with Mali, Senegal, and Mauritania, Guinea was a charter member. Beginning in 1975, he moved to improve relations with all his neighbors and sought to rejoin the OERS. But his unpredictability, the conditions he posed, and his attempt early in 1976 to form an organization of "progressive" African states as a rival to the Organization of African Unity (OAU), as well as the discovery of still another plot against him, have done little to lessen his isolation. More successful, however, has been his recent role in helping to settle disputes between Mali and Upper Volta and between Togo and Benin (formerly called Dahomey).

Touré's revolutionary stance and his promotion of state agencies characteristic of Communist countries seem to imply close relations with the Soviet Union, but in fact a bitter controversy arose between the U.S.S.R. and Guinea in 1961 regarding an anti-Touré plot in which the Soviet ambassador appeared to be implicated. In this instance, relations were successfully patched up, but Guinea has been careful to balance Soviet aid with aid it has received from China, and relations with both countries now seem cooperative. Not surprisingly, Touré has been less successful in winning the confidence of liberals in Western countries because of his arbitrary imprisonment and, in some cases, execution of prominent Guinean opponents, and because of their sympathy for the thousands of Guinean exiles now living in France, Senegal, and Ivory Coast.

Despite Guinea's revolutionary socialist postures and policies, its relationship with the United States has been fairly smooth. Guinea's rich mineral deposits, chiefly bauxite and iron, have attracted considerable American private investment, and this fact, coupled with its strategic location, makes it one of the more important countries of West Africa.

On the whole, Guinea's socialist experiments have not been outstandingly successful, notably in the agricultural domain, partly because of inadequate planning and probably even more because of inefficient administration. There is little evidence, however, that socialist experimentation has been abandoned in Guinea; hence the country continues to serve as an interesting and, to sympathizers, disconcerting example of the difficulties associated with such efforts on the part of a developing country.

The pages that follow provide a careful, scrupulously fair account both of Guinea's weaknesses and failures and of its strengths and achievements. Whether one is in favor of or opposed to what President Sékou Touré is attempting to accomplish, Guinea is a sufficiently important country to warrant concern. It is likely to become even more so in the future.

GWENDOLEN M. CARTER

Indiana University

Contents

Foreword, by Gwendolen M. Carter	7
Preface	13
Abbreviations	17
1. Wealth in Diversity	23
2. The Road to Emancipation	51
3. Building a Revolutionary State	83
4. The Perennial Plot	121
5. Balanced Neutralism	141
6. National Resources and Individual Poverty	172
7. The Strategies of National Integration	210
Conclusion	238
Bibliography	247
Index	253

Tables

1. Sociocultural characterization of Guinean peoples   34
2. Foreign agreements, 1958–1963   157
3. Public finances of Guinea, 1964–1973   174
4. Guinea's foreign trade in selected years, 1964–1972   178
5. Trade with Guinea's major suppliers and customers   179

Chart

1. Political and administrative organization of the
    Republic of Guinea   98

Preface

Anyone who would try to find a clue to the destiny of a country by studying the etymology of its name would be properly regarded as scientifically inept for undertaking a project that smacks of magic. Yet without claiming this to be more than an intellectual exercise, looking into the history of a word may disclose analogies with the history of a people. If nothing else, the word's striking oddities could cast light on what we have chosen to explore in this study: the present experience of a people, or at least the very recent past, for the present has already vanished into thin air, like Daphne at the moment when Apollo believed that he had captured her.

Just as *Sudan* derives from the Arabic word for blacks, so the name *Guinée* probably comes from the Berber *aginau,* or *agnau,* signifying a mute or a person whose language is incomprehensible; the designation has been applied particularly to the blacks living south of the Sahara. Early in the first half of the twelfth century, the Arab Al Zukri spoke of the country of Kanawa (perhaps a corruption of *Ghana,* about which El Bekri wrote at length in the eleventh century), and Dulcert, circa A.D. 1340, identified it as the country of the blacks. In the fifteenth century, the Portuguese took over the name Guinea, and maps of that period applied it to all of the southern region lying between the mouths of the Senegal River and Gabon, where the kingdom of Manicongo had its beginning.

Toward the end of the nineteenth century, certain colonizing powers each carved out its own Guinea along that coast. There were the Guinea of Portugal, with Bissau as its capital; that of France, whose capital city was Conakry; and that of England, Sierra Leone (which the French called English Guinea), whose capital is Freetown. Spanish Guinea, lying in the hollow of the Gulf of Guinea, was partly insular (Fernando Po) and partly continental (Rio Muni); its capital was Santa Isabel. These Guineas gave their name to a New Guinea in distant Oceania. The term "guinea" also applied to the piece of cotton cloth used as money by the English traders in their dealings with the West African coast natives. Subsequently, the term was applied to the gold coin that represented the value of a piece of cloth. After 1661, during the reign of Charles II of England, gold began to be imported from the Guinea region. The name "guinea" was also applied to the English gold coin called a sovereign.

Today each of the meanings has certain overtones. Until after World War II, French Guinea continued to be as mute and anonymous as it had been under the French colonial empire. Since it has won independence many political scientists have admitted that they cannot understand the language employed by the government of Guinea, whose tactics and fitful or surly moods bewilder the logicians of politics. Many Americans and Europeans still find it difficult to place Guinea among the African nations. Those who know its geographical location might well envisage the country as colored bright red on the map, like the Soviet Union. Certainly, red is the right color for Guinea, but it is the tint of the blood of its slaves in the eighteenth century or that of the flames that twenty years ago consumed the scarecrow of colonialism on its soil.

Ahmed Sékou Touré, an admirer of Nkrumah and of the same stamp as he, aimed to link the destiny of the new Guinea

Preface

with that of the new Ghana, after he had become the supreme leader of the former country following France's grant of a semi-independent status in 1957. A breach was made in the French colonial bastion of Black Africa on September 28, 1958, when Guinea voted in favor of independence, and in so doing showed the way to its former brothers. At first they were shocked, although Ghana the year before had set the example for the Anglophone African countries without, however, leaving the Commonwealth.

Thereafter, Guinea became the land of the blacks, the champion of nascent African unity and also of the Africanization of the highest posts, after the French who had occupied them fled the country in disarray. From the whole Guinea Gulf area and beyond, black revolutionaries came to help a mobilized people to build their nation. Of all the countries called Guinea, as well as other African territories, the new Republic of Guinea alone has distinguished itself by adopting a constitution bearing the imprint of the French republic which had been its—at times unfeeling—guardian.

Just as events have gradually restricted Guinea's scope for expansion, so the new state's first experiences have delimited the range of its political maneuvering. They have also clarified the extent of Guinea's real economic potential in relation to the welter of options generated by its people's impulses and aspirations. For its currency, Guinea in 1960 created the autonomous Guinean franc, which was replaced by the sily in 1972. Thereafter exports of Guinea's gold, which had been coveted by Arab rulers and, not long ago, by European powers, gave way to those of aluminum. Cotton goods, however, are still bartered for raw materials in an economy that remains predominantly agricultural and that is still feeling its way. Will the permanent mobilization of a people, of and by itself, suffice to ensure an economic take-off, or will it engender more lethargy and illusion than enthusiasm?

This book aims to provide the basic elements needed to answer that question by studying the history of a people, a party, and a leader, and by assessing Guinea's choice of political and economic policies as well as the transformations that have been altering Guinean society.

Chapters 2, 4, 5, and 6 appeared originally in Nos. 68, 95, 107, and 114 of *Revue Française d'Etudes Politiques Africaines* and are reprinted by permission of Société Africaine d'Edition, 32, rue de l'Echiquier, 75010 Paris; Tables 3, 4, and 5 are reprinted from *La Guinée Libre,* February and March 1974, with the permission of Abou Soumah.

CLAUDE RIVIÈRE

Paris, June 1976

Abbreviations

AGRIMA	Société Nationale de Matériel Agricole
AID	Agency for International Development
ALCAN	Aluminium of Canada, Ltd.
ALCOA	Aluminum Company of America
ALIMAG	Magasin d'Alimentation en Gros
BAG	Bloc Africain de Guinée
BATIPORT	Société Nationale d'Importation de Matériel pour le Bâtiment
BPN	Bureau Politique National
CAP	Coopérative Agricole de Production
CATC	Confédération Africaine des Travailleurs Croyants
CER	Collèges d'Enseignement Rural (later, Centres d'Enseignement Révolutionnaire)
CFA franc	Colonies Françaises d'Afrique (later, Caisse Franco-Africaine) franc
CFAO	Compagnie Française d'Afrique Occidentale
CFTC	Confédération Française des Travailleurs Chrétiens
CGCE	Comptoir Guinéen du Commerce Extérieur
CGCI	Comptoir Guinéen du Commerce Intérieur
CGT	Confédération Générale du Travail
CGTA	Confédération Générale des Travailleurs Africains
CNR	Congrès National de la Révolution
COFICOMEX	Compagnie de Financement du Commerce Extérieur
COPAC	Coopérative de Production Agricole et de Consommation
DSG	Démocratie Socialiste de Guinée
ENTRAT	Entreprise Nationale d'Acconage et de Transit
FG	Franc Guinéen
FIDES	Fonds d'Investissements pour le Développement Economique et Social

FNLG	Front National de Libération de la Guinée
FO	Force Ouvrière
FWA	French West Africa
GUINEXPORT	Société Guinéenne d'Exportation
IFAN	Institut Français (later, Fondamental) d'Afrique Noire
IOM	Indépendants d'Outre-Mer
JRDA	Jeunesse de la Révolution Démocratique Africaine
LAMCO	Liberian American-Swedish Minerals Co.
MIFERGUI	Minerais de Fer de Guinée
MSA	Mouvement Socialiste Africain
OAU	Organization of African Unity
OBETAIL	Office de Commercialisation du Bétail
OBK	Office des Bauxites de Kindia
OCAM	Organisation de la Coopération Africaine et Malgache
OECD	Organization for Economic Cooperation and Development
OERS	Organisation des Etats Riverains du Fleuve Sénégal
PAI	Parti Africain de l'Indépendance
PAIGC	Partido Africano da Independencia da Guinée Cabo Verde
PDG	Parti Démocratique de Guinée
PPA	Parti Progressiste Africain
PRA	Parti du Regroupement Africain
PRG	Présidence de la République de Guinée
PRL	Pouvoir Révolutionnaire Local
PUNG	Parti de l'Unité Nationale Guinéenne
RDA	Rassemblement Démocratique Africain (in Guinea, it became Révolution Démocratique Africaine)
RPF	Rassemblement du Peuple Français
SADA	Société Anonyme pour le Développement de l'Industrie de l'Aluminium de Tougué-Dabola
SBD	Société de Bauxites de Dabola
SCOA	Société Commerciale de l'Ouest Africain
SFIO	Section Française de l'Internationale Ouvrière
SIFRA	Société Industrielle des Fruits Africains
SIP	Sociétés Indigènes de Prévoyance

Abbreviations

SMDR	Sociétés Mutuelles de Développement Rural
SOGUINEX	Société Guinéenne d'Exploitation du Diamant
SOGUIP	Société Guinéenne des Pétroles
SOMIGA	Société Minière Guinée–Alu-Suisse
SONATEX	Société Nationale de Textiles
SOTRAMAR	Société de Transports Maritimes
UDSR	Union Démocratique et Socialiste de la Résistance
UGTAN	Union Générale des Travailleurs d'Afrique Noire
USCG	Union des Syndicats Confédérés de Guinée

GUINEA

The Mobilization
of a People

CHAPTER 1

Wealth in Diversity

Because traditions of the two great empires of Mali and of the Fouta Djalon still influence the sociopolitical behavior of two-thirds of the Guinean population, and because the head of state, Ahmed Sékou Touré, is a descendant, on his mother's side, of the great *almami* of Wassulu, Samori Touré (who personifies the bravest resistance to the progress of French colonialism), it might be assumed that this heritage would intensify political life for present-day Guineans to a degree commensurate with their glorious past. Also, the diversity of its regions —savanna, forest, mountains, plains, and swamps—provides Guinea's farmers, planters, and herders with every opportunity for developing complementary economies. Furthermore, Guinea possesses West Africa's great source of water—the Fouta Djalon—as well as the world's largest bauxite resources. It might be hoped that, with all these assets, Guinea's economic development would be on a scale with its political fervor.

Before judging to what degree the reality corresponds to these expectations, it is advisable to examine all the favorable factors. A Guinean proverb observes that the *balafon* player tests his instrument, verifies its tone quality, and tries out his rhythms before playing his showpiece. An analysis of Guinea's basic geography, demography, ethnography, and history makes it easier to understand the hopes, resentments, vacillations, and decisions of its people.

Lands and Peoples

Situated on the West African coast between 7°10′ and 12°30′ north latitude, and between 8° and 15° west longitude, Guinea covers 245,857 square kilometers (95,100 square miles). It is bounded by Guinea-Bissau on the northwest, Senegal and Mali on the north and northeast, Ivory Coast on the east, and Liberia and Sierra Leone on the south. Guinea's western side fronts on the Atlantic Ocean. Its width from east to west is 800 km. and its length from north to south 550 km. However, its circular form and the layout of its means of communication are such that Nzérékoré, the forest zone's principal town, is 1,200 km. by road from Guinea's capital, Conakry, whereas it is only 360 km. from Liberia's capital, Monrovia.

Like the rest of West Africa, Guinea's ethnic geography defies the administrative frontiers that were carved out by the diplomacy of the colonial powers. Various Franco-British agreements gave to France the Rivières du Sud (June 28, 1882), which later that year (October 12) became a colony and was divided into several territories. To one of them, French Guinea, Dr. Noël Ballay was named governor by a decree of December 22, 1891. After the agreement that established Guinea's frontiers with Sierra Leone (January 21, 1895), others followed: a Franco-Portuguese accord, ratified July 28, 1888, defined the boundaries of Portuguese Guinea with Senegal and French Guinea; the Franco-British agreement of April 8, 1904, ceded the Los Islands to France; and there was one between France and Liberia on January 13, 1911, relating to boundaries. None of the separate territories established by these treaties took into account linguistic realities, cultural entities, or ethnic divisions.

Coniagui and Bassari tribesmen in Guinea have "brothers"

in Senegal and Guinea-Bissau. The Kouranko and Kissi-Sherbro peoples have one foot in Sierra Leone and the other in Guinea. In the forest zone, the Guerzé-Kpellé and the Toma (or Loma, as they call themselves) straddle the frontiers of Liberia and Guinea. The Malinké, who trade throughout West Africa, are to be found in Ivory Coast, Senegal, and Mali, among the Bambara, from whom they differ more in religious organization than as to their history. Finally, the Peul of the Fouta Djalon feel less akin to their Manding neighbors than to the Peul of the Senegalese Fouta or of Macina. It was from Macina that they emigrated in two waves during the fourteenth century and again in the seventeenth and eighteenth centuries, pushing back or subjugating the native peoples. Despite frontiers that are apparently insecure because they separate peoples of the same ethnic origin or social structure, Guinea took on a distinctive character both during the colonial period and after independence, when the Parti Démocratique de Guinée provided a strong cohesive force. Although its boundaries are artificial, Guinea is, on the one hand, predisposed toward close economic relations with the rest of West Africa, and is also, on the other hand, exceptionally accessible. This permeability of its frontiers was accentuated by Guinea's withdrawal from the CFA-franc zone on March 1, 1960.[1]

Guinea's diverse cultural areas in the hinterland reflect fairly closely its administrative and geographic divisions. Indeed, its variations in altitude and the diversity of its climates and vege-

[1] Originally, the value of the Colonies Françaises d'Afrique (CFA) franc was double that of the Metropolitan franc. With the French government's creation of the "heavy franc" in 1960, the CFA franc's value became 2 French centimes or about 0.4 U.S. cent. The Guinean franc (franc guinéen or FG) officially retained its parity with the CFA franc until 1972, when it was replaced by the sily, worth 10 former Guinean francs or 4 U.S. cents.

tation divide Guinea into four natural regions which, by and large, correspond to its major tribes. The country derives its wealth from the wide range of its mineral, agricultural, animal, and human resources.

Lower or maritime Guinea, inhabited mainly by Susu and related tribes (Baga, Nalou, and Landouman), is the alluvial basin of the coastal rivers—the Rios Componi, Nunez, Kapatchez, Pongo, Konkouré, Mellacoré—which fronts on the Atlantic for 300 km. and extends as far as the foot of the Fouta Djalon cliffs to a distance of 50 km. toward the north and 90 km. toward the south. From the air, the meandering course of these streams, the swampy estuaries, the mangrove growths, and the smattering of islands (of which the best known are the Los, called in Portuguese Ilhas dos Idolhos) beyond the extremity of the Kaloum Peninsula on which Conakry is located offer what appears to be a splendid lacework of land, greenery, and water. In this amphibious plain, the humidity reaches saturation point, the temperature remains constant between 24 and 30 degrees centigrade and rainfall totals more than 5 meters a year at the foot of Mt. Kakoulima during the rainy season (*hivernage*), from May to October. This is the region where the subsistence crops of swamp rice, oil and coconut palms, and the cola bush are grown, as well as the export crops of bananas and pineapples.

Middle Guinea, or the Fouta Djalon, is made up of primary mountains and plateaus. The massifs of Dalaba to the south and of Mali to the north (Mt. Loura is 1,515 meters high), and the high central plateaus of Pita and Labé, deeply eroded, form highlands at altitudes of 600 to 1,500 meters. To the northwest, the crests of this dorsal range give way to a gentle slope. Tectonic breaks in this tight-knit network exist wherever the many watercourses which have their source in the

Fouta flow across the sandstone, schists, and dolerite, at different levels. These streams are the Gambia, the Komba, the Bafing (which becomes the Senegal River after its juncture with the Bakoy), and the Niger with its tributary, the Tinkisso, the Konkouré, and the Kolenté, or Grande Scarcie. Monsoon rains come from the west during the northern (boreal) summer, but the arid harmattan blows in the region from December to February. Thanks to the altitude, the tropical climate here is transformed into various microclimates. Because of its dry and cool air, Dalaba has become a well-known health resort. Alongside the region's lateritic plateaus, which are the source of Guinea's bauxite and where many herds graze, there is a great variety of terrain and of landscape—grassy plains, fields of millet (*fonio*) and local beans (*niébé*), orange groves, vegetable gardens in the hollows, and hard, burned soil on which gnarled bushes grow. Here in the Fouta Djalon the Peul herders settled, making this massif into a great fief of Islam.

Upper Guinea is savanna country of terraced plateaus, which lie 200 to 400 meters above sea level and whose more or less eroded buttes break the monotony of a slightly rolling landscape. It is there that the Niger and its tributaries have created inundated plains, which are bordered with terraces that can be converted into rice fields. About 1.50 meters of rain fall between June and October, but during the long dry season crop yields are meager (except in the plains of Siguiri, Kankan, and Kouroussa) because much of the soil is poor and the area's continental location makes for extremes of temperature. This area is inhabited by the Malinké, who are related to all the great clans that formed the empire of Mali.

Guinea's forest zone, to the south of upper Guinea, is wedged between Sierra Leone, Liberia, and Ivory Coast.

Tropical forest covers the imposing massifs of Mts. Nimba (1,752 meters) and Simandou (Pic de Fon, 1,656 meters), which contain rich iron deposits. The density of its vegetation makes for a uniform temperature and constant humidity. Also it has long protected the small autonomous villages of the Kissi rice growers, as well as the Toma, Guerzé, Manon, and Kono populations, against intruders. Their resources, besides subsistence crops, consist of plantations of coffee, oil palms, and cola bushes.

Population densities in these regions differ markedly, decreasing from the Fouta Djalon to the forest zone, and from lower to upper Guinea. According to the only valid censuses (those of 1955 and 1967), and the estimates of averages (based on those data as well as on hypotheses concerning the birth and death rates) made by the demographic expert Julien Condé, Guinea's population has grown as follows since 1955:[2]

[2] The following figures (published in decree no. 145/PRG of July 22, 1973) are those of the census of December 30, 1972:

Lower Guinea	1,572,660
Middle Guinea	1,483,400
Upper Guinea	1,012,328
Forest zone	1,055,896
Total	5,124,284

This census cannot be taken seriously because it implies an annual growth rate of 5.7 per cent, which is scientifically impossible, as such growth has never been experienced by a population even for a short period, much less over a span of seventeen years. Julien Condé, a demographic statistician, demonstrated in an article published in the February 28, 1974, issue of *La Guinée libre,* how wholly unscientific was the 1972 census, which was carried out with no serious preparation by the Party organizations. Because the census register was unrelated to the tax rolls, the population figures could be deliberately exaggerated so that they might serve as the basis for a region's obtaining loans or investments. Moreover, the Party's services doctored these figures so as to include Guineans living in exile, with the aim of giving Guinea greater weight in comparison with Senegal and Ivory Coast.

1955	2,570,000
1960	3,072,000
1965	3,510,000
1970	4,069,000

Projections give an estimated population of 4,833,000 in 1975 and of 5,656,000 in 1980.

The census taken from May 19 to 21, 1967, indicated a total population of 3,784,786 at that time, and an annual growth rate of 2.7 per cent, which suggests that the number of Guineans will double in twenty-five years. Compared with Senegal (3.8 million inhabitants in 1968) and Ivory Coast (4 million in 1965), Guinea seems to be relatively populous. Yet, with an average density of 15 to the square kilometer, it is underpopulated for the purpose of intensive development of its economic potential. Upper Guinea, in particular, with 6 inhabitants to the square kilometer, appears to be almost deserted compared with the Fouta Djalon, which has 18 to the square kilometer. The contrasts are even more marked when one examines the extremes in density of the 29 administrative regions, which range from 5 to 42 to the square kilometer. Among their 220 *arrondissements,* there is a demographic spread ranging from 3 to 70 inhabitants to the square kilometer.

If one considers that Dakar doubled, Douala tripled, and Abidjan quadrupled their respective populations between 1950 and 1960, the pace of Conakry's growth—from 26,000 inhabitants in 1945 to 78,000 in 1958 and to 197,000 in 1967—is not surprising. Furthermore, it reflects the extent to which the country's economic life has become centered around the Kaloum Peninsula. Following Conakry, the largest towns are Kankan (60,000), Kindia (45,000), Labé (25,000), and Mamou and Nzérékoré (15,000 each). Less than 10 per cent of Guinea's population lives in settlements of more than 10,000 inhabitants. Urbanization, only recently introduced, has not yet attained significant scope. Nevertheless, one should not underestimate its effect on the economic, political, and social planes in such phenomena as acculturation and deculturation, employment problems, and political indoctrination. On several occasions, the government has had to take arbitrary measures (a decree of January 1963 and police sweeps in 1965) to try to check the rural exodus, directed mainly toward Conakry. More than 85 per cent of Guineans are still country dwellers. As elsewhere in Africa and with similar consequences, there is a gap between the urban and rural segments, although in each segment there exist certain cleavages between the educated and the illiterate, the wage earner and the peasant, and the modernist and the traditionalist.

Without being related to those cleavages, ethnic and linguistic differences are no less important—particularly because they reflect very diverse forms of agriculture, including animal husbandry, and cultural customs, which vary greatly with the population and the geographic setting. The people's cultural and ecological characteristics give rise not only to differences among them but also to a form of regional isolation that is accentuated by the factors of distance, difficulties in communication, and the remoteness of the capital. To carry out a policy of regionalization, designed to utilize to the maximum an area's economic development in terms of its needs, land regime, and customs, the governors of each of Guinea's thirty-four (formerly twenty-nine) administrative regions have been vested with considerable authority. Nevertheless, in the exercise of that authority, they are responsible to the minister-delegate in each of Guinea's four natural regions. The close-knit organization of the PDG facilitates the execution of a policy of national integration.

Wealth in Diversity

Although Guinea's population is far from homogeneous, it does not form an ethnic mosaic of such extreme diversity as, for example, that of Ivory Coast. If one takes language, customs, organizational forms, and traditions as the criteria, there are only slightly more than twenty ethnic groups. Bernard Charles has based his demographic studies on the 1955 census, the only one that has recorded ethnic data separately. He has corrected population estimates by allowing for the inaccuracy of some tribal classifications caused by the fact that the census takers used as their basis the language spoken by the individuals polled. He concluded:

In 1955, the Peul, or Fula, were probably the most numerous single tribe (735,000), outranking the Malinké (576,000), Susu (326,000), Kissi (192,000), and Guerzé (108,000), to mention only the most sizable groups. To these may be added the 600,000 "miscellaneous" persons constituting some sixteen secondary ethnic groups. However, if one takes into account the related tribes (Baga and Landouman assimilated to the Susu), as well as the existence of subgroups (Kouranko, Lélé, and others related to the Malinké), the proportions would turn out to be different. In that case, the Malinké and those assimilated to them would total 30 to 34 per cent and thus be the largest group numerically, with the Peul and Toucouleur (comprising 29 to 30 per cent) following close behind. Next in importance would be the Susu and assimilated tribes, and the forest people (a term used to include ethnic groups living in that region), who represent 17 to 18 per cent of the total. The uniqueness of Guinea's ethnic composition lies in the fact that it comprises two dominant groups of almost equal importance and two secondary groups also approximately equal in size. Without being homogeneous to the same degree, they nevertheless are sufficiently distinctive in their characteristics that they counterbalance each other, neither being able to claim a clear-cut numerical preponderance. Nevertheless, there exists a danger in excessive regionalization. More than 90 per cent of the forest people live in the forest zone, at least 80 per cent of the Peul are in the Fouta Djalon, and over 75 per cent of the Susu are settled in lower Guinea. Only the Malinké, being less concentrated geographically, are dispersed to a considerable degree in three of the four natural regions.[3]

A synthesis of the four principal ethnic groups is given in Table 1.

Historical Setting

Stone carvings found in the grottoes of Kakimbon near Conakry, and of Santa near Kindia, show that Guinea must have been inhabited at least as early as the Neolithic period. Other finds of lesser importance discovered in the regions of Pita, Télimélé, and Gaoual in the Fouta Djalon are evidence of man's presence there in very ancient times. It would be pointless, however, to confuse these original inhabitants with Negrillos by giving credence to oral traditions concerning primitive undersized hunters and fishermen or to legends about the Fadube of Fouta, cave dwellers and sorcerers of former epochs. It would be equally unprofitable to speculate about the similarities between the soapstone *pomdo* statuettes of the Kissi and the sculptures produced by the Nok civilization of Nigeria, for that would place them in the same era (280 B.C.), whereas recent scientific analysis indicates that the former do not antedate our millennium.

Modern Guinea entered the historical period with the empire of Mali, whose primitive nucleus and first capital, Niani, was situated on the Sankarani, a tributary of the upper Niger near the Malian frontier. In the mid-eleventh century, the power of the Ghana kings was at its height though nearing its

[3] Bernard Charles, *La République de Guinée* (Paris: Berger-Levrault, 1972), pp. 9–10.

decline, for the town of Ghana (present-day Koumbi Salah) fell into the hands of Muslim Almoravides in 1077. At that time, tradition has it that Baramendana, a sovereign of Mali, was converted to Islam, although most of his subjects remained animists. Toward the end of the eleventh century, the Saracolé and the first Dioulas whom they converted to Islam moved into Guinea, from the northeast spreading their religion in the Fouta as well as nearer the coast and on the borders of the forest along the cola-trade routes. In 1203, the blacksmith-king of Sosso, Sumaoro Kante, or Sumanguru, gained control over Ghana and crushed Mali. It was at that time that the Keita dynasty which governed Mali first appeared on the scene. Sundiata Keita (who died in 1255), grandson of the dynasty's founder, decisively defeated the king of Sosso at Kirina in 1235, after beating off his attacks. Sundiata then established Manding supremacy in West Africa from lower Gambia to Djenné and from Oualata to the Fouta Djalon.[4] The reign of one of his successors, the emperor Kanku Mussa, from 1312 to 1335, marked the apogee of the Manding empire and created, during his pilgrimage to Mecca in 1324, the Sudanese zone's reputation in the Arab world for being rich in gold. Kanku Mussa's generosity in distributing gold was so lavish that the value of gold (in relation to silver) in Cairo declined for more than a decade, according to the Arab historian Al Omari. At that time, the Mali empire included the three great gold-producing regions of Galam, Bambouk, and Bouré.

During the growth of the Manding empire, its political organization was first created as a military reaction to the con-

[4] Djibril Tamsir Niane, *Soundjata ou l'épopée mandingue* (Paris: Présence africaine, 1960); *Recherches sur l'empire du Mali au moyen-âge* (Conakry: Institut National de Recherches et de Documentation, 1962).

Table 1. Sociocultural Characterization of Guinean Peoples

Characteristics	Peul	Malinké	Susu	Forest peoples
General psychological characteristics	Devoted to cattle; of noble character; respectful of chief's authority; suspicious; discreet; individualistic	Trading ability; ingenuity; leadership qualities; accustomed to farming and mining	Adaptable; conciliatory but at times belligerent; exuberant; garrulous; indolent	Hard-working; morally upright; true to ancestral customs; crude in manner; terrified of the supernatural
Social stratification	Society strongly hierarchized into nobles, freemen, craftsmen, and serfs	Distinctions based on occupations as farmers, traders, and artisans, and according to generations	Accessible to outside influences; no strong traditional divisions; adapt easily to modern economy	Democratic institutions; important roles played by hunters, sorcerers, secret societies
Family structure	Patriarchal, albeit allowing women relative independence; considerable inbreeding	Patriarchal; families customarily submissive to their chiefs	Intense community feeling; frequent crossbreeding; lax sexual morality	Age-oriented, domination by elderly; matrilinear traces; important role of maternal uncle
Village organization	Loose-knit; villages of freemen and of slaves, economically interdependent	Descendants of original inhabitants hold highest rank	Strong solidarity; open-minded; cooperative	Integrated, but within narrow framework of village and family
Major occupations	Seminomadic herding; cultivation of *tapades* (small gardens)	Food-crop farming; plantation agriculture, using draught animals; trading	Food-crop and plantation agriculture (bananas, pineapples, palm kernels); sea and river fishing; wild-produce gathering	Farming in forest clearings by slash-and-burn method; coffee culture; gathering of wild palm kernels and colas
Principal crafts	Leatherworking;	Blacksmith work;	Dyeing; basketry;	Basketry; weaving,

	woodworking; embroidery	jewelry manufacture; pottery; weaving	crafts such as cabinet-making, mechanics; upholstering	on vertical looms; arms manufacture
Nourishment	Meager; *fonio*, curdled milk, honey, sweet potatoes	Average; rice, millet, corn, shea butter	Varied; rice, fish, cassava, palm oil	Varied; yams, corn, rice, tubers, caterpillars, game
Housing	Scattered dwellings despite fairly dense population; family compounds, with small, separated, circular houses; shepherds' huts	Big villages composed of family compounds of spacious fenced-in houses	Large communal barracks open to countryside; small villages dotted along roads; good household equipment	Tiny villages dispersed in forest, off beaten track; separated according to clans; small round huts of clay and straw; grain storage under thatched roofs
Aesthetics	Women style-conscious—special hair style, skin incisions at outer eye corners	Highly developed musical art; instruments are *balafon* and *cora* (lute); many *griots* (minstrels)	Important expensive ritual festivities of baptism and marriage, with dancing	Drumming and whistling style of guttural communication, more rhythmic than melodic in sound; fetishist initiation rites in sacred forest; masks
Language	Poular, with one vocabulary of respect, the other for ordinary speech	Mandé-tan	Mandé-fu; poorer vocabulary and simpler grammar than Mandé-tan	Various paleonegritic languages; some similarities to Mandé-fu
Predominant religion	Islam widespread; main brotherhoods Tidjaniya, Qadrya Bekkaya near Touba; many Koranic schools	Archaic form of Islam; Qadrya and Tidjaniya brotherhoods; influence of Kankan; vestiges of fetishism	Modern Islam; mainly Qadrya Bekkaya brotherhood; lax religious practices; fetishist residue	Fetishism diluted by Islam and even more by Christianity

quest of Ghana, and later developed as an institutionalization of its political apparatus. The rulers' use of force facilitated the capture of slaves and maintained the allegiance owed by artisans (*nyamakala*) to the nobles (*horon*) who protected and supported them. Meanwhile, changes in the hierarchical structure of clans and of lineages resulted from Islamization and from Sundiata's conquests. These changes included domination of the animists by the Islamized clans and of all the clans by the Keita dynasty. Concurrently there developed the administrative machinery required for the continuity and guidance of the empire by the warrior chiefs and the *fama* (officials who administered the provinces in the sovereign's name). The empire's economy, however, prevented those favored persons from accumulating great wealth, the political hazards precluded their retaining their privileges indefinitely, and customs based on lineal descent hindered them from making their power hereditary.[5]

Mali's decadence began early in the fifteenth century. Then, Niani was sacked by Songhaï warriors. Sundiata's heirs, beset by fratricidal struggles, gradually lost their international standing, particularly in the Arab world, and ruled over a progressively shrinking area until 1645, when the empire was broken up.

The collapse of that empire occurred at a time when migrations in the Sahel zone shifted the focus of Guinea's recorded history to the Fouta Djalon. When the animist Peul herders first reached the Fouta during the fourteenth century they encountered Dialonké tribesmen of Manding origin. In small family groups, the Peul immigrants established themselves among the indigenous farmers and then tried to drive out their erstwhile hosts. Under orders from the Toucouleur chief

[5] Claude Rivière, "Genèse d'inégalités dans l'organisation sociale malinké," *Cultures et développement*, 5, No. 2 (1973), 273–313.

Bamba Diadé, they began the conquests that culminated in the creation by his great-grandson, Koli Tanguella, of a military state in the Guinean Badiar at the beginning of the sixteenth century, and later in the founding of a kingdom in the Senegalese Tekrour (1559) freed from vassalage to Mali. The Peul influx continued throughout the seventeenth century. The *tariks* of Timbo (annals in the Peul language but written in Arabic script) noted that in the year 1105 of the Hegira (A.D. 1694), a large band of Islamized Peul from Macina, led by two brothers, Séri and Sédi, sons of Mamadu Muktar of Tichitt, arrived in the Fouta. Tradition has made one of their descendants a legendary figure.[6]

Alfa Ibrahima Sambegu, also known as Karamoko Alfa, was the great architect of the nine-province confederation of the Fouta, the nucleus of the Fula kingdom. The provincial chiefs, meeting at Fugumba in 1727, decided to exclude the animists totally from power and to establish Islam definitively in the Fouta by means of a holy war. Their primary target was the animist Peul chief, Dian Yero, who had come with the first wave of immigrants. Then they intercepted at Horé the caravans bringing supplies from Senegal for the Dialonké chiefs. The latter, in collaboration with the animist Peul chiefs, launched a powerful army against the Muslims but were defeated in the battle of Talansan in 1750. Karamoko Alfa, chosen by his political and religious peers as their leader, had already placed his cousin, Ibrahima Sori, in command of the holy war (*jihad*). That bold warrior led victorious campaigns against Kondé Burama, chief of the Fouta animists and of the Malinké of the Niger, and also against the Wassulunké and the Sulima. In 1766, the warrior Sori succeeded the scholarly Alfa as the supreme imam (the sovereign of the Fouta is called

[6] Paul Marty, *L'Islam en Guinée* (Paris: Leroux, 1921).

almami or *al imam*). After further fighting and the death of Sori in 1793, the supreme power rotated every two years between two rival families, albeit with some difficulty and resistance. These families were the Alfaya, whose ancestor was Karamoko Alfa, and the Soria, descendants of the warrior Sori.

The Peul empire continued to expand throughout the Fouta during the nineteenth century. Raiding provided it with slaves and grain taken from the infidels, on whom a regular tribute called *sagalé* (derived from the Arabic *zakhat*) was imposed in the name of the Koran. The Peul's political domination, which was the basis of their comparative prosperity, enabled them to trade with the petty kings and merchants of the coast, where they exchanged slaves and produce for imported European merchandise.

The early Portuguese explorers of the West African coast were Nuno Tristao, in 1447; Nuno Fernandez, who gave his name to the Rio Nunez a few years later; Pedro de Sintra, who reached Cape Verga and Cape Sagres (Kaloum) about 1460; and Valentim Fernandes, in 1508. These explorations enabled the Portuguese to establish a profitable trade in slaves, gold, ivory, and spices.[7] However, it was the English, firmly entrenched in Sierra Leone, who got the upper hand about 1820, when the small forts as well as persons of mixed African and Portuguese descent in coastal Guinea were abandoned.

In December 1816, two British officers, John Peddie and Benjamin Campbell, journeyed to Rio Nunez, and in 1818 the Frenchman Gaspard Mollien reached Timbo by way of Senegal. They were followed in 1827 by René Caillé, who aimed at getting to Timbuktu via Rio Nunez. These expeditions ushered in a period of treaty-making with the coastal kings which was

[7] Claude Rivière, "Le Long des côtes de Guinée avant la phase coloniale," *Bulletin de l'IFAN*, 30, B.2 (1968), 727–50.

to open up the hinterland to colonization. A naval lieutenant, Louis-Edouard Bouët-Villaumez, was charged by the French king, Louis-Philippe, with keeping a close watch on the slave traders. On behalf of some Bordeaux merchants, the lieutenant made treaties with the local potentates which permitted establishment of the trading posts known as the Rivières du Sud (1837–1842). In the hinterland the Toucouleur chief, El Hadj Omar Tall (1797–1864), installed himself at Dinguiraye in 1850 for the purpose of propagating in the Fouta Djalon the Muslim practices of the Tidjaniya brotherhood and of conquering the land to the north. Meanwhile, the number of French merchants in the estuaries of the Rio Nunez, the Rio Pongo, and the Mellacoré increased, despite fierce competition from English, Belgian, and German traders who kept their grip on that area for the purpose of winning concessions elsewhere. On January 21, 1866, French troops captured Boké on the Rio Nunez, where they set up France's first military post.

In 1880 and again in 1888, Olivier de Sanderval, an adventurer obsessed with the dream of creating an African kingdom, passed through Boké en route to Timbo, where he obtained important concessions from the *almami*. And a welcome also awaited the Bayol-Noirot mission, which traveled from Boké to Timbo in 1881 with the aim of obtaining the *almami*'s confirmation of French rights. On July 5, 1881, a treaty of friendship was signed that assured respect for the rights of Frenchmen to trade and send their caravans to the coast. The Fouta Djalon thus came under the protection of France, but its *almami* specified that Fouta should belong to the Peul just as France belonged to the French, even though the stronger of the two nations was giving help to the weaker. Nonetheless, Guinea's fate seemed to be sealed, and the grip of colonialism grew stronger everywhere. On December 21, 1890, the dispute between the Nalou chiefs Dina Salifu and Bokari for the chieftaincy of the Nunez was settled in Bokari's favor when the Salifu capital of Sogoboli was bombarded by the gunboat "Le Mésange."

From 1881 to 1896, the Fouta lived under a protectorate regime, after which it yielded to armed pressure by the colonial power. Almami Bokar Biro's refusal to retire after his term of office expired, and his take-over of Timbo, provided the pretext for French intervention. Supported by chiefs of the Alfaya clan and by the army of Sanderval, French troops occupied Timbo and defeated Bokar Biro at Porédaka on November 14, 1896. Alfa Yaya, one of the Alfaya chiefs, who had initially favored the French, soon changed his mind, but his opposition to the French in 1905 and 1911 culminated in his arrest and deportation. Also in 1911, Tierno Aliou, the wali of Goumba, suffered the same fate.

The strongest resistance to colonization came from the northwest, where Samori Touré (born about 1840), after he had exchanged his peddler's pack for the soldier's sword, built himself an empire called Wassulu. His campaigns, which combined raids with military operations, lasted for five years (1870–1875). During that period, Samori consolidated his rule over many tribes which had been torn by continuous warfare. After capturing Kankan in 1879, Samori set up his capital at Bissandugu, his native land.[8]

A bold strategist as well as a clever and tenacious politician, Samori gave himself the title of *almami* in order to consolidate his authority. He divided his domain into 162 cantons (*kafu*), organized into ten provincial governments (*jamana*) at the

[8] Yves Person, *Samori: Une révolution dyula*, 2 vols. (Dakar: IFAN, 1969).

head of each of which he placed either a relative or a loyal friend. With the support of a warrior chief or a *marabout* (holy man), these administrators collected taxes and dispensed justice. They also forced each village to farm a field for the benefit of the government, and to supply grain and livestock for the needs of the military garrisons. Slaves captured in raids were traded for horses sold by Moors of the Sahel and for European firearms and ammunition (in Sierra Leone or through the agency of the Peul of the Fouta Djalon). These arms were used by the warriors (*sofa*), who formed a permanent body of crack troops, which in time of danger were reinforced by militiamen sent by the villages.

After concluding a peace treaty with France in 1886, Samori moved against Tieba, the king of Sikasso, and unsuccessfully laid siege to that town. In answer to Tieba's appeal for help, the French sent a military mission to Sikasso. Samori, claiming that this violated the agreements made by the French, declared war on them and tried vainly to enlist aid, first from England and then from the kings of Ségou and Sikasso (after the last-named had quarreled with the French). Intermittently for seven years, beginning in 1891, Samori fought the expeditionary forces led by Colonels Louis Archinard, Georges Humbert, and Antoine Combes. The scene of combat shifted from the frontiers of Mali and upper Guinea to Ivory Coast and the Black Volta, and the fighting was marked by temporary alliances, by victories, and by defeats. When the populations that Samori had forced to follow in his train were exhausted and when his retreat to the east was cut off, he tried to negotiate a peace. But during a surprise attack by Captain Henri Gouraud's troops, Samori fell into the hands of the French at Guélémou on September 29, 1898. Deported to Gabon, he died there in 1900.

The resistance in the north by the Coniagui ended with the battle of Ithiou (April 1902). That in the south by the Toma, led by Kohko Tolno Onivogi and Nzebela Tokpa, ended with the capture of Boussedou in 1907; there a revolt by the Guerzé and Manon against the French army's exactions lasted from August 1911 to March 1912. Thus ended what is called, sometimes ironically, the "French pacification"; the colonial system had already been installed in Guinea.

The Colonial Regime

On August 1, 1889, the Rivières du Sud was freed from the administrative control of Senegal, and in July 1890, Dr. Noël Ballay disembarked at Conakry as head of a mission. In December 1891 he was formally named governor when the colony of French Guinea was officially created. His main tasks consisted of supervising construction of the territorial capital, developing the means of communication needed for commerce, and establishing and guiding an effective administration and judiciary. Under his government (which lasted until 1900) and that of his successors, the system known as "direct administration" was instituted progressively at the turn of the century. Guinea was divided into *cercles*, each headed by a French commandant. The *cercles* were divided into cantons placed in the charge of native chiefs appointed by the governor. In 1921, the *commandant de cercle* (district officer) was empowered to name the canton chiefs, subject to the governor's approval. At the head of each village in his canton, the chief placed one of his ablest aides.

In taking over the administration of Guinea, the colonial power was confronted with two choices: either it could destroy the authorities whose rule was sanctioned by the population but might compete with that of the administration, or it could confirm them in their posts with a view to utilizing them as auxiliaries. As the latter solution seemed less risky, one of the administration's first tasks was to find collaborators who could be used as intermediaries between itself and the native peoples. Preference was given to functioning Notables, in order to cause the least disturbance to the established order and lessen the risk of a popular uprising that might prove hard to suppress.[9] However, difficulties arose because the new cantons did not necessarily correspond to the traditional jurisdictions, and the old chieftaincies differed greatly in size and authority from region to region. In the Peul kingdom of the *almami* of Fouta, the chieftaincies were united and powerful; in the *kafu* and settlements of the Manding, they were based on lineage; in the forest zone they were limited to villages; and in coastal Guinea they were of recent date and acculturated. Despite these differences, the colonial power delegated its authority only to those who, after being chosen by the Notables from among rival contenders, were officially registered as chiefs in the territorial units that it had itself created. Its first step was to take away from the people their right to choose chiefs, who thenceforth were appointed and dismissed solely by the administration. The great pseudo state of Fouta was dismembered by abolishing the highest symbols of authority, such as the title *almami* (in 1912), and by recognizing only individual forms of power at the expense of collective institutions of authority. Chiefs who opposed the colonizing power were removed; others had their authority reduced (as was the case with the *almami* of Timbo, whose authority became limited to the three provinces of Timbo, Bouria, and Kolen). Labé province was divided into three *cercles,* and Dalaba and Ditinn became important

[9] Jacques Lombard, *Autorités traditionnelles et pouvoirs européens en Afrique noire* (Paris: Armand Colin, 1967).

cercles. In 1912, the evicted *almami* of Labé had to settle in Mamou and that of Timbo in Dabola—in both cases near the railroad, for easy surveillance.

Inasmuch as settlements in the forest zone comprised no more than three or four villages, the civil and military authorities divided such settlements among cantons as they pleased. The chieftaincy problem was resolved there either by choosing individuals for investiture as chiefs from among the masters of the land and warrior or religious chiefs those who appeared to the authorities to be Notables, or by naming as "straw chiefs" men who had been useful to the colonial cause but who possessed no traditional influence (as in the case of the Malinké clan, Camara, among the Toma). This new method of selecting individuals for the chieftaincy ignored the hierarchical order, the rights of certain families, the qualifications required by tradition, and the support of the elders. It brought forth a multitude of ambitious or intriguing candidates and gave rise to such disregard for democratic legitimacy that the African masses were increasingly alienated from their chiefs. Suppression of the canton chieftaincy in accordance with the *loi-cadre* of June 23, 1956, aroused no regrets among the population.

What was the impact of this administrative organization and colonial policy on the officially proclaimed French civilizing mission? Its positive accomplishments can be termed relatively meager. With regard to education, progress was fairly slow. In 1953, for example, only 6,558 students (in a population of two million) were attending thirty-four primary schools, and secondary education was nonexistent. Beginning in 1947, when Guinean students numbered 11,084, and until 1958, when there were 42,543 and progress was steady, fewer than 10 per cent of the school-age population attended school. Hospitals, like education, were available only to a few privileged Guineans. Even in 1935, there was in all Guinea only one hospital, which had been built at Conakry in 1901. The director of the Institut Français de l'Afrique Noire, Maurice Houis, noted that after sixty years of colonization the campaigns against epidemics and trypanosomiasis, as well as a native medical service, had not moved beyond the stage of projects. "Outside Conakry," he wrote, "there are in fact only four maternity clinics, three dispensaries, and four buildings with hospital facilities."[10] No more than that!

Guinea's rail network had not progressed beyond the 662 km. of track laid in 1914. Domestic slavery (a status midway between old-fashioned slavery and medieval serfdom) had not diminished in the Fouta, although the slaves there were now described as sharecroppers. It was to the interest of the colonizer to maintain the *status quo,* both to develop the land at little cost and to avoid alienating the established chiefs, whose prestige the colonizer could use to his own advantage to facilitate the requisitioning of labor. Some chiefs even preferred to send their slaves instead of their sons to the white man's school or to serve in the army, when they were required to recruit students or conscripts. During World War I, slaves made up three-fourths of the conscripts from the Fouta. Yet emancipation made headway among the Manding during the first quarter of this century. In short, everyone knows that at the outset no form of colonization is ever primarily a "charitable work." At most, colonization was beneficial—economically and politically—to the ruling power.[11]

---

[10] Maurice Houis, *La Guinée française* (Paris: Editions Maritimes et Coloniales, 1953), p. 57.

[11] See Jean Suret-Canale, "La Guinée dans le système colonial," *Présence africaine,* 29 (December–January 1960), 9–44.

By the general introduction of a market economy and currency circulation, the definitive establishment of colonial authority progressively undermined traditional trading, which until then had been oriented toward the coast. It also laid down the geographical and juridical boundaries of trade. There is no doubt that for the Africans the development of commerce was not related primarily to their need for certain products (a need that long remained very limited) but to their need for the money required to pay taxes.[12]

By a local regulation of December 28, 1897, the payment of the head tax (two francs for all natives of both sexes above the age of eight) was made obligatory throughout the colony, which had just been enlarged by the addition of the Fouta Djalon after the battle of Porédaka. Beginning in 1900, the sums realized from the head tax topped all other budgetary resources, and by 1928, the tax accounted for 70.8 per cent of Guinea's revenues. The percentage dropped to 46 in 1940, when the "war effort" necessitated the supply of many raw materials. From the end of the nineteenth century onward, the taxpayer had to meet his fiscal obligations by supplying the trading economy with wild produce, mainly rubber and palm kernels. At Pita, beginning in 1908, even the land, traditionally inalienable, had to be sold by Africans to their compatriots for the same reason.

The circulation of currency, stimulated by tax obligations, led to the excessive development of commerce. From 1895 to 1914, rubber was the basic item in the trading economy (it accounted for four-fifths of the value of Guinea's exports in 1898). To gather rubber, the population had to go far afield after the rubber-yielding vines near the villages were exhausted. Transporting latex was the occupation of the Dioula

[12] Claude Rivière, "Les Bénéficiaires du commerce dans la Guinée précoloniale et coloniale," *Bulletin de l'IFAN,* 33, B.2 (1971), 257–84.

merchants until the price fell, between 1909 and 1915, when the start of production from hevea trees in the Far East affected the entire rubber trade.

To meet the demands of colonial trading in Guinea, the infrastructure required to handle imports and exports was developed. In 1895, the first pier was built at Conakry, just at the time when that town was being laid out like a checkerboard and the Conakry–Niger road was being constructed. The improvement of Conakry's port concentrated commercial operations in the capital and brought such activities to a standstill in the Rivières du Sud. Construction of the railroad from Conakry to Kindia and its extension to Mamou in 1908, to Kouroussa on the Niger in 1910, and to Kankan in 1914 had the same effect: it facilitated the movement of the hinterland's produce to the coast, thereby enhancing the importance of Conakry. Formerly the trade of Fouta and upper Guinea had been drawn to Bamako, Freetown, and Nunez.

Three firms soon cornered the largest share of the market. These were the Compagnie Française de l'Afrique Occidentale (CFAO), the Société Commerciale de l'Ouest Africain (SCOA), and the Compagnie du Niger Français (which in conjunction with the Paterson-Zochonis Company took over some old-established Manchester firms). The trading companies of Bordeaux, along with some others, continued to operate but were relegated to secondary rank. Usually, Syrians and Lebanese, who were installed in the small towns, served as middlemen between the big trading houses and the native population by collecting the produce that was useful to the French economy and selling imported European goods. At Conakry, the Levantines numbered three hundred in 1903 and seven hundred in 1905; at Mamou they increased from two in 1906 to six hundred in 1912.

After World War I, no single product filled the gap left by

the decline in rubber output, and the Dioulas supplied the trading firms with palm kernels, honey and wax, gum copal, and cowhides. In the Fouta Djalon, aside from the production of orange essence by the Compagnie Africaine des Plantes à Parfum (which was established near Labé in 1928), the sale of cattle, land, and Korans supplied most of the money with which taxes were paid. In upper Guinea, the traditional panning of gold in Bouré province was revived, and through the agency of the Dioulas, it supplied the domestic market as well as foreign trade. Between 1920 and 1930, from 50 to 300 kg. of gold a year were exported.[13] Because of the worldwide depression, there occurred a gold boom that increased the value of the metal in relation to the falling prices for agricultural produce. According to the official figures, 4,750 kg. of gold were produced in 1936. This caused a spurt in the contraband trade—impossible to estimate but appreciable—until 1939, when the war effort revived the payment of taxes in kind, as well as portage and forced labor.

After shortages and quotas ended, public investments under the four-year plans of 1948 to 1952 and of 1953 to 1958 triggered an upsurge of the economy. At first this benefited European opportunists, but the Dioulas too saw a potential windfall in the development of small African banana and coffee plantations. They continued to serve as commercial middlemen just at the time when an increase in the head tax necessitated increased trading in local produce. (In 1956, the head tax for every individual between the ages of fourteen and sixty ranged from 812 to 1,085 CFA francs, depending upon the *cercle,* and it was imposed on a population whose average annual per capita income was estimated at about 10,000 CFA francs.)

The movements of labor followed the evolution of the econ-

[13] Claude Rivière, "L'Or fabuleux du Bouré," *L'Afrique littéraire et artistique,* 23 (June 1972), 41–45.

omy throughout the colonial period, and they promoted the mingling of tribes. Although the scale of such movements has never been computed, they can be summarized as follows:

(1) The development of Conakry between 1890 and 1900 encouraged the immigration of Limba and Temne tribesmen from Sierra Leone as clerks in trading firms and as masons and laborers in public works, of Senegalese as builders and industrious craftsmen, and of Gabonese as cabinetmakers. After 1930 came the Togolese to fill administrative posts and the Dahomeans as government employes. More recently, after 1955, they were joined by Hausa traders and Ghanaian fishermen.

(2) Construction of the Conakry–Niger railroad stabilized laborers and track supervisors between 1900 and 1910 but caused the displacement of traders.

(3) The annual migration of *navétanes* (seasonal migrant workers) between Senegal and Guinea during the 1930–1940 decade involved some thirty thousand Guineans, of whom the majority were Peul and Malinké. This movement continued until independence.

(4) About 1935, the banana plantations on the lower coast began to attract the forest people and the Fula. At the peak of production in 1955, more than ten thousand agricultural workers were employed in the banana groves.

(5) There was a gold rush to the Bouré placers until they were exhausted about 1949. As of 1937, some hundred thousand panners worked in the Siguiri placers.

(6) After World War II, there was a concentration of labor in the diamond-bearing regions of Beyla and Kérouané.

(7) During this same period, many Malinké moved into the forest region, where they traded in coffee, palm kernels, and colas.

(8) The Peul of Fouta migrated to the Malinké areas, seek-

ing employment as herders, butchers, and tailors. They also moved into lower Guinea to find work as cooks and unlicensed peddlers, and to Sierra Leone, where they could most profitably sell their cattle.

(9) Various tribesmen were attracted to the bauxite mines at Kassa (1952) and to the iron mines at Kaloum (1953). Beginning in 1957, they worked on building the alumina plant of the Fria Company.

The participation of two societies—the colonized and the colonizer—in Guinea's economic structure promoted the exploitation of new raw materials, which was related to the growth of industrial capitalism; at the same time that participation modified the means of production and modernized techniques. With respect to Guinea's social structure, the repercussions of the colonial situation have been even more marked. It damaged social relationships, combined different ethnic groups within the same territorial framework, made French the vehicular language among educated Guineans, gave rise to new social classes such as clerks, planters, wage earners, and the like, disseminated democratic concepts and the examples provided by Metropolitan politics, and incited the development of organized labor in the modern sector. The circulation of men and ideas—thanks to the market economy, the increase of public and private services, and the sending of African soldiers to France—brought about the great political awakening of 1945.

CHAPTER 2

The Road to Emancipation

The holy trinity of colonialism—Europe, Christianity, money—revolutionized African attitudes. Those elements seemed to possess a permanent validity, and it also appeared likely that the colonial empires would long continue to bask in glory. Then, somewhat unexpectedly, World War II broke down the myth of the invincible father figure—the European.

From that period dates the great political awakening of Black Africa. Postwar colonial policy became noteworthy in several respects. Economically, a start was made toward industrialization and the development of mineral resources, along with agricultural improvements. There was also a considerable increase in job openings as well as wages, and also an expansion of education. As for the administration, the powers of colonial governors were increased. What was most characteristic of the postwar period in Guinea, however, was political agitation, which led in 1958 to independence. The concurrent activities of organized labor and political parties were of primary importance in promoting Guinea's total emancipation, and they are the subject of this chapter.

Unionism, a Decisive Force

Historically, this period can be divided into three main phases. During the first, from 1945 through 1952, a sociovocational form of trade unionism emerged and developed. As for the political parties, they were above all committees more or less with an ethnic basis, formed during election campaigns; in trying to achieve cohesion they disintegrated under the pressures to which they were subjected. The second phase, from early 1953 to June 1956, foreshadowed specialization in African trade unionism, while a branch of the Rassemblement Démocratique Africain (RDA), the Parti Démocratique de Guinée (PDG), gradually assumed the dominant position on the political scene. The third phase, which lasted from the *loi-cadre* to the PDG's assumption of power on September 28, 1958, was that of Pan-African labor organization.

In Guinea, organized labor was a decisive force in forming national consciousness. The solidarity it created through strikes proved to be the most effective instrument in promoting nationalistic aspirations. Through the very form they assumed, these aspirations tended to orient the labor movement toward its identification with a leader and a party. This was carried to such lengths that it could be said that the PDG was the offspring of the labor movement, insofar as the party was created by the labor leader Sékou Touré and received from him its socialist ideology and centralized organization. Consequently, and for convenience in explaining this evolution, we shall begin by studying the role of organized labor before investigating that of political parties, and start with these historical observations:[1] (1) Two factors affected the emergence of labor unions: the state of the economy and colonialism, both of which continued to influence wage earners' movements until the achievement of independence. (2) However, in the evolution of organized labor, two other elements were decisive: the relations between the African unions and their Metropolitan headquarters, and those between the labor movement and

[1] See Jean Meynaud and Anisse Salah-Bey, *Le Syndicalisme africain* (Paris: Payot, 1963), pp. 87–94.

the political party. (3) A dominant labor organization and a dominant party corresponded to the undivided authority exercised by the colonial regime, suggesting a trend toward unity. (4) The PDG's adoption of a progressive ideology facilitated its integration with the labor movement and its acceptance of charismatic leadership. (5) That the unions served as a school for training the party's cadres explains in part its utilization of the labor movement. The cadres, after assuming political responsibilities, would not necessarily be radical or extremist.

It was not until the end of World War II that wage earners were organized. This came about through a weakening of colonialism's repressive aspects, as a result of the moral obligation felt by the authorities toward African colonial peoples because of the contribution they had made toward the war effort. Parties and unions, sometimes with the same leaders, were formed during this era, and both were fully aware of the Africans' condition of dependency in material respects. But it is worth noting that it was the most active labor leaders who made wage earners conscious of their economic strength and who, as heads of the RDA, won the assent of most of the population to their policy.

The two principal forces for independence—the RDA and the French Confédération Générale du Travail (CGT)—put down their deepest roots in the soil prepared by the French Communist Party.[2] This single source of their inspiration and

[2] In the 1950s, three trade-union federations dominated the labor scene in France, and sought to create branches in Africa. The General Confederation of Labor (CGT), founded in 1895, was the largest and had followers in all categories of workers. Early in the Cold War between the East and the West, many non-communist reformers, who were a minority compared with the number of those imbued by Marxist ideology, broke away from the federation. Under the banner of anticommunism, they initiated on December 18, 1947, the CGT-FO (Worker

the identity of their leadership meant that the benefits accruing from a struggle that had been spearheaded by the CGT were likewise credited to the RDA.

From the chronological standpoint, it was the professional unions that provided the basic organization for the movement. Among the Africans, civil servants in the communications service were the first to organize and to act effectively, because it was they who maintained links with the outside world and between the country's different regions. Postal workers led the way by organizing within the framework of the CGT, and then railroad employees formed an autonomous union. Wage earners in the public services, employees in trading firms, and artisans in small enterprises followed their example. Finally came the organizing of employers' associations, aimed at defending their interests rather than redressing grievances, and these were joined by entrepreneurs and artisans who worked for themselves.

Soon the diversity of the unions showed the need for a program of common action. This was the goal set by the union created at Kankan early in 1946, comprising all the labor sectors of that town and region. But unions with a limited geographical base could not so effectively press their demands as the large labor organizations. In March 1946, the CGT, informed of this need for a program of joint action, sent two of its officials on a labor mission to French West Africa (FWA).

Force), which was formally constituted at a congress in April 1948. The FO opposed any political orientation, and it gained many members among the civil servants in France. The French Confederation of Christian Workers (CFTC), formed on November 1, 1919, professed an ideology and a program derived from the social creed of the Catholic Church; it opposed the class struggle. After World War II, the CFTC tried to increase its membership among other religious faiths, but its most zealous militants came from Catholic-action movements.

They convened a congress at Dakar attended by thirteen European and twenty-one African delegates, who among other accomplishments formed the Union des Syndicats Confédérés de Guinée (USCG), headed by five Europeans and five Africans. This organization decided to affiliate each of its vocational unions with its Metropolitan counterpart. Two delegates, one a European (Maurice Guignouard) and one an African (Sékou Touré), were chosen to represent the new organization at the twenty-seventh CGT congress at Dakar in 1947. At that meeting, Sékou Touré praised the unions' merger but voiced his regret at the reluctance of many European and African workers in the private sector to join the new confederation.

This expression of regret revealed the existence of significantly divergent views, notably between the Catholic Confédération Française des Travailleurs Chrétiens (CFTC) and the Socialist Force Ouvrière (FO). From the time it was constituted in Africa in April 1948, the FO was able to recruit European members, thanks to the support given it by high-ranking French officials. On the other hand, the Guinean branch of the CFTC, which had been founded in 1946 with the rather reluctant consent of Monseigneur Raymond Lerouge, bishop of Conakry, aimed at competing with the CGT, established there the previous year. Under the leadership of David Soumah, aided by Antoine Lawrence, Firmin Coumbassa, and Marius Sainkoun, the CFTC in Guinea was handicapped (just as that labor organization was in the rest of FWA) by the fact that its membership was small and dispersed. As of 1954, the CGT had five times as many members as the CFTC.

In the struggles led by the civil-service unions, as well as by those of the private sector, a wage increase was the principal objective, as it was in Europe. After 1950, labor's demands gave priority to the elimination of auxiliary (contract) workers, the admission of Africans to certain posts through competitive and professional examinations, an improvement in working conditions (an eight-hour working day, paid vacations, family allowances, and workers' accident compensation), and the creation of a single cadre in which, notably, discrimination in pay between European and African workers could be ended. European wage earners, who were divided into six categories, benefited from automatic promotions, paid trips home for themselves and their families, cost-of-living allowances, and lodgings. Africans, on the other hand, who were classified into eleven or, in some cases, fifteen categories, enjoyed none of the foregoing advantages. Moreover, they earned three to four times less than Europeans with equal qualifications.

These cumulative grievances motivated the most serious of the strikes that occurred between 1945 and 1952—that of June 1950.[3] This was a strike by wage earners of the public sector, which soon spread to those in private employment and also to domestic servants. Its broad goal was a revision of pay scales, and this was the first step toward achieving a labor code. The June 1950 strike proved the fighting spirit of the unions, widened the gap between Europeans and Africans, and, to some degree, discredited an administration that showed itself incapable of imposing arbitration. Emboldened by this success, the unions thenceforth often used the strike weapon, especially at Conakry during 1952, at the time when the mining of bauxite at Kassa and of iron at Kaloum was beginning. As a result, there was a general rise of 20 to 25 per cent in wages that year.[4]

[3] Alpha Condé, *Guinée: L'Albanie de l'Afrique ou néo-colonie américaine?* (Paris: Git-le-Coeur, 1972), pp. 54–55.
[4] *Ibid.*, p. 57.

The adoption on December 15, 1952, of a labor code for the French colonies marked the end of union activity geared to special-interest objectives. This, however, was primarily because the adoption of that code virtually coincided with two other major events. One of these was the election of the outstanding labor leader, Sékou Touré, as territorial assemblyman from Beyla (on August 2, 1953). The other major event was a two-month-long strike (from September 21 to November 25, 1953), in which workers of the public and private sectors joined forces. Although the Overseas Labor Code was not immediately enforced, its application led to a general adaptation to organized labor's demands, which theretofore had given priority to the enactment of a labor code. As for the election of Sékou Touré to the territorial assembly, it provided the labor movement with a platform for political action and also promoted the merging of the unions' economic and political demands in their struggle against the colonial regime. Finally, the success of the general strike led by the unions during the last quarter of 1953 redounded to the credit of the PDG, the party most active in the anticolonial struggle. At the same time it reinforced the solidarity between members of the unions and of Sékou Touré's party. The peasants went so far as to collect rice for striking workers.[5]

The colonial administration had suddenly realized that the organizing of labor was the first step toward nationalistic demands because it helped to underscore the link between economic exploitation and political domination. Consequently, for as long as possible, the administration tried to discourage the organizing of labor until it was overborne by the workers' awareness of their strength, brought about mainly by the 1952 strikes and by promulgation of the Overseas Labor Code. It

[5] Sékou Touré, *L'Afrique et la révolution* (Switzerland, 1966), XIII, 60.

then was forced to come to terms with the unions, which used the parties as their spokesmen. Political demands underlay all the economic demands by the trade unions regarding employment, for each move by organized labor showed more clearly that colonialism by and of itself gave rise to injustice. Every reform in colonial policy could be interpreted as a confession of error, and, like the 1940 Franco-German armistice, a symptom of the weakness of the colonizer and the vulnerability of his policy. Still another factor contributed to the combining of economic with political demands. As of 1953, almost half the urban wage earners in Guinea were employed in the public sector. Consequently, they had to submit their grievances to the administration, which was both the defendant and the ruling power.

Those rising leaders who were trying to combine union with party action began to assess the labor movement's ideological, organizational, and technical dependency on the Metropolitan confederations as a genuine obstacle to acquiring experience in specifically Guinean terms. So they played up their grievances against the CGT, which they accused of relegating its branches in Africa to a subordinate position in its hierarchy. They also charged the CGT with deliberately using the African unions to increase its influence, with imposing its authority by assimilationist tactics, and with failing to do its duty in helping to train African wage earners. As a result, it was chiefly workers in the tertiary sector (administration, trade, and transport) who filled the union cadres. Furthermore, by stressing the class struggle, the CGT allegedly was deflecting the true course of African labor's struggle and was guilty above all of stratagems and sins of omission. In correcting these errors by Africanizing the labor movement, the union leaders achieved their second great success after passage of the Overseas Labor

Code: they won independence for Guinean organized labor.

In 1955, Sékou Touré, Seydou Diallo, and Bassirou Guèye (all CGT secretaries) began their campaign to downgrade the CGT. At the RDA coordinating committee's meeting in Conakry that July, the subject of disaffiliating African labor federations from their Metropolitan headquarters was placed on the agenda. The process of transforming the African CGT into an autonomous union began in November with the inauguration of its first territorial branch in Guinea. However, the Confédération Générale des Travailleurs Africains (CGTA) was not officially created until January 1956.[6]

The year 1956 marked the real break between the African and the Metropolitan labor movements. As soon as the CGTA was officially launched, with a membership taken largely from the CGT and the FO, a congress was held at Ouagadougou, Upper Volta, in July which transformed the CFTC into the Confédération Africaine des Travailleurs Croyants (CATC). Once union autonomy had confirmed the African character of the labor movement, the unions, in order to make it more effective, had to unite. This was the objective of the congress held at Conakry in October 1956. On November 24, David Soumah signed the interunion protocol agreement for the CATC, as Sékou Touré had done for the CGTA and Abdoulaye Diallo for the CGT. Although the Cotonou, Dahomey, conference of January 1957 was tumultuous, it succeeded in constituting the first truly African labor confederation—the Union Générale des Travailleurs d'Afrique Noire (UGTAN), which was largely the handiwork of Sékou Touré, who became its general secretary.

Strengthened by its unity, Guinean trade unionism thence-

[6] See Condé, *op. cit.*, pp. 76–83; *Afrique nouvelle*, Feb. 21, May 22, and June 26, 1956; and *La Liberté*, Dec. 11, 1956.

forth became wholly a political organ. This was the result of combining syndicalism with political functions in the person of the general secretary of the UGTAN, who was then also vice-president of the territorial assembly. This transformation of a labor union into an organization for political activity initially became apparent at the first congress of UGTAN cadres, held at Bamako, Soudan, in March 1958.[7] There the problem of the compatibility of union operations and political responsibilities was debated, and the report made by Sékou Touré advocating a single labor movement dominated by the Party was accepted as a directive. This evolution was evidenced by the stand taken by the UGTAN in favor of a negative vote in the referendum on the constitution of the Fifth Republic, whereas all the parties of French-speaking Black Africa except the PDG favored an affirmative response.

In most African countries, many of the labor leaders who had been elected in 1957 to the territorial assemblies gave up their union posts. In Guinea, on the contrary, the same man represented concurrently the PDG and the UGTAN. Above all, he demonstrated his power by putting a stop to the demands of the railroad employees and the teachers, meeting at Mamou. Indeed, after the *loi-cadre* those unions had reproached the former labor leaders who became members of the government with having betrayed the ideals of the labor movement. Specifically, they were accused of having become accomplices of the colonial regime, of seeking to gratify their personal ambitions, and of removing the most aggressive leaders from responsible union posts.

To disguise a "personalization" of power, Sékou Touré was already using the alibi that unity was indispensable for better economic and political management of the territory. After in-

[7] Meynaud and Salah-Bey, *op. cit.*, p. 115.

The Road to Emancipation

dependence this insistence on unity was to lead to his asserting a monopoly of ideology and suppressing the militancy that marks trade unions in capitalist countries, where they play a part in the balance of socioeconomic forces. Submissive to the PDG, as were the women's and youth movements, the Guinean unions were thenceforward to have no functions besides serving as the communications medium between business firms and the central power. Consequently, the PDG forbade labor agitation by the trade unions.

This rapid survey of the labor movement's evolution shows how agitated was the political history of Guinea. Turning now to the political parties, the elections, and the administrative reorganizations that have taken place since 1940, we shall try to present an over-all view of Guinean political life without identifying it—as has often been done for ideological reasons—solely with the rise of the PDG.[8]

Political Awakening

During World War II, an embryonic Gaullist movement in Guinea was quickly crushed by the pro-Pétain agents of the administration. They executed the mulatto Adolphe Gaétan, who had joined the Gaullists of Sierra Leone in resisting the Vichy government in Guinea. But political activity revived with General de Gaulle's formation of African battalions for the liberation of France and, above all, following the Free French Brazzaville Conference on Africa of January 30 to February 8, 1944. Guinea was not represented at that confer-

---

[8] Most of the sources cited by Ruth Schachter Morgenthau in Chapter 6 of her *Political Parties in French-Speaking West Africa* (Oxford: Clarendon Press, 1964) come from the PDG press. Consequently, they have already been subject to interpretation. Nevertheless, in this book the major problems of the period are well stated.

ence because the post of governor of the colony had no incumbent at that time.

In the elections to the first constituent assembly in Paris, open to FWA citizens (thanks to General de Gaulle's statute of August 22, 1945), candidates generally competed as individuals, although some of them had the support of organized groups. Thus Yacine Diallo, the first black director of a Conakry school, who was backed by the Amicale Gilbert Vieillard (whose members were principally Peul) was elected in the runoff of November 4, 1945, as deputy of the second (or African) college to the French constituent assembly. Maurice Chevence, manager of the newspaper *Combat,* represented the first electoral college, composed of Guinea's white residents. Subsequently, Yacine Diallo was hailed by the native population as one of Africa's liberators. It was during his term as deputy that the French Constituent Assembly voted, as a sequel to the Brazzaville Conference, for abrogation of the *indigénat*[9] regime and its penalties (decrees of December 22, 1945, and January 20, 1946), elimination of forced labor (law of April 11, 1946), institution of a single college that would not discriminate between black and white voters in elections for deputies to the French National Assembly (law of April 13, 1946), and the grant of French citizenship to the former subjects in overseas France (law of May 7, 1946).

Nevertheless, the Africans, when called upon to participate effectively in political life, remained divided along ethnic lines. Until the dominant party finally gained control in Guinea in 1957, ethnic differences continued to breed dissension, and

---

[9] Under this regime, the administration exercised excessive powers. The *indigénat* was based on the concept of the native African as a child, who required training including punishment and who owed goods and services to the administrator (or chief representing him).

they led to the resignation of militants and to local clashes, despite temporary agreements.

In the first postwar years, electoral committees rather than political movements were formed, for elections provided the means of satisfying the ambitions of a man or of a region. Moreover, political activity was restricted to defending individuals in trouble with the administration, and party programs were aimed mainly at improving living conditions for a party's constituents, membership being determined by ethnic affiliation, tribe, and language. The lack of democratic practices and of continuity in action also characterized this type of adventitious political movement. It was led by a very small intellectual elite who exploited popular emotions during the infrequent public meetings that were held.

An effort was made, however, to move beyond such haphazard activity and to integrate French Black Africa's diverse peoples. In Paris, on September 18, 1946, after the final debate on the new French constitution, the Africans who had been elected to the assembly convened a big conference of French-ruled black Africans to be held at Bamako on October 18. Its purpose was to define a common platform and to plan concerted political action. Guinea sent ten delegates to this constituent congress of the RDA. Three were members of the Parti Progressiste Africain (PPA), founded by Madeira Kéita in April 1946, and one was chosen from each of the following groups: Mouvement de la Réforme Démocratique, Union du Mandé, Amicale Gilbert Vieillard, Union Forestière Guinéenne, Union des Métis, Comité d'Union de Basse Guinée, and Groupe d'Etudes Communistes.[10] The official program of the RDA, drafted on October 21, 1946, was purported to harmonize with the constitution of the French Union. Yet the exist-

[10] Sékou Touré, *L'Afrique et la révolution*, p. 40.

ence of a common determination to fight colonial oppression was already evidenced by the RDA's demand that the territorial assemblies become sovereign bodies.

Nevertheless, the legislative elections of November 18, 1946, for the French National Assembly showed that the African political movements were still poorly organized, and this favored the candidacy of individuals. The first vote encouraged candidates to consolidate their own forces and, in some cases, to withdraw. Consequently the election of Yacine Diallo, candidate of the Amicale Gilbert Vieillard, and of Mamba Sano, the RDA's candidate, revealed the existence of two trends. Yacine Diallo's party was affiliated with the socialist Section Française de l'Internationale Ouvrière (SFIO), whereas Mamba Sano's party aligned itself with the French Communist Party. The left wing, which was dominant in postwar France, attracted most of the African elite, except for some veterans of the Resistance who favored the Gaullist Rassemblement du Peuple Français (RPF). Because membership in a French party entailed distinct advantages, the Africans gladly joined such parties, even though the latter were more concerned to swell their own ranks than to cope with the problems of Black Africa.

Yacine Diallo, the socialist Peul deputy, supported by Senator Fodé Mamadou Touré, of Susu origin, defended the assimilationist policy of the SFIO in Diallo's periodical, *Le Progrès africain,* founded in August 1947. In the 1950s, Diallo also led a campaign for the recall of Governor Roland Pré, for he disapproved of the governor's administration and of his projects for the economic development of Guinea, which he held responsible for the territory's financial deficit. The Guinean branch of the RDA, the PDG, which was founded on May 14 and officially constituted on June 20, 1947, also criticized the governor. But the PDG was then undergoing a crisis brought on by internal dissensions, spectacular resignations of members, and very strong opposition to the local administration.

In contrast to the wave of political agitation in 1945–1946, the period following the founding of the PDG was euphoric. This enabled the PDG to consolidate its position, thanks to the support of the rank and file and of leaders of some regional and ethnic groups, as well as of the cadres of the Parti Progressiste Africain. The PDG's prestige was further enhanced by the visits to Conakry of certain RDA deputies (Mamadou Konaté of Soudan and Ouezzin Coulibali of Ivory Coast, accompanied by Doudou Guèye and Joseph Franceschi), who tried by their presence to offset the influence of the SFIO deputy, Yacine Diallo.

Beginning in June 1947, Paul Ramadier, then head of the French government, parted company with his communist ministers, and this forced the RDA into the ranks of the opposition. Consequently the RDA began to encounter hostility from the administration, which proceeded to arrest RDA members in Ivory Coast and Soudan. Nor did the administration spare Guinea, where it tried to destroy the newborn PDG-RDA by exerting its influence on leaders of ethnic groups. It thus brought about the withdrawal of the Union du Mandé from the RDA in April 1948, and of the Union Forestière three months later. Those who remained staunch RDA militants were subjected to harassment.

The administration's hostility took various forms: the removal from the civil service of the pharmacist Abdouramane Diallo, member of the PDG directorate; the sentencing to two years in prison, on March 23, 1950, of Ray Autra and Ibrahima Ciré Cissé, who handled RDA funds; the dismissal of RDA members who were employed by private firms; and the arbitrary transfer of such civil servants as Madeira Kéita, general secretary of the PDG-RDA, to a post in Dahomey. About three years later, Ray Autra (whose prison sentence had been annulled) was similarly transferred. Further evidence of the PDG's disintegration was provided by the sensational resignations of such outstanding members as the deputy Mamba Sano. Some of them joined the Indépendants d'Outre-Mer (IOM). Formed in Paris in 1948, the IOM was affiliated with the Mouvement Républicain Populaire until the legislative elections of June 17, 1951.[11] Even the RDA's disaffiliation from the communists at its second congress, held at Conakry on October 17, 1950, did not alter the local administration's attitude toward the leaders of the PDG. The French authorities were hardly reassured by the RDA's anticolonialist statements and the labor-union activities of Sékou Touré—who became the foremost leader of the PDG in 1950, after Madeira Kéita's exile from Guinea, and who received financial support and political protection from Félix Houphouët-Boigny, RDA leader in Ivory Coast.

Above all, the disintegration of the PDG was accentuated on July 1, 1949, by the formation of the Comité d'Entente Guinéenne, composed of RDA deserters and members of the Union du Mandé, Union Forestière, Amicale Gilbert Vieillard, and Comité d'Union de Basse Guinée. The declared objectives of the entente committee, which was affiliated with no Metropolitan party, were to strengthen the fraternal bonds uniting Guinea's regional groups and to enter into contact with the French administrators, with a view to studying together, in a spirit of comprehension, ways of raising the country's economic and social standards.

[11] Sylvain Camara, "Le conflit franco-guinéen" (unpublished doctoral thesis, University of Paris, 1974; mimeographed), p. 42.

Beginning with the first issue of its press organ, *La Voix de la Guinée*, the entente committee praised France's civilizing mission and the benefits brought to Guinea by French colonization. It also took the side of Governor Roland Pré, whom Yacine Diallo and the PDG opposed. It attributed the territory's budget deficit simply to the rise in the administration's operating expenses and massive increases in pay. Supporting the chieftaincy, the entente committee campaigned against what its manifesto called agitators inimical to law and order—in other words, the RDA, which it proceeded to ridicule as the Rassemblement de Démagogues Africains. Naturally, the RDA replied in kind, accusing its adversaries of being merely dummies, of defending the sordid interests of the feudal system and regionalism, and of closing their eyes to the peasants' misery. The RDA also charged the committee with falsely proclaiming that everyone in Guinea was free, whereas the only freedom enjoyed by the Guineans was "to be without a job, to provide the chiefs with milk, calves, and money, and to die of hunger."[12]

On June 17, 1951, the three deputies elected to the National Assembly in Paris were Yacine Diallo and Mamba Sano (who was re-elected), and Albert Liurette, an African doctor. Diallo and Liurette were sponsored by the SFIO, whereas Mamba Sano ran on the Union Forestière ticket, belonged to the entente committee, and was backed by the IOM. The PDG-RDA fell victim to the administration's repressive measures and won no seat, gathering only 14.3 per cent of the votes cast. In the elections of March 1952, the PDG took one of the fifty seats in the territorial assembly, but its candidate, Amara Soumah, withdrew from the RDA after his election.

[12] *La Voix de la Guinée* (first issue of the periodical of the Comité d'Entente Guinéenne), July 1949; *Coup de bambou* (PDG periodical), April 1950.

Yet it was in that year that the RDA got a new lease on life through its affiliation with the Union Démocratique et Socialiste de la Résistance (UDSR). This occurred on February 6, 1952, thanks to the initiative taken by François Mitterrand, who was joint leader of the UDSR with René Pleven.

The new party connection, followed by the strikes for higher pay that year and the passage of the Overseas Labor Code by the Parliament on December 15, 1952, reinvigorated the PDG. Three years earlier, the PDG had to some degree withdrawn to Conakry and its Kaporo headquarters near there. A handful of party stalwarts had remained at Labé, and new blood had been injected into the PDG by the arrival at Nzérékoré of some twenty Guinean members of the RDA who had been living in Ivory Coast. Up to that time there had been no question that the PDG could win over members other than those of the labor unions. In fact, it was by using the unions as a spearhead that the party began to expand from 1952 on.

In the by-election of August 2, 1953, held to fill the seat of Paul Tétau, the recently deceased assemblyman from Beyla, Sékou Touré was elected to Guinea's territorial assembly. For once the administration refrained from intervening in the election, believing that after his election Sékou Touré, in his capacity as general secretary of the local CGT, could be persuaded to cancel the strike order issued for September 1. The failure of the administration's maneuver aroused the wrath of officialdom. Trade unionism, by its advocacy of unity, was beginning to triumph over Guinea's ethnic and class divergencies.

The death of Yacine Diallo on the night of April 13/14, 1954, brought about a major change in the political scene in Guinea. The election for his replacement was held on June 27. In preparing for it, the parties opposing the PDG-RDA created a coordinating committee composed of representatives from the regional groups. It conceded to the Peul chiefs of the Fouta Djalon the privilege of naming a "territorial" candidate, in return for which the chiefs allowed regional groups in lower Guinea to choose candidates for the posts of second-college senator and French Union assemblyman. Fodé Mamadou Touré was chosen for the former post and Karim Bangoura (later Guinea's ambassador to Washington) for the latter. Upper Guinea was represented on the coordinating committee by Framoi Bérété, president of the territorial assembly's permanent committee, and by Koumandian Kéita, general secretary of the union of primary-school teachers.[13] After consulting the canton chiefs, the *almami* Ibrahima Sory Dara, spiritual leader of the Fouta Djalon, supported the candidacy of Diawadou Barry, son of the *almami* of Dabola, to succeed Yacine Diallo. Diawadou was elected, but the PDG-RDA slate of candidates received 34.6 per cent of the votes.

Under the above-mentioned leaders, the coordinating committee was transformed into the Bloc Africain de Guinée (BAG), composed of the Comité d'Union de Basse Guinée, the Foyer des Jeunes de Basse Guinée, the Union Forestière, the Union du Mandé, the Amicale Gilbert Vieillard, and the Union du Fouta. The conservative views of this new party, which aligned itself with the Radical Party in France, became the favorite target for RDA attacks. Until 1956, however, the RDA spared the Démocratie Socialiste de Guinée (DSG), the name assumed on October 28, 1954, by the Guinean branch of the SFIO. The DSG's leader, Ibrahima Barry (called Barry III), unlike Yacine Diallo, was an opponent of the chieftaincy.

Barry III was affectionately called Silyoré, or Little Elephant, by the women of lower Guinea, while the name Sily

[13] *La Presse de Guinée* (organ of the European colonial milieux), June 15, 1954.

(Elephant, in the Susu vernacular) was applied to both Sékou Touré and the RDA. The socialist militants belonging to the CGT unions aligned themselves with Sékou Touré. At one time, it looked as if the Guinean branch of the SFIO might join with that of the RDA. The latter even sent a delegation to the first congress held by the DSG at Dixinn, a suburb of Conakry, from November 20 to 22, 1955.[14] The platforms of the two parties were similar: reforms, opposition to the war in Algeria, and the evolution of Black Africa toward a federal structure. But the authority of the self-educated Sékou Touré was unacceptable to Barry III, a university graduate, as well as to the BAG president, Koumandian Kéita, a primary-school teacher. Furthermore, because the PDG-RDA's strategy consisted of sabotaging other parties for its own benefit, the DSG ended up drawing closer to the BAG. This process culminated in a merger between the DSG and BAG in 1958, and together they formed the Guinean section of the Parti du Regroupement Africain (PRA).

Party Rivalry

These developments among the PDG's rivals between 1954 and 1958 had several causes: the evolution of French policy during that period;[15] a change in the attitude of the administration toward the RDA; the conservatism of the BAG in alliance with the chieftaincy; and the shrinking constituencies of both the BAG and DSG. In the 1956 elections, however, it was above all the success of the PDG's policy of violently attacking the chieftaincy and conservative programs that gave the party a 62 per cent majority of the votes.

[14] *Ibid.,* Dec. 1, 1955.
[15] This policy has been ably described in Ernest Milcent, *L'AOF entre en scène* (Paris: Editions Témoignage chrétien, 1958).

Beginning in 1954, party rivalry in Guinea lost its tribal character and assumed a political—at times even an ideological—cast, but this evolution brought violence and bitterness in its wake. Goaded by their leaders and dissatisfied with receiving only 34.6 per cent of the votes in the June 1954 legislative elections, the PDG-RDA militants decided to break their ties with the BAG. In so doing they were indirectly backed by their DSG allies, who were themselves opposed to the conservative BAG. At its first congress, held in Conakry from August 4 to 7, 1955, the BAG passed resolutions inspired by the confirmation of a drastic change in RDA policy. This new orientation had been announced at the RDA meeting of July 8 to 11, 1955, by Houphouët-Boigny, who sought to disarm the administration's hostility by asserting the RDA's support for a federal French Union and a policy of dialogue in North Africa. In conformity with the RDA's reorientation, delegates to the BAG congress denounced the PDG-RDA for trying to "take the place of the legally constituted authority by means of terrorism and lying propaganda." They demanded that "valid traditional social structures be retained" but drew "the attention of the native chiefs to the opportunity they have to adapt themselves to the exigencies of modern life." The BAG defined its program as attachment to the "one and indivisible" French Republic, decentralization of the administration, transformation of the FWA government-general into a coordinating and managerial organization, and reinforcement of the powers of the territorial assemblies.[16] A few months later, the BAG assumed a pro-West stance.[17]

No more was needed to exasperate the PDG, which or-

[16] *La Presse de Guinée*, Aug. 9 and 11, 1955; *Afrique nouvelle*, Aug. 16, 1955.

[17] *Marchés tropicaux et méditerranéens*, Sept. 29, 1956.

ganized village and urban ward committees everywhere. This was done despite the influence of the canton chiefs, who had armed guards (called *batula* in the Fouta Djalon) at their disposal as well as support from the gendarmerie. The PDG decided to eliminate the BAG followers by force and to attack the very institution of the chieftaincy. From 1955 to 1958, the PDG-RDA sent veritable commandos to take on the *batula* and, by publicly beating up some of the chiefs and burning their houses or their fields, showed how vulnerable the chieftaincy was. At the same time, the PDG press, first the *Coup de bambou* and then *La liberté,* reiterated its verbal attacks on the chieftaincy. The PDG's adversaries counterattacked, sometimes taking the offensive, and blood was shed throughout Guinea. The most noteworthy such incidents occurred in 1955 and 1956. In February of the former year, the PDG heroine M'Balia Camara was killed, while nursing her child, in a clash with David Sylla, canton chief of Tondon in Dubréka *cercle;* violence also occurred in May at Macenta, in July at Boké and Conakry, and in September–October at Coyah and Conakry. In 1956 there were similar outbreaks between the PDG-RDA and the DSG in March at Conakry and Coyah, in August at Macenta, and in September at Nzérékoré. During May 1958, there were clashes almost everywhere in the country, especially at Conakry.[18]

PDG militants required all Guineans to buy the PDG party card, but they attacked only those who refused to obey their orders. At the outset, the Conakry clashes pitted the Susu and Baga youth and women militants of the PDG against their Notables, who had remained members of the opposition parties. The Peul chiefs also opposed the PDG and thus made common cause with their Susu and Baga counterparts. Un-

[18] Camara, *op. cit.,* p. 167.

like them, however, the Peul chiefs kept their followers politically in line, even in Conakry. Because the Peul living there were a minority, they suffered severe losses at the hands of the PDG militants in May 1958.

If it had been only a matter of ethnic differences, the Peul would have "invaded" Conakry to avenge "their dead," or retaliated against the Susu minority in middle Guinea. But they did nothing of the sort, because the conflict was not tribal but partisan. Parties fought each other on behalf of ideas, and of Guinea, and of Africa, but this did not mean that ethnic divisions were the decisive cause of their mutual opposition. In fact, the BAG and DSG, like the PDG, were multitribal parties.

During this period of great political agitation the PDG was making headway in taking power. It did so by combining violent tactics with a tactful handling of those chiefs who had rallied to the PDG banner; by carrying on vigorous propaganda and activities designed to emancipate the population; by flouting the established authorities and desecrating the traditional values of tribal solidarity and respect for elders; and, finally, by isolating and sometimes winning over its opponents. A spectacular example of such a change-over was the shift by Ouremba Kéita, treasurer of the territorial assembly, from membership in the BAG to the PDG; it was an important factor in shaking the morale of the former party in 1956.

Now that they had become minority parties, the BAG and DSG decided to turn the tables on the PDG, and they adopted the latter's favorite practices of violence and demagogy. The semiautonomous government council formed in May 1957 (under PDG auspices) collided with an opposition inspired by the thirst for revenge. Opposition took the form of disparaging the big industrial projects promoted by the PDG, and of censuring its cooperation with capitalism. Diawadou Barry, Barry III, and Abdoulaye Diallo (a territorial assemblyman) tried to regain control over the masses in the Fouta Djalon by inciting them to default on their taxes and to commit acts of civil disobedience, and by fostering Peul ethnocentricity. The success of the meetings that they organized at Conakry grew in proportion to the difficulties the PDG was encountering in its exercise of power. Together with the CATC, the BAG and DSG voiced disapproval of Sékou Touré's combining political with trade-union officeholding. Eventually, however, the absence of a civic spirit among the forces opposing the PDG-RDA made that party more acceptable to the resident Europeans, who had formerly been opposed to it. After the legislative elections of January 2, 1956, had given a majority to the PDG-RDA, that party now appeared in their eyes to be the best guarantor of the execution of French West Africa's industrialization program.

Those elections, which ushered in the PDG's triumphal period, were a good test of the representativeness of Guinea's political parties, because of the extent of popular participation[19] and the neutrality of the administration. For all French West Africa, the number of deputies elected to the National Assembly in Paris were seven for the RDA (compared with two in the 1951 elections), six for the IOM (nine in 1951), and two for the SFIO (three in 1951). In Guinea, Diawadou Barry was re-elected, but the coalition that he headed was defeated by the PDG, whose candidates won the other two seats. One of those seats went to Sékou Touré, general secretary of

---

[19] "The number of subscribers rose from 131,309, in 1946 to 476,503 in 1954 and to 976,757 in 1956." Jean Suret-Canale, *La République de Guinée* (Paris: Editions Sociales, 1970), p. 161.

the party, and the other to Saifoulaye Diallo, its political secretary, whereas no DSG candidate was elected to the French National Assembly. On a regional basis, the two major parties in the January 1956 elections won the following percentages: lower Guinea—RDA 87 per cent and BAG 9 per cent; middle Guinea (Fouta Djalon)—RDA 41 per cent and BAG 36.8 per cent; upper Guinea—RDA 80 per cent and BAG 17 per cent; and the forest zone—RDA 65 per cent and BAG 29 per cent.[20] In Guinea as a whole, the PDG garnered nearly 62 per cent of the votes cast.

That it continued to hold the confidence of the masses was shown by the municipal elections of November 18, 1956. At Conakry, the new deputy, Sékou Touré, also became mayor of the capital, and the PDG carried the mayoralty in Guinea's four other full communes—Mamou, Kindia, Kankan, and Nzérékoré. Successive elections strengthened the self-confidence of the RDA. Thus in the territorial elections of March 31, 1957, the PDG won fifty of the sixty seats at stake; the DSG three seats, notably that of Pita, Barry III's native region; and the remaining seat (Dinguiraye) was taken by an independent, Habib Tall. The BAG's failure was complete—even at Dabola, fief of the canton chief who was the father of Diawadou Barry. In his own birthplace, Diawadou received only 2,332 votes, as against 4,464 for the RDA candidate.[21] Two months before the May 1958 elections for the circumscription councils, the merger of the BAG with the DSG to form the local branch of the PRA did not reverse this trend. In those elections the PDG-RDA received 690,216 votes and

[20] *La Presse de Guinée,* Jan. 7, 1956; J. Beaujeu-Garnier, "Essai de géographie électorale guinéenne," *Cahiers d'Outre-Mer,* 44, (Oct.–Dec. 1958).

[21] *Afrique nouvelle,* Apr. 2 and 9, 1957.

its adversaries only 93, 397,[22] and the former carried all of the 526 seats contested.

The PDG Take-over

To understand thoroughly the events that transpired between 1956 and 1958, one must not only take into account the methods used by the PDG-RDA but must also consider them in the socioeconomic context of that period. Even before a *loi-cadre* for Africa was envisaged, a climate favoring decolonization had been created by black students in France, African teachers and trade unionists (most of whom were civil servants), and many deputies. These elements were highly sensitive to the repercussions of the war in Algeria and to the evolution of colonial problems. That evolution was marked by the Afro-Asian Conference at Bandung and the revolt led by the Union des Populations du Cameroun in 1955; the independence of Tunisia and Morocco and the autonomy granted to Togo and to the eastern and western regions of Nigeria in 1956; and the Gold Coast's achievement of sovereignty as Ghana in 1957. Because the RDA was the most effective element in checkmating France's colonial policy and in bringing about improvements in the status of African workers and peasants, it was supported by the majority of Guineans.

Believing that the proposal—made by Gaston Defferre when he was Minister for Overseas France—to transfer certain powers to the colonies marked the first step toward autonomy, the PDG-RDA and also the BAG favored the *loi-cadre* after it was voted by the Parliament on June 23, 1956. This law aimed at decentralizing power and it was to be applied through decrees. Along with the state services that still depended on the French government and were run by its agents,

[22] *La Presse de Guinée,* May 22, 1958.

territorial services were created. These services were administered by a local executive—the government council—and by the territorial assembly acting under the governor's supervision.[23] By law, the governor was also president of the government council.

The territorial reorganization took place in April and May 1957, after elections for new territorial assemblies had been held on March 31. But as soon as the new institutions began to function, the locally elected representatives began showing their annoyance at the limitations placed on their powers, which led Sékou Touré to start as early as June 1957—just one month after the government councils had been elected—to severely criticize the *loi-cadre*. Yet it was he, of all the African vice-presidents of the government councils, who derived the greatest benefits therefrom. By his reforming zeal, Sékou Touré transcended even the spirit of the *loi-cadre* and in so doing furthered the growth of nationalism.

Hardly had the government been set up in Guinea than it moved to reorganize the administration. At a meeting in July, the *commandants de cercle* (district officers) came out in favor of eliminating the post of canton chief. The cantons had been headed by chiefs chosen by the administration on the basis of their loyalty to the colonizing power rather than the prestige conferred by tradition and competence. On December 31, therefore, the cantons were eliminated, at the same time as a plan to reorganize the territory was carried out. Guinea's villages were transformed into 4,723 "rural communes" administered by councils of five to fifteen members elected for a five-year term. Council presidents were given the title of village chiefs, or mayors in the case of urban centers. The twenty-

[23] *Le Monde*, June 24, 1956; *Marchés tropicaux et méditerranéens*, Sept. 29, 1956.

five *cercles* were renamed circumscriptions (after independence they became known as "administrative regions"), and they were also provided with councils and were administered by officials named by the government according to the law. Ninety-three administrative units, later known as *arrondissements*, were created as dependencies of the circumscriptions. Thanks to the system of electing circumscription councilors from a single slate of candidates by a majority vote in an election without any crossover or runoff, the PDG acquired control of these assemblies. That party also controlled the municipal councils in all the main towns except Dalaba and Labé, where the DSG was victorious in the municipal elections of 1956. Furthermore, the PDG dominated most of the general administrative services, to which African cadres were promoted after undergoing rapid training in a Territorial School of Administration.[24]

The administrative reorganization having been carried out, the new government moved to reinforce its authority by designating African civil servants as deputies to the circumscription chiefs, so that the French administrators felt themselves hemmed in by political commissars. To acquire the maximum political power as quickly as possible, the PDG tried to restrict the role and authority of the governor[25] and to place party representatives in positions at all levels of the administration. Allotment of these posts also served to insure the loy-

[24] *Guinée nouvelle* (news bulletin issued by the Ministry of Interior), No. 1 (Apr. 1, 1958).

[25] Governor Jean Ramadier played an ambiguous role in Guinea. He was named to that post so as to offset the preceding governor's failure to halt the progress being made by the PDG-RDA. Using all the leeway provided by the *loi-cadre* of 1956, Ramadier covertly became a rival to Sékou Touré under the guise of maintaining excellent official relations. Similarly, he seemed to be supporting the PDG while at the same time trying to win over its leaders, who had severely criticized French colonialism, by offering them money, posts, cars, and villas.

alty of party cadres. By means of this over-all reform, the PDG rapidly created conditions conducive to gaining independence with minimal confusion to the administration. The power of the PDG was confirmed at the same time that Guinea was moving toward a single-party regime.

Now that the PDG, virtually alone, had come to control Guinea's destiny, the other parties were gradually abandoned by their followers and consequently sought outside help. Barry III aligned his DSG with the Mouvement Socialiste Africain (MSA), which had been created in October 1956 with the aims of building a single African political movement and of liberalizing the French Union. The BAG leader, Diawadou Barry, however, drew closer to but did not join the federalist program of the Convention Africaine, which had come into being in January 1957 through the initiative of Léopold S. Senghor of Senegal and had won the favor of the elite.

The fear of balkanizing Africa just at a time when the *loi-cadre* was accentuating territorial divergencies underscored the need for African solidarity. Sékou Touré therefore proposed establishing a federal executive at Dakar, first at a meeting of the FWA Grand Council late in August and then at the second PDG territorial conference in Kankan on September 22–23. Also in September, a new Marxist party came into existence on the eve of the RDA's third congress at Bamako. This was the Parti Africain de l'Indépendance (PAI), promoted by young university graduates who forcefully demanded immediate independence for the African territories.

It was at that time that political parties began vying with each other in a series of sparring contests that ended only with the constitutional referendum of September 1958. First the RDA tried to outbid the Convention Africaine and then the former's radical wing, led by Sékou Touré, pursued the same strategy vis-à-vis the followers of Houphouët-Boigny, president and founder of the whole movement. The BAG and the DSG, increasingly aware of their own weakness, the result of desertions by their members and of electoral defeats, joined the PRA, which had been founded at Dakar on March 26, 1958, through a rapprochement between the Mouvement Socialiste Africain and the Convention Africaine. Only the RDA remained solitary and faithful to its own standard.

Proponents of the two main political trends at that period in Guinea tried to settle their accounts in a final outburst of violence. On May 2 and 3, 1958, rioting caused blood to flow in the Guinean capital: depending on the source, either 23 or 30 persons were killed and 140 or 200 were wounded. Stabbing, poisoning, pillaging, and arson took place. David Soumah, head of the CATC, the rival of Sékou Touré's union, saved his life only by taking flight. Others, like Moussa Kéita, fought off the PDG militia with a gun. Several opponents of the majority party sought refuge in Dakar and Abidjan.[26] Since clashes between parties were aggravated by ethnic and personal animosities, the PDG used its power and the foregoing events to appeal strongly for tribal unity and an end to regionalism. The real leaders of the Guinean branch of the PRA, at its constituent congress held at Cotonou in July 1958, tried to outflank Sékou Touré on the left by rallying to the slogan of immediate independence. All the conditions propitious for achieving national unity were met when the PDG decided to reject the constitution of the Fifth French Republic on September 14, 1958. (After independence, the PDG insisted on dissolution of the Guinean branch of the PRA (BAG and DSG)', which had already lost popular support.)

Nevertheless, the decision to opt for independence caused disagreements and misunderstandings. Inside the RDA, Houphouët-Boigny clashed with Sékou Touré on April 9–10,

[26] Camara, *op. cit.*, p. 172.

1958. At that time, the former advocated a union between France and each territory within the framework of a federal Franco-African Community, whereas Touré considered the stand taken by the Ivory Coast representatives as inopportune and contrary to the wishes of the African masses.[27] This dissension came to a head on October 9, when the coordinating committee of the RDA decided to exclude the PDG from its membership. A few days later, the PDG announced that it considered itself to be no longer a branch of the RDA but its "natural ally." The root cause of this schism was Guinea's decision to go it alone by voting no in the referendum proposed by General de Gaulle.

Political problems, arising largely from the Algerian war, had led to a crisis in France early in 1958. It was not resolved until the President of the French Republic called on General de Gaulle to head the government. Once in power, de Gaulle decided to give the French Republic a new constitution. The African colonies were to choose between a Franco-African Community and total independence. On August 25, however, during de Gaulle's trip to Africa, his susceptibilities[28] as well as those of the Guineans became mutually exacerbated. When General de Gaulle was received on that day by the Guinean territorial assembly at Conakry, Sékou Touré stated that Guinea favored the new constitution only if it would proclaim the Africans' "right to independence" and recognize the "right to divorce" in a Franco-African "marriage" as well as the "active solidarity existing between the Associated States and the populations."[29]

[27] *Afrique nouvelle,* Apr. 11, 1958.
[28] B. Ameillon, *La Guinée: Bilan d'une indépendance* (Paris: Maspero, 1964), p. 61.
[29] Sékou Touré, *Expérience guinéenne et unité africaine* (Paris: Présence africaine, 1959), p. 80.

To this statement General de Gaulle replied:

> France proposes this community and no one is compelled to belong to it. Independence has been mentioned. I say more loudly here than elsewhere that independence is available to Guinea, and can be obtained by voting no on September 28 to the proposition under consideration. In such an event, I pledge that the Metropole will place no obstacle in the way. To be sure, France will draw its conclusions but will place no stumbling blocks in the way. Your territory can, if it so desires and under the circumstances it prefers, follow the path of its choice. . . . Vote yes in the interests of all. I have spoken. You must reflect.[30]

Was this bitterness, born of wounded pride? Perhaps. Or was there pressure from the French industrialists and financiers in the Fonds d'Investissements pour le Développement Economique et Social (FIDES), who wanted de Gaulle to use his influence so that Guinea would become a member of the Community and their investments in Africa would pay off? Such a hypothesis cannot be ruled out.

In the ensuing weeks, Guinea gradually became isolated from the RDA and other African parties, contrary to its professed goal of African unity. The Guinean moderates engaged in some delaying tactics, but the temptation to opt for independence carried the day. At their first national conference, on September 14, 1958, the cadres of the PDG decided to vote no, thereby making the most important decision in their history. Even though the PDG conducted no campaign and simply issued directives, 1,134,324 negative to 56,981 affirmative votes were cast in the referendum of September 28, 1958. On October 2, the Republic of Guinea was proclaimed and the territorial assembly became the national legislature.

[30] *Ibid.*, pp. 83, 84.

CHAPTER 3

Building a Revolutionary State

The first breach in France's over-all colonial policy had been made. In Paris, *Le Figaro*'s commentator wondered if "Guinea would become a people's democracy" and stir up the world's illusions: "Behind Sily, the elephant mascot of the PDG, appears the snout of a bear." And a few days later, *Le Figaro* commented that "Sékou Touré has placed a revolutionary red bonnet on the kinky hair of the Guinean Marianne."[1]

Knowing that his country's decision was considered by France as secession, the head of the young republic nevertheless sent a cable to the former Metropolitan power urging it to make cooperation agreements with Guinea and to grant it protection. He did this even though the French administrators and technicians had been asked immediately after the referendum to return to their country. Some of them had destroyed equipment before they left, others had carried away their files, and the soldiers at Dalaba had set fire to their barracks. Despite pressure from France, combined with the inducement of compensation to expedite the departure of French nationals, some of those under contract with the local government—including one-third of the teachers—stayed on, in order to help the country whose potential they knew take its first steps. Some private individuals also remained to salvage as much of their property as they could.

[1] Louis Marin, *Le Figaro*, Sept. 29 and Oct. 3, 1958.

To make an example of Guinea for the African countries of the Community that had shown fidelity to France (and whose leaders would have found the encouragement of Guinea's dissidence incomprehensible), Paris suspended all financial aid provided to Guinea by the FIDES except the fund for improving the aluminum port of Fria.

Guinea was so irritated by the French attitude that it became exceedingly meticulous and suspicious in its dealings with all whites. Statues of former governors were pulled down and carted away. However, before giving vent to his ill humor, the Guinean president made conciliatory gestures both locally and on the international scene. At a meeting organized by the Chamber of Commerce on October 4, 1958, he said: "Our determination to be independent should not be interpreted as a desire to break off relations with France."[2] His feigned good will, compared with what B. Ameillon calls the "obstinacy of General de Gaulle,"[3] enabled Sékou Touré to achieve three objectives: first, to obviate a sudden disruption of Guinea's economy by reassuring businessmen, while at the same time pursuing a policy of "positive neutralism" generally favorable to the socialist countries and nationalistic regimes of Africa; second, to discourage vindictive moves on the part of the French government by appealing for sympathy to the French public—attributing the Franco-Guinean conflict to such classical causes as lost opportunities, psychological errors, and the like; and third, for the purpose of enhancing his own prestige, to court world opinion by claiming that Guinea had been ostracized because it was the sole member of overseas France that dared to challenge General de Gaulle.

[2] B. Ameillon, *La Guinée: Bilan d'une indépendance* (Paris: Maspero, 1964), p. 86.
[3] *Ibid.,* p. 98.

Fernand Gigon, in his *Guinée, Etat-pilote*,[4] has given a lively and colorful description of the merry-go-round of missions and delegations from all countries that came to Guinea, the beating of drums to incite voluntary labor, the club of cronies that constituted the cabinet, and the ideological choices of *"homo africanus."* Perhaps the euphoria of independence inspired an outlook that took into account only the immediate future. In any case, Guinea's policy was already determined, even if reviving the national economy was proving to be difficult.

On the domestic front, total unity was essential for consolidating the new power. This was facilitated by the unanimous support given it by all the Guinean parties prior to the referendum. The BAG and MSA were immediately integrated into the PDG, and their respective leaders became ministers in the new Guinean government. The diverse fortunes of those leaders culminated twelve years later, when all of them had been physically liquidated. For the time being, the most pressing task was to strengthen the nation as much as possible by providing it with adequate institutions and reorienting its economy. The politico-administrative organization and the economic revolution will be examined here; the country's social transformation will be taken up in another chapter. However, to understand the direction taken by Guinea politically and economically, one must first consider the man responsible for it and the ideological model he followed.

Sékou Touré and the PDG's Ideology

Sékou Touré, the son of a poor peasant, who came to emulate his reputed ancestor, Samori, was raised in a Muslim family and

[4] Fernand Gigon, *Guinée: Etat-pilote* (Paris: Plon, 1959).

married a Christian mulatto. At one time a modest government employee, he was later described by his party as "the supreme revolutionary authority." After studying Marxist doctrine, he gained through his own efforts an intellectual independence which made him unique. Sékou Touré molded his life dialectically by reconciling contradictory theories and formulating his own synthesis from them. He did not belong to the group of pioneers of more or less aristocratic origin, or to that of the activist teachers at the William Ponty normal school, but should be classified among the revolutionary trade unionists.

Born in 1922 at Faranah, Sékou Touré grew up as an *enfant terrible*. After finishing primary school, he was admitted to the Georges Poiret Vocational Training School at Conakry in 1936. Dropped from that school the next year because of poor grades, he continued his studies by correspondence. At the age of eighteen he was employed by the Compagnie du Niger Français. The following year, when he was working as an assistant in the postal service, he passed an examination that gave him clerical status. As of 1945, he was general secretary of the union of employees of the postal service and helped to found the Guinean branch of the CGT. Having successfully competed for admission to the financial services, he entered the treasury administration in 1946. He became general secretary of its employees' union and a founding member of the RDA at the constituent congress of that movement. Dismissed from the treasury service for his political activities, Sékou Touré devoted himself exclusively to trade unionism. After being named general secretary of the Guinean sector of the CGT in 1948, he established contact with its French leaders, Benoit Frachon and Louis Saillant. Two years later he became general secretary of the Coordinating Committee of the CGT unions of French West Africa and Togo.

Feeling ill at ease within the French Communist Party, the RDA broke away from it in 1950. Although Sékou Touré publicly supported the stand taken by Houphouët-Boigny, he continued to follow the Communist Party line within the framework of the CGT. At the same time, by hinting that he might join the CGT-FO, he established relations with the leaders of that labor federation in Senegal.

It was during this period, when his role on the local and federal levels was growing in importance, that Sékou Touré became politically ambitious and began to hope that someday he might be elected to Parliament. After becoming general secretary of the PDG in 1952, he was encouraged in such aspirations by the growing benevolence of Bernard Cornut-Gentille, High Commissioner of French West Africa and advocate of a policy of salvaging and utilizing the RDA. By this time, Sékou Touré had already got rid of some competitors, notably Madeira Kéita, his rival in the PDG secretariat, whom he had persuaded Cornut-Gentille to transfer to Soudan. Without Cornut-Gentille's protection it might perhaps have been harder and slower for Sékou Touré to win popular acclaim. His popularity was shown by his election to the territorial assembly from Beyla in 1953, as well as by the showdown of a two-month-long strike at Conakry.

At the same time that he created the CGTA, Sékou Touré's political career was furthered by his election as deputy to the French National Assembly in 1956. Moreover, on November 18, 1956, he was elected mayor of Conakry. During the next year he garnered more honors as well as heavier burdens—as founder of the UGTAN, vice-president of the government council of Guinea, and vice-president of the RDA. He was expelled from the RDA post in September 1958, the very month when the independence of Guinea brought him the presidency of the new republic.

Those who have been close to Sékou Touré entertain no doubts as to the sincerity of the campaign he led and of the austerity of his life style—qualities which he has tried with little success to inculcate in his aides. Although he did not emulate Ghana's Kwame Nkrumah, his former model and eventual protégé, by calling himself the Redeemer (Osagyefo), he took pride in his work, as he did in his "philosophy." No one would dream of pointing out to him that he had made mistakes, or simply that he might be fallible—on the part of an ordinary citizen, this would be taken as impertinence; from a minister, indebted as he was to Sékou Touré for his post, it would be inadmissible; and from a foreigner it would be considered as meddling in the state's internal affairs. It is generally believed that the touchiness and obstinacy of the head of state have greatly restricted Guinea's margin of maneuver and compromised any chance of its resuming relations with those who have recently become its adversaries. Moreover, Sékou Touré's constant preoccupation with a possible attack by the imperialists, and his obsessive fear of a domestic counterrevolution, apparent on every page of his book *Défendre la révolution*,[5] could hardly promote fraternal cooperation with other states. At every turn, their leaders risked being accused of helping imperialism, or tolerating neocolonialism, or trying to undermine Guinea internally, either by giving asylum to Guinean émigrés or by plotting to wreck the Guinean revolution. Sékou Touré's permanent fear of counterrevolution explains his many appeals for vigilance and firmness.

Sékou Touré was self-educated, though any resulting intel-

[5] Sékou Touré, *Défendre la révolution* (Conakry: Imprimerie Nationale, 1969).

lectual handicap was outweighed by his youthful ambition and determination. After having tried to give form and substance to the concepts of Marx, Jaurès, and Nkrumah, Sékou Touré evolved a strongly pragmatic system of thought. Its logic might be defective, but it was dynamic because it derived from his powerful intuitive sense and an open-mindedness in making judgments.

In the author's view, however, Sékou Touré's strongest point was his remarkable tactical ability. Impulsiveness, fantasy, and caprice undoubtedly played a part in the decisions made by this man who controlled the republic's destiny. Yet one cannot deny his mastery of the art of reconciling a theoretical ideal and the realistic social evolution of a people still weighed down by traditions, or the skill with which he tempered firmness with concessions, or his astuteness in accepting what was traditional insofar as it did not hamper the development of new policies. The priority which he gave to the practical over the theoretical accounts for the revisions made in operating the political system, as well as for those made in basic economic doctrine. His balanced policy, during the first years of independence, was to promote the interests and aspirations of each of the nation's groups, at the same time as he imposed on the country a rational plan for orderly growth. Later, because of some blunders, the interests involved proved to be so contradictory and divergent that Sékou Touré perforce resorted to authoritarian measures and forceful methods. Because of this, his initial flexibility was obscured, and the impression was created that Sékou Touré was no longer listening to his people and had finally become a despot. As a matter of fact, he was practicing two contradictory and competitive forms of government. There is no doubt that his exercise of power became progressively harsher, yet it cannot be denied that the head of the Guinean state took advantage of every opportunity to disguise the arbitrary nature of a decree. He knew how to utilize successive periods of social fervor, which recurred as regularly as malaria, for the purpose of trying out a new remedy—all the while knowing that the "patient" would fairly soon put it on the back of the shelf. At these times, the people expressed thanks to their temporary healer, even though they must have been fully aware that his release of stocks of rice and textiles on the eve of major holidays was merely bait.

Insofar as he uses oratory as an instrument of political action, Sékou Touré's speeches disclose his strategy to those who grasp its essence, which is that of the African rhetorician whose aim is to influence opinion abroad and to persuade his own countrymen of what he wants them to believe. The world view on which his thought is predicated stresses certain general ideas as they relate to news and current events. He argues by analogy and glosses over the gaps in his thought so as to disguise its sophistry. In the long run, it is more by the firmness of his arguments than by his verbal excesses that he is persuasive.

If one can make an honest judgment that distinguishes between the plan for economic development and that for social change, without ignoring the relationship between them, one must admit that Guinea, in the person of Sékou Touré, had a resource which in and by itself was worth a revolution.

Although such men as Madeira Kéita and Saifoulaye Diallo may have influenced the formulation of the PDG's ideology in its early stages, it is evident that the final statement of this ideology was above all the brainchild of the Guinean leader who had been trained in three schools of thought—those of Africa, the West, and Marxist socialism. The basic aim of Sékou Touré's socialism or noncapitalist approach (for it was not until 1962 that the term "socialist path" was used), is to alter the relationship between human beings. This is to be done by decolonizing their viewpoints and attitudes, and by creating a new man freed from a system of capitalistic exploitation and participating with all his strength in the development of his nation. Here nationalism transcends socialism, just as support for the regime has priority over promotion of the revolution. As preached by Sékou Touré,[6] the revival of authentic African values was not to be achieved through *négritude,* which he regards as a form of abdication and a tacit admission of the white man's superiority.[7] Rather, the revival was to come through the restoration of African culture by renewing popular art forms, relating formal education to life, fostering literacy in the national languages, and glorifying African heroes. In this way it would serve as a moral and spiritual bulwark for a hybrid society passing through a period of crisis.

Behind this loyalty to Africa—first strongly expressed in the preamble to the constitution—lies the conviction that renewal can be achieved through action, the content of thought, and the structure of institutions. History is conceived as leading to the future rather than as clinging to past events. It upgrades the struggle against colonialism, depicted as the classical means of effecting cultural alienation, and plays down intertribal wars. Nor was there any question of the class struggle until 1967, for in a newly independent country the contrasts between social classes should not be artificially aggravated. Furthermore, it was assumed that such differences would disap-

[6] Yves Bénot, *Idéologies des indépendances africaines* (Paris: Maspero, 1969).
[7] Sékou Touré, *La Négritude et la cinquième colonne* (Conakry: Imprimerie Nationale, 1971).

pear in a revolutionary and democratic state through the action taken by a single party—the party of all the people.[8]

The PDG ideology offers its own method of interpreting sociohistorical realities. This method delves deeper than the Party's political doctrine, whose slogans (unity and dignity) and whose aims (industrialization and autonomy) have a profound appeal for Africans. The Party's ideology goes beyond a synthesis of its objectives and basic themes (such as revolutionary action, positive neutralism, African unity, national independence, democratic centralism, social justice, and priority to production and African culture), which sometimes suffice to dazzle and guide the masses and to lessen their centrifugal tendencies. The method adopted by the PDG analyzes phenomena at three different levels—those of the Party line, of its organization, and of human beings.[9] By drawing such distinctions, blunders can be camouflaged. All criticism in any form of the three- and seven-year plans, of state-controlled trading, or of educational reforms can be blamed on individuals and, in part, on the organizational structure. Accordingly, mistakes result from a compromise between the ideal and unalterable circumstances. On the other hand, the Party line, as the president's brainchild, is always correct and just. In Sékou Touré's view, its absolute validity is guaranteed by its objectivity and by faith in his own oracular powers.

In its contentious and optimistic aspects, this vigorously propagated ideology undoubtedly meets basic African psychological needs. Its aggressiveness, formerly expressed in the conflicts between clans and tribes and then damped down by

[8] Sékou Touré, *La Révolution guinéenne et le progrès social* (Conakry: Imprimerie Nationale, 1963), pp. 208–245.
[9] Sékou Touré, *L'Afrique et la révolution* (Switzerland, 1966), p. 125.

colonization, revived in the struggle for independence. Thereafter it was sublimated through an ideology vehemently opposed to imperialism, colonialism, and neocolonialism. At the same time as it freed the Guineans from their chains, this ideology assured them that after the revolution succeeded they could look to a happy future in a prosperous nation free of any class struggle. Its lack of realism and verbiage added to the seductiveness of this ideology by satisfying the African taste for sheer oratory. New words and concepts gained currency and became stereotypes: puppets, revolutionary thought that continually outran itself, sudden qualitative changes, climax of an historical process, organized and informed producers, and the like. They served as verbal tools for those who felt they must engage in public speechmaking to demonstrate their fidelity to the Party, and for those who required prefabricated ideas to give themselves the illusion of thought. This writer believes that the true interpretation of the PDG's ideology and the explanation of its hold on the population can be found in its sublimation of the Guinean's frustrated desire for dignity, its projection of his basic ego, and the escape it offers him into a new and apparently rational kind of mythology.

Potent as the effect of this ideology may be, it is but one of the means used to promote national integration, and it is one not used by many African nations. On the other hand, an administrative organization and political institutions that regulate the exercise of legislative, executive, and judicial powers are absolutely vital for the effective functioning of any regime.

The Political Regime

From the early days of the Guinean republic, the PDG politburo quickly showed its preference for those institutions that would confirm the state's sovereignty. As its two mainstays it chose the constitution of November 10, 1958, slightly modified by the law of October 31, 1963, and the Party statutes. Drafted in ten days and comprising fifty-three articles divided into twelve sections, the constitution is remarkably succinct. Its preamble affirms Guinea's adherence to the United Nations Charter and the Universal Declaration of the Rights of Man, and it proclaims the "equality and solidarity of all nationals without regard to race, sex, or religion." Its basic principles of "government by, of, and for the people" were reflected in its denomination as a "democratic, lay, and social republic." The motto it adopted was "work, justice, and solidarity." Civil and political liberties, the freedom to organize trade unions, and immunity from arbitrary arrest were recognized as the rights of its citizens. The privacy of homes and of correspondence was assured (Art. 43), as was the right to vote and to be elected to office (Art. 39); freedom of the press, speech, assembly, and conscience was proclaimed (Art. 40), as was freedom to participate in processions and demonstrations; discrimination on racial or religious grounds was forbidden (Arts. 41 and 45); and the right to work, rest, social assistance, education, and to engage in strikes (Art. 44) was guaranteed. In regard to most of the specified rights, except those relating to social assistance, education, and nondiscrimination, one has only to assume the exact opposite of the constitution's provisions in order to grasp the reality.

The executive power is exercised essentially by the president of the republic, who is the head of the state, the government, and the armed forces (Art. 20). He is elected by universal suffrage for seven years and is eligible indefinitely for re-election (Art. 22). Sékou Touré was elected on January 15, 1961, by 1,576,580 of the votes cast by 1,576,747 electors, and was re-elected in January 1968 and December 1974. His prerogatives (listed in Articles 23–27) are extensive: it is he who executes the laws, fills all public offices and military posts (Art. 25) and initiates laws concurrently with the national assembly (Art. 14); he negotiates Guinea's international treaties (Art. 32); the ministers he appoints are responsible solely to him (Arts. 23–24), and they can neither serve as deputies nor carry on any private professional activity (Art. 27).

Deputies to the national assembly (75 until December 1974, and 150 thereafter) do not carry on political campaigns but are elected by universal suffrage for five years from the single list drawn up by the Party.[10] Their legislative role is reduced to voting the budget (Art. 16) and the laws (Art. 9) which are initiated and drafted by the head of state alone. Most legal measures are promulgated by decree,[11] so the assembly's functions are as minimal as its two annual sessions are brief. The only laws passed concern the ratification of international treaties, taxation, and public finances. Moreover, there is no genuine debate nor, *a fortiori*, any control over the budget as laid down in the constitution. Moreover, the assembly is not empowered to handle the expenditures for equipment that are financed by foreign loans, the national banking system, or subsidies from abroad. Nor can the deputies exercise control over the budgets of state enterprises or those of the administrative regions. Questioning the policy of the president of the republic remains merely a theoretical privilege, for it lacks any practical application. Furthermore, it is in the annual Party congresses and not in the assembly that the president, in a mara-

[10] After independence, the territorial assembly became the national assembly, and the first legislative elections were held in 1963.
[11] For example, in 1960, 20 laws and 331 decrees were promulgated; in 1961, 23 laws and 477 decrees; in 1962, 58 laws and 471 decrees; and in 1963, 60 laws and 636 decrees.

thon speech, discloses his policy. Everyone knows that the only authority other than the president's is held by the National Politburo. The weakness of the assembly as a rubber-stamp body led Bernard Charles to conclude that the men drafting Guinea's constitution "borrowed from the American system everything that concentrated power in the hands of the president, while ignoring all the checks and balances designed theoretically to prevent a strong regime from becoming a dictatorship."[12] Inasmuch as no Supreme Court or economic and social council has been created, the regime has neither judges nor advocates. One minister remarked that by initialing the budget, the state civil servants were charged with defending the revolutionary truth, but no more than that.

That the constitution could not be amended and was full of loopholes seems to have caused Guinea's leaders little concern, whereas the Party's statutes have been revised several times and abound in precise details. Although in theory Guinea could have a multiparty system, the PDG monopolizes all the political, judicial, administrative, and technical authority, controlling all the state functions and public affairs. It directs the state's policy and even manages its operations. The Party's general secretary is at one and the same time prime minister and president of the republic. The National Politburo (Bureau Politique National or BPN), the Party's highest authority and its executive organ, handles all questions involving appointments to the bureaucracy, the management of state enterprises, the delimitation of administrative regions, economic planning, international relations, and the like. It supervises the justice dispensed in the people's courts, assesses direct taxation, and controls prices as well as the commercial agencies.

[12] Bernard Charles, *La République de Guinée* (Paris: Berger-Levrault, 1972), p. 23.

Building a Revolutionary State

To carry out its multiple tasks, the Party is provided with a strongly hierarchized structure. As of 1974, the country's 29 administrative regions were identical with the Party's federations. Their 220 *arrondissements* correspond with the same number of federation-controlled sections. All of Guinea's 4,000 villages have their Pouvoir Révolutionnaire Local (PRL), which constitute the Party's base, replacing the former village or urban district committees. At all levels except that of the village, the congress (composed of sectional, federal, and national congresses) represents the highest political authority: conferences are held in the intervals between the congress sessions. It is in these congresses and conferences that the Party's political line is defined, proclaimed, or ratified, and it is there too that the Party leaders are elected. To be elected to the PRL directorate, a candidate must have been an active Party militant for three years. Candidates for election to sectional managing committees are required to have carried on such activities for five years. Members of the federal bureau are chosen from among the heads of sectional committees, and those of the BPN are elected from among members of the federal bureaus.

The very uniqueness of the single party and the osmosis between the political and administrative functions were justified by the need to preserve the revolution's dynamism, make the anticolonial struggle effective, and economize on cadres in a country so underdeveloped as Guinea. At the same time, this situation helped to reassure those Guineans who were concerned about their nation's instability. The Party, which claimed to reflect the collective Guinean viewpoint, tried to inject a militant spirit into the entire population. If one can accept the PDG's claim to being the "gauge of Guinea's public health," then it can be considered successful as a mass or national party. Its dues-paying membership rose from 300,000

Chart 1. Political and administrative organization of the Republic of Guinea

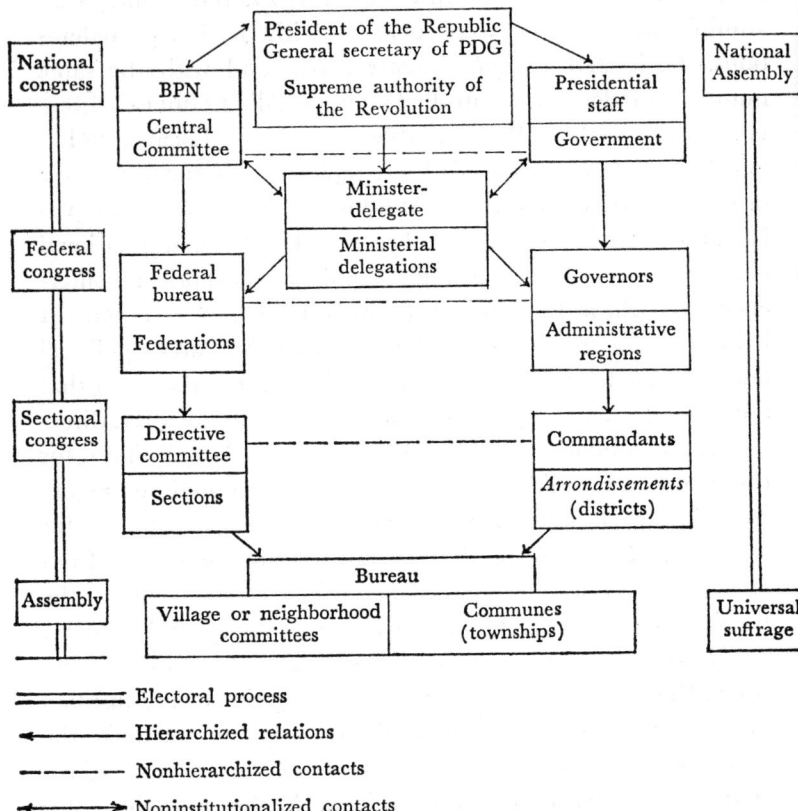

Source: Bernard Charles, *La République de Guinée* (Paris: Berger-Levrault, 1972), p. 26.

in 1955 to 800,000 in 1959 and to 1.8 million in 1962. Inasmuch as the population totaled some 3 million in 1962, the PDG comprised virtually all Guineans over the age of fifteen. The better to keep a tight rein on the masses, the PDG increased the number of its sections from 43 in 1959, to 167 in 1963, to 180 in 1966, and to 220 in 1974.

At the eighth Party congress, in 1967, membership in the BPN was expanded from seventeen to twenty-five and a special six-member committee was set up and given authority over the BPN. Women, youths, and trade unionists each have their own organization inside the Party. By frequently convening the base or PRL committees (weekly meetings), sections, federations, assemblies, commissions, inspectorates, congresses, and national conferences, all the country's political life is kept under close supervision. Control is exercised over the Party militants' civic activity as well as the administrative cadres' competence and their ability to mobilize the masses and to maintain respect for the technical organizations, to such a degree that very few individuals can escape this network of revolutionary vigilance. The Party's supremacy over all institutions in every domain, the indivisibility of responsibilities and the lack of any separation of powers, exact from all citizens at least outward obedience. The fact that no jurisdiction is empowered to hear complaints about the abuses of power seriously impairs the Guineans' freedom to act at the same time as it checks any deviationism. This corresponds to the constraints imposed by custom in traditional society to prevent any manifestation of individualism, in the social sense of the term, under pain of death.

Whether Sékou Touré describes his regime as a "popular dictatorship" or as a "democratic dictatorship" does not alter what all observers believe to be "the fluctuation of his regime between a monocracy ruled by partisans and the personalization of power."[13] Nevertheless, what Sékou Touré terms "democratic centralism" limits its dictatorial aspect. Theoretically, the base cells elect their leaders, discuss economic plans, and

[13] Seydou Madani Sy, *Recherches sur l'exercice du pouvoir politique en Afrique noire: Côte d'Ivoire, Guinée, Mali* (Paris: Pedone, 1965), p. 206.

participate in their execution; the organized agencies distribute governmental directives; and the constituents can control the leaders they elect. In practice, however, there is no division of authority. The elected leader is the Party's candidate; PDG organs control every aspect of national life, censor the news, propose themes for meditation, and stifle many complaints.

This overpoliticization, which was simply burdensome in its early stages, has now alienated the population. In 1965, Victor DuBois noted:

> While it is hazardous to attribute the decline of a nation to any one specific cause, available evidence strongly suggests that Guinea's major problem was overpoliticization and the sacrifice of national planning to political expediency.

The advantages which accrued to the PDG from the intense politicization of the country—not only popular assent to its programs but also widespread popular participation—were the positive side of the coin. There was also a negative side. The plethora of base committees,[14] regional committees, sectional committees, youth and women's committees, and government councils meant a political system top-heavy with notables of one sort or another. The maintenance of this array of government and Party officials demanded vast amounts of time, energy, and money. Moreover, while the establishment of party cells at the neighborhood and village levels provided a means for popular participation in government, it also created a vast bureaucratic apparatus which taxed the financial resources of the state, bogged down the decision-making process, and retarded the implementation of policy.[15]

With the application of the *loi-cadre* of 1956, there was a general rush for the jobs in the new political and administra-

[14] In 1957, there were 3,500 base committees; in December 1961, 7,626; and in December 1962, 10,225.

[15] Victor DuBois, "The Decline of the Guinean Revolution," *American Universities Field Staff Reports,* West Africa Series, 8, No. 7 (1965), p. 5.

tive organization that were handed out by the PDG. The first beneficiaries were Sékou Touré's companions-in-arms. When independence led to the precipitate departure of the French administrators and technicians, the middle-ranking cadres who had acquired some knowledge and experience in management had to take charge of most of the government services. African and international solidarity helped with this effort to put the country back on its feet as quickly as possible. Aid was given in the form of money, economic agreements, and experts, cadres, and friendly professors and technicians. The first to arrive were from the former French West Africa, the Antilles, Haiti, and even France, and after 1960 others came from the socialist countries and North Vietnam. The administrative posts were reserved for nationals, hence low-ranking Guinean bureaucrats, instructors, and clerical staff were promoted to responsible positions. The PDG, for its part, chose its top officials from among the few doctors, veterinarians, school principals, technicians, and accountants in the middle ranks. Sékou Touré described this upgrading of the civil servants as follows:

In 1958, there were barely 6,000 government servants, including members of the local cadres, in a total of 62,000 to 70,000 wage earners throughout the country. In 1965, government servants numbered 25,000. The analysis of these figures indicates that, compared with the 7,000 auxiliary employees in 1958, we had at least 17,000 in 1965, without taking into account all the unofficial appointments to the civil service made by the governors. By 1965, the number of those employed in the local cadres had risen to nearly 6,000, almost twice as many as the 3,000 thus employed in 1958. Here I am referring to shipping clerks, nurses, etc. As to the agents in the higher or general cadres, they numbered slightly fewer than 965 in 1958; by 1965, there were 4,600. The social implications of this upward evolution are easy to grasp. During those seven years, nearly 3,700 members of the local cadres were promoted to the higher ranks. Thanks to the various competitive examinations, assistant instructors, shipping clerks, nurses, and customs officials from the local cadres improved their status, and those already in the higher ranks were promoted to the general cadres. The number of those benefiting by such promotions was five times larger than the total in 1958.[16]

As happened in many other African countries, the bureaucracy expanded inordinately because far too many persons had been appointed to carry out the commonest tasks. This resulted from a general policy of combating unemployment, the favoritism shown by bureau chiefs, and the employees' lack of zeal for their work. It also derived from the habit acquired during the colonial period of multiplying the number of messengers and clerks to the point where three were hired to do the work of one. While taking into account the excessive scale of these cut-rate promotions, it should also be noted that the need to measure up to their duties—under pain of being severely criticized or dismissed—induced many of the cadres to train themselves for their jobs. They had to learn the rudiments of managing enterprises, how and when to import merchandise, and the difficult task of managing millions of francs honestly when they had formerly dealt only in centimes. Thus, in many cases, far more was involved than a simple rise in official rank. Furthermore, it was with this new personnel that the national economy was launched.

The Decolonization and Socialization of the Economy

Moderation characterized the first economic measures taken during the months following the referendum, despite the excitement generated by the novel situation. Fully aware that

[16] Sékou Touré, *Défendre la révolution*, p. 244.

local savings were nonexistent, Sékou Touré had no intention of overturning the existing structure. He kept Guinea in the franc zone, respected the commitments made with the firms mining bauxite at Kassa and Fria (where the plant was in process of construction), and retained the tax system which brought in revenues for the budget without jeopardizing investments. At the same time, however, he insisted on widening the scope of his international contacts.

By decree No. 89, November 20, 1958, an Interministerial Economic Committee was created to advise the government about reorganizing Guinea's economy. One month later, the repercussions of the French franc's devaluation on the CFA franc forced the government to freeze prices. For lack of official controls, however, this measure proved ineffectual, but at the same time, the first installment of a 10-million-pound loan granted by Ghana from its Cocoa Marketing Board funds on November 23, 1958, temporarily protected Guinea from experiencing a serious shortage of currency. This money, instead of being invested, was used to meet operating expenditures. Inasmuch as Guinea's embryonic industries were still in French hands, very little revenue could be expected from that source unless the orientation of Guinea's foreign and domestic trade were changed. As a matter of fact, such a reorientation was the prerequisite for the country's economic decolonization.

The Guinean authorities launched their economic socialization policy by eliminating private wholesale trading at the same time as they instituted currency controls.[17] Rigorous planning was initiated in June 1959, as proposed by the Marxist economist, Charles Bettelheim. His advice, with some modifications, was given serious consideration by the government,

[17] *Journal officiel de la République de Guinée*, No. 3/93 (1959), avis 326.

whereas the not-often-disinterested offers of aid made by many Western and Communist experts were ignored. As for the hasty suggestions made by the agronomist René Dumont after a quick trip to Guinea,[18] these were judged by the Guinean leaders as impracticable. Guidelines of the reforms proposed by Bettelheim included control over trade, currency, credit, and prices; expansion of state enterprises; nationalization of private concerns distributing water, gas, and electricity; and reforms in the structure of agriculture through the agency of cooperative societies.

The Reorganization of Trade

To apply this type of socialistic development policy, the new state of Guinea decided to decolonize rapidly the existing commercial structure and circuits. The two principal procedures followed for this purpose were (1) the creation of a strong public sector that would have a quasi monopoly of imports and exports, a total monopoly of the wholesale trade, and a partial control of the retail trade (in which model stores would offer goods for sale at the official prices); and (2) the organization of production and sales cooperative societies, which would be allotted the major role in distributing merchandise and in selling produce at the village level.

By leaving most of the semiwholesale and all of the retail trade to private merchants, the government leaders hoped that they were taking into consideration both the potential of the public sector, in process of formation, and their revolutionary principles. Those principles admitted as desirable the accumulation of a certain degree of wealth on the part of the formerly oppressed population and small-scale merchants. As for

[18] René Dumont, *Reconversion de l'économie agricole: Guinée, Côte d'Ivoire, Mali* (Paris: Presses Universitaires de France, 1961).

the village cooperative societies, their function was to bring together, insofar as possible, both consumers and producers with a view to assuring the latter of a market for all their output at remunerative prices.

The nonmaterialization of projects and the frequent revisions of policy that were evident until 1964 can be explained by the urgent need to create new commercial agencies after the abortive attempt of the colonial trading monopolies to boycott Guinea's trade and by the decline in value of the Guinean franc that resulted from the flight of capital.

First of all, by requiring all the commercial and industrial enterprises to transfer their headquarters before July 1, 1959, to Guinea, where their operations could be controlled, the government attempted to repair the breakdown in the country's traditional flow of trade. Foreign capitalists were greatly disturbed by this move, which they took to be the forerunner of a policy of nationalization. An even more important move to break the monopoly of the trading companies was the creation, on January 24, 1959, of the Comptoir Guinéen du Commerce Extérieur (CGCE) to handle imports and exports.

Reorienting Guinea's trade toward the Eastern bloc required granting to the CGCE a total monopoly of commerce with the socialist countries, as well as that of the importation from any source of prime necessities such as rice, sugar, flour, cement, beer, and matches. All exports of peanuts, 75 per cent of those of palm kernels, 50 per cent of bananas, and 30 per cent of coffee shipments were placed under control. Moreover, permits for importing merchandise from the franc zone were issued by the CGCE only upon presentation of the requisite documents.

Concurrently, important markets were opened up with new trading partners (the U.S.S.R., North Africa, the U.S.A., and the U.A.R.), at higher prices for Guinean products than those paid by France. Contracts were signed for the importation of prime necessities from new sources. In two respects the terms of these agreements were very favorable to Guinea: either they reduced the cost of living for its consumers or such imports were sold at the same prices as before for the benefit of the state, which thereby acquired the funds needed for investing in projects of general interest. In practice, however, the anarchic situation caused by burdening the CGCE with so many duties led to disarray among Guinea's trading partners abroad.

Certainly the lack of an over-all development plan that might have given trading by the state a chance of survival was a major handicap. An even more serious obstacle was the juxtaposition of the state system and the capitalist one, for the latter deliberately operated in such a way as to hinder the functioning of the former. In fact, the CGCE depended for its provisions on the good will of private enterprises. At the same time, Guinea's continued affiliation with the franc zone and the financial operations of the locally established foreign banks paralyzed state trading in its attempt to organize.

Had the government not simultaneously monopolized both foreign trade and banking, it would have risked aggravating the difficulties it was encountering at this time—the flight of capital, the reckless importation of certain consumer goods, and the expansion of private capital that escaped the controls set up under the plan. To combat the adverse effects of uncontrolled foreign trading, the government had available only such means as a licensing system (which for lack of foreign currency could neither prevent abuses nor carry out its objectives) and tariff barriers (which proved ineffectual because the industrial concerns could always grant subsidies and price reductions to their own customers).

In order to establish a tight control over private activities, liberate itself from France's financial grip that prevented the young republic from making free use of the loans it received, and no longer be subjected to perturbations in the French economy, such as those caused by the franc's devaluation on December 28, 1958, the government issued a decree on February 29, 1960. This decree, which surprised all the banks, created a national currency, the Guinean franc (FG), at parity with the Colonies Françaises d'Afrique (CFA) franc, and it also established the Bank of the Republic of Guinea. When this measure came into force on March 1, 1960, it was found that the funds available, which had been estimated at about 9 billion CFA francs, totaled only 6.7 billion because most of the liquid capital held by companies and wealthy individuals had already been transferred out of the country. The French trading concerns, now unable to repatriate their large profits, closed most of their local offices. Thereafter their activities were limited to maintaining a central office at Conakry in a state of suspended animation.

Normal trading circuits were obstructed by the sudden eviction of the commercial companies and by the fact that the CGCE was burdened with too many responsibilities, so that an immediate reorganization of domestic trade was necessary. To that end, the Comptoir Guinéen du Commerce Intérieur (CGCI) was created on May 11, 1960. It was empowered to carry out all sales operations, represent foreign firms in Guinea, make a study of potential markets, collect and stock the produce placed at the CGCE's disposal, take steps to preserve perishable goods, standardize products offered for sale, and supply repair and maintenance services for all kinds of equipment. The CGCI was further required to gather information related to provisioning programs and to set the prices for merchandise.

The organizational measures resorted to during the second

half of 1960 failed to remedy the prevailing trade dislocation. According to the official analysis, its major causes were the congestion of Conakry port; the immobilization and sometimes the destruction of stocks; the devastation of farinaceous foodstuffs by weevils; the shortages of certain goods; the importation of items wholly unsuited to Guinea (such as bidets and screw-base light bulbs; the inadequacies and irregularities in provisioning the domestic market; and the refusal to permit private merchants to handle merchandise, even if they agreed to pay cash for it and to ship it themselves. By its failure to deal effectively with these difficulties, the government jeopardized the help it might have received from the private sector, without at the same time providing for its replacement.

This deplorable state of affairs can be attributed to causes more deep-rooted than the circumstances which forced Guinea into acting precipitately. These were the inadequacy of the transport infrastructure, a defective accounting system, the uneconomic and plethoric distribution network, and human incompetence. The deficiencies of the cadres were due not simply to their inexperience, but even more to their pilfering, corruption, and aspirations to improve their social status.[19] The unexpected rapidity with which this last-mentioned tendency developed can be clearly seen from the data for 1961 issued by the National Statistics Office in regard to imports (by value, in Guinean francs):

Description	Consumer goods	Equipment goods	Total
Program as planned	6,335,000	4,765,000	11,100,000
Expenditures	9,402,912	6,199,922	15,702,634
Disparity	3,067,712	1,534,922	6,026,634
Percentage of disparity	+ 48.4%	+ 32.2%	+ 41.4%

[19] Claude Rivière, "Les Conséquences de la réorganisation des circuits commerciaux en Guinée," *Revue française d'études politiques africaines*, 66 (June 1971), 74–96. "Les Mécanismes de constitution

The fact that the goals set were exceeded by 41 per cent is the more serious in that the most notable success was registered in the category of consumer goods, especially of textiles and shoes (99 per cent) and automobiles and motorcycles (104 per cent). Inasmuch as those fishing in troubled waters profited most from the general confusion, there was a rush beginning in 1961 to enter the commercial field. This was furthered by a psychosis caused by shortages.

New developments between 1961 and 1963 followed failure of the experiments with the *comptoirs*. On the one hand, an accentuation of regionalism benefited the administrators of state trading companies, while, on the other hand, the Guinean private sector was in the process of absorbing the public sector. The more liberal policy inaugurated at the sixth Party congress, reflected in a 10 per cent reduction of prices, not only failed to check inflation but even aggravated the confusion and the race to make money. Exports declined instead of expanding. Farmers and merchants went to Liberia and Ivory Coast to sell their rice and coffee (two-thirds of the 1963 crop was exported) to acquire hard currency and consumer goods that were not available in Guinea.

To do away with such trading practices, a return to state controls was imperative. This was the aim of the *loi-cadre* of November 8, 1964, which restored the state's monopoly over foreign and wholesale commerce, strictly curtailed the number of merchants, laid down rules for trading, and instituted a commission to allocate merchandise and control prices. However, none of these measures either slowed the rate of inflation or abated the evils to which it gave rise—smuggling and the black market.

---

d'une bourgeoisie commerçante en Guinée," *Cahiers d'études africaines,* 11, No. 43 (1971), 600–25.

The seventeen specialized state organizations that had been formed to replace the CGCE and the CGCI[20] in 1961 acquired greater authority as a result of this fairly radical reform. Furthermore, by 1961 those enterprises or privately managed sectors of the economy that had failed to carry out the plan's objectives or to meet their obligations had already been nationalized. Such was the fate of the companies that had supplied water, generated and distributed electric current (February 1, 1961), mined gold and diamonds (March 1, 1961), handled sea shipping and lighterage (August 1961), and managed the bauxite concessions at Kassa and Boké held by the Bauxites du Midi Company (November 1961).

At the outset, all the measures instituting state controls and nationalization were part of a development strategy that was to be carried out in three stages: basic reforms, 1958–1960; execution of the three-year plan, 1960–1963; and realization of the seven-year plan, 1963–1971. By then, Guinea's economy should have reached the take-off point, after which it was expected to move forward under its own momentum.

The Three-Year Plan

Guinea's first (three-year) plan was drawn up at the April 1960 Party congress in Kankan and inaugurated officially on

[20] For exports: GUINEXPORT (agricultural products); Prodex (other local products);

For imports and distribution: ENIMOB (furniture); SONATEX (textiles); Confection (ready-made clothing); EMATEC (electrical supplies); LIBRAPORT (books, stationery, office equipment); ONAH (hydrocarbons); Droguerie de Guinée (household goods); Quincaillerie de Guinée (hardware); TRANSMAT (motor vehicles, tires); ENTRAT (shipping, lighterage, handling); BATIPORT (construction); AGRIMA (fertilizer, farm supplies); DIVERMA (miscellaneous materials); ALIMAG (foodstuffs); PHARMAGUINÉE (pharmaceuticals, medical and surgical equipment).

July 1. Its objectives were an improvement in the population's living standards, economic decolonization, and Guinea's transformation into an up-to-date country.[21] The attainment of these goals required a modernization of the country's infrastructure (housing, roads, railroads, seaports, airports, school facilities, and hotels); a rapid increase in farm output by modernizing and mechanizing agriculture and a collective utilization of the equipment owned by the agricultural cooperative societies (of which there were 295 by April 1961), the creation of collective farm tracts and of centers of rural modernization (in effect, state farms); and finally, the launching of consumer-goods industries in conjunction with a price policy designed to raise living standards.

Of the investment funds required to carry out the foregoing plan, 23 billion FG were to come from abroad, 6 billion from the CGCE's profits, and 10 billion from an increase in agricultural exports. "Human investment," a form of voluntary labor promoted by the Party, was the means through which a number of projects for which no sizable investments had been scheduled were to be executed.[22]

Three main themes characterized Guinea's ideology of development. The first was to mold the economy by subordinating what would be economically profitable to what was politically desirable—in other words, to nip Guinean capitalism in the bud, lest it harm national unity and the goal of equitably distributing the country's resources. Secondly, to achieve self-

[21] N'Famara Kéita, "Le Plan triennal de la Guinée," *Afrique-Documents*, 55 (1961).

[22] The plan comprised 171 projects divided as follows: 56 for the infrastructure (100 kw. radio broadcasting station, printing plant, port, airports, hotels, railroads, roads); 62 for agricultural and industrial production; 53 for educational establishments (including a polytechnic institute for 1,500 students) and for health and social affairs.

sufficiency by increasing production, which assumed that all creative and executive talents would be fully employed for that purpose, and that the output would be of such quality as to reduce dependence on foreign aid as quickly as possible. The final leitmotiv was to promote group participation in the drafting and execution of projects. However, this attempt to devise and discuss activities at the various Party levels gave few positive results. Too many disparate proposals and too few qualified experts were the major handicaps to systematic and coherent planning.

At the outset, the three-year plan may have satisfied the ambitions of the country's leaders, but it bore within itself the seeds of failure. These consisted of an oversimplification of the measures needed to resolve Guinea's economic problems; misapprehensions about the human capital available to carry out the plan, including the lack of enough trained and competent personnel and an overestimation of Guineans' zeal and capacity for work; and the failure to provide the country with an adequate infrastructure to begin with. Often it was because they neglected to assign priorities and to respect a timetable for the execution of projects that the agricultural and industrial enterprises encountered so many difficulties in their operations. To set up a cannery without products to can, a textile factory that lacked cotton supplies, a cigarette factory without sufficient locally grown tobacco, and to develop agriculturally a forest region that had no roads and trucks to carry its output and lacked the trading goods that could have served as an incentive to the peasantry—all these were gambles taken by utopian idealists and ignoramuses.

The number of haphazard activities grew in proportion to the availability of foreign aid and easy loans. They were undertaken without determining how to get maximum returns for minimal production costs, and those who wasted available funds were not punished. That no more consideration was given to economic feasibility than to the actual costs of production[23] can be accurately deduced from the following tabulation, derived from the report of Saifoulaye Diallo, Minister of State, to the Congrès National de la Révolution (CNR), April 16, 1964:

Expenditure (millions of FG)

Unit	Estimated	Actual
P. Lumumba Printing Press	700	1,226
Water supply and dependencies	2,100	2,552
Conakry airport runway	690	2,126
Equipment for regional public works	0	1,226
Maritime shipping	500	1,446
Kobaya Brick Factory	600	892

Public works were undertaken without regard for planning, each government service jealously and selfishly striving to get the largest allocation of funds, and individual enterprises as well as the national economy ran deficits. The result was widespread disorder and a consequent reduction in investment funds for production (from the budget allotment of 47.6 per cent to 29 per cent) and for the social services (from 15.9 per cent to 13 per cent). Its corollary was a rise in operating expenditures (57.4 per cent instead of the anticipated 36.4 per cent in the administration and in transportation) and, even worse, disastrous returns from the state enterprises.

Within three months of the plan's official completion, the state enterprises had turned over to the planning budget no more than 4 billion FG, whereas they should have contributed 5.3 billion FG from profits that had been expected to amount

---

[23] The considerable sums wasted cannot be assessed. The budget of the plan rose from 39 to 43 billion FG and then to 46 billion, of which more than 80 per cent came from foreign sources.

to 7 billion FG. It should also be noted that the loans made by the national bank to the state trading and industrial companies totaled 30 billion FG instead of the 10 billion allotted for that purpose. Dishonesty and careless management eroded the plan's funds, even if one concedes that 80 per cent of its projects were carried out. This writer might well be accused of painting too black a picture of Guinea's chaotic planning were it not for the criticisms voiced by the Minister of State, Saifoulaye Diallo, at the CNR on April 16, 1964.[24]

To carry out its plan, Guinea had also counted heavily on "human investment"—that is, collective voluntary labor. To be sure, it had been a highly successful venture in 1959–1960, when the enthusiasm engendered by independence was at its peak. In those years, improvements were made in secondary roads serving the villages, town streets were cleaned up and repaired to the accompaniment of joyful songs, and schools, dispensaries, and Party assembly halls were also built. However, very few workers devoted themselves to collective farming, improvements in plantations, and a fight against soil erosion that might have increased production. Within four years of independence, the early zeal for "human investment" had been completely dissipated. In terms of money, the most favorable evaluation of such activities between 1959 and 1963 would total 3 billion FG. Guinea's more far-sighted leaders deplored the squandering of an immense amount of labor and good will on poorly conceived undertakings, some of which involved the destruction of capital. Such waste was particularly grievous where schools and dispensaries were built without teachers and nurses to staff them.

---

[24] Sékou Touré, *Plan septennal, 1964–1971* (Conakry: Imprimerie Nationale, 1967), pp. 60–72.

Reforms in the Land Regime and in Rural Development

In the first years after independence, great hopes had been placed in making rural society more dynamic. To that end, the land system was revised and collective farms and agricultural productive cooperatives were created. If one were to evaluate the results of all the ensuing measures and experiments, high marks would be given to the land regime but low grades to the cooperative societies.[25]

By a series of decrees, that of October 20, 1959, being the most important, all the land in Guinea became public domain. Nevertheless, this take-over by the state was not tantamount to nationalization. Through the first of these regulations, the state regained control of the plantations, market gardens, and lodgings that had been abandoned by European officials and technicians and by one-fifth of the French planters in the general exodus that occurred toward the end of 1958. However, the land that had been so vacated was distributed to those wanting to develop or build on it, and these recipients were often the Party cadres. Those laying claim to a piece of land under customary law could confirm their title to it by registration. The aim of that provision was to prevent speculators from reaping profits from the land, as well as the possible formation of big estates. Beginning with the decree (No. 242) of October 20, 1959, the sale and lease of plots of land were regulated. Landowners who sold, mortgaged, or gave away their property without permission from the lands service (Service des Domaines) of the public works ministry were liable to the cancellation or confiscation of their titles.

An even more drastic law was promulgated in 1961. Prop-

[25] Claude Rivière, "Dynamique des systèmes fonciers et inégalités sociales: Le cas guinéen," *Cahiers internationaux de sociologie*, 54, (1973), 61–94.

erty owners who had let their land remain unproductive for more than three years were now required by the state to develop it for a period of at least six months. Real property not improved through cultivation or by the construction of a house would revert to the state. By laying down regulations for settling land disputes, this decree prevented high-placed chiefs from attempting to appropriate property by invoking their former status. However, this law did not apply to those who enjoyed usufruct rights on huge family domains. It aimed to foster the collective utilization of pasture land that was often nonarable, such as the Bowé area in northwestern Fouta Djalon, but there was considerable flexibility in interpreting the law.

In granting land to those who cultivated and needed it, the state was pursuing two objectives. It aimed first to give an incentive for agricultural labor, and second, to encourage the stabilization of landless peasants who had become seasonal migrants. Still another government aim was to eliminate unjustified claims to land: those receiving grants of arable land did not thereby acquire permanent rights to it. If an owner died without bequeathing his property, abandoned it, or failed to develop it, such land became state property. Thereafter the elected representative of the region in which the land was situated had charge of it. In practice, this very often gave preferential treatment to the chairman of the local Party Committee or his close relatives.

To consolidate the socialistic basis of the peasant economy, Guinea's lawmakers were not satisfied with simply declaring land to be state property. They also sought to set up communal cooperative institutions, including farming at the village level, as the first step toward collectivization. In this respect, the law was doubly innovative. First, because in traditional society land was indivisible only if it was owned by the joint family.

Second, Guinean villagers did not own herds or equipment in common. The mutual aid initially provided by the age groups for the benefit of their elders preserved the right of an individual or a family to enjoy the products of their collective toil on the land allotted to them by the community.

Had these experiments not failed, it would be pointless to dwell on them at length. The government came to realize that wherever collective farms had been set up between 1961 and 1964 they were more poorly maintained and gave poorer yields than did family-owned land. Furthermore, the area collectively farmed was very limited. As the best land was monopolized by farming families, the collectively cultivated fields were those with the poorest soil.[26] In part the meagerness of the yields from collective farming could be attributed to soil deficiencies, but these could not wholly account for the experiment's failure and for the peasants' lack of maintenance and scant enthusiasm. Indeed, the experiment in collective farming suffered from its association with forced labor. This was a legacy from the past, when villagers had had to produce millet to feed Samori's mounted warriors (the *sofa*) and later cultivate a field for the benefit of the canton chief, and finally were forced to grow rice during World War II.

As for the Coopératives Agricoles de Production (CAP), their membership fell from 60,000 in 1962 to 34,413 in 1964, so that at most they included only about 4 per cent of the active farming population. In 1964, the total area under CAP cultivation was 2,200 ha., or one-fourth of the area farmed by the 559 CAP in 1962. These cooperatives had to contend with geographical, ecological, economic, technical, and human obstacles. They failed for many reasons, of which the most

[26] *Rapports 1962 et 1963 de l'inspecteur général de l'agriculture,* Archives du Ministère de l'Agriculture, Conakry.

frequent was poor management. Other causes were the failure of the responsible political and administrative authorities to provide the aid they had promised, their imposition on the population by force, or their deflection from the purpose for which they had originally been founded.[27] Sékou Touré realized that in the region of Beyla, for example, the cooperatives' managing committees, on pain of being deprived of provisions, were pressured by Party leaders determined to win first place in the competition for so-called human investment. He also admitted in several National Congresses of the Revolution that the cooperative producing societies had become cooperatives of a different type. Inasmuch as the Party leaders were not accountable to the managing committees, composed for the most part of illiterate members, they were able to utilize the funds, machinery, seed, and other equipment of the Centers of Rural Modernization and to sell the societies' output for their own benefit.[28] For easily understandable reasons, other than discretion, there are no official statistics for those societies. Nevertheless, a clue to the situation is provided by the decline, over a five-year period, in exports of the cooperatives' two main products, as disclosed by the National Statistics Office:

	Exports (tons)		
Commodity	1960	1962	1965
Bananas	55,000	44,000	37,000
Coffee	14,000	8,000	7,000

Guinea's ineffectual agricultural policy, foundering trade, money-losing national industrial enterprises, and defective

[27] Henri de Decker, *Nation et développement communautaire en Guinée et au Sénégal* (Paris: Mouton, 1968), p. 171 *et seq.*
[28] Sékou Touré, *Plan septennal,* pp. 260–66.

planning are only symptoms of a deeper disorder—the inflationary situation. Its dimensions can be grasped by noting the increase in the quantity of money in circulation between the end of 1960 and June 1965—a rise from 14 billion FG to 37 billion. Over the same period, bank deposits grew from 5.1 to 37 billion FG, and bank loans from 10 to 46 billion. However, the basic cause of the inflation itself was the country's unhealthy finances. As of September 1967, Guinea's foreign debt stood at 344 million dollars (86 billion FG)—in other words, it was four times as great as the state's annual revenues.[29]

Guinea's indebtedness increased its dependence on the outside world. This became more and more obvious to those who think in financial terms and who take into account the source of and the returns on funds, and the need to repay the cost of building the small industries of which Guinea is proud. By the end of 1964, the state enterprises on which the government had founded its hopes for economic development had contributed no more than 2 per cent to the national revenues. And in 1968 they were operating, on the average, at only one-fourth of their productive capacity.

Guinea ranks very high among those African countries which have received aid from foreign sources. Between 1962 and 1965, such aid totaled 270 million dollars, or an annual average of 40 million dollars (which works out to 16 dollars per capita of the population). Of this sum, 120 million dollars came from the Eastern European bloc. It was used in part to build such more or less productive projects under the three-

---

[29] Sources for 1960–65: Jean Suret-Canale, *La République de Guinée* (Paris: Editions Sociales, 1970), p. 214; for 1967: Alain Cournanel, "Planification et investissements privés en République de Guinée" (Paris, unpublished doctoral thesis, University of Paris, 1968), (mimeo.).

year plan as the stadium, the polytechnic institute, the Hotel Camayenne, and the airport runway. In this way, Guinea became heavily burdened by debt. Between 1966 and 1972, it was committed to repay about 8 million dollars a year to China and the Eastern bloc, although an agreement made in 1967 gave Guinea a reprieve. The 80 million dollars which Guinea owed to the Western bloc was also due for repayment in annual installments of 7 to 8 million dollars. By this time, the profits Guinea received from the Fria company—the goose that laid its golden eggs—had been mortgaged, and the cost of that company's infrastructure had risen to three times more than the original estimate. In brief, Guinea's economy cannot be described as self-generating or self-sufficient, let alone dynamic.

To resolve these problems Guinea had two choices. A massive increase in production was unrealistic, given the lack of incentive other than revolutionary oratory. The alternative was a drastic devaluation of its currency, which would please the well-to-do but create hardship for the mass of the population and also have no beneficial effect on an economy only slightly oriented abroad. Because Guinea had not achieved economic independence, its political sovereignty could not be other than vulnerable. The story of Guinea's successive plots shows how pervasive was this feeling of insecurity.

CHAPTER 4

The Perennial Plot

Accounts of *coups d'état* or plots are regular features of the news from African nations. Although, as of 1976, Sékou Touré is dean of the functioning heads of sub-Saharan states with respect to the duration of his rule, his regime has been beset by many internal conflicts. A number of these have been dealt with by what has become a ritual of announcing genuine or fictitious plots. Even if the interpretation of these plots against the Touré regime does not lead to a theory explaining them, it should at least show that to grasp the structure of these crises the high points in Guinea's political life must be followed in the order in which they occurred, and the explanation of the forces behind them must be sought in the long-term sequence of sociohistorical events.

As in many newly independent African states, the main conflicts stem from a double contradiction. The first is between the tendency of modern forces to unite in centers of comparatively independent power and the ambition of the ruling elite to control as many of those forces as possible. A second contradiction pits the use of national resources for the general improvement of the economy against their use to reward supporters of the existing power structure.

These contradictions explain to some extent the driving forces in Guinean society. A group has acquired power by being provided with all the services needed to attain it. Yet none of those services has been given free of charge. If the ruling group fails to recompense its servitors to their satisfaction, it risks alienating them. The chronicle of the most outstanding successes registered by the Touré regime seems to substantiate the interpretation that they were the result of an exchange of gifts or payoffs:

(1) The intellectuals, notably primary-school teachers, have been the purveyors of the PDG's ideology to the mass of the population and to its youth. If they had not been accorded a fair share of the posts assigned in the years following the *loi-cadre* and especially after independence (1957–1961), there was the risk that they would react unfavorably.

(2) Secretly, the merchants had promoted the rise of the PDG with funds and the loan of their trucks. As was shown by their resentment against the CGCI and the economicopolitical changes of November 8, 1964, they detached themselves from the PDG after its nationalization of the wholesale trade and regulation of retail business had threatened to paralyze private commerce.

(3) The peasants and wage earners formed the base of the party which sought to defend their interests. But the PDG, through its defective economic system, the shortage of consumer goods, and its failure to improve living standards, provoked a typical peasant reaction. The peasants refused to increase their output for export and to support the Party politically, and they left the country in large numbers.

(4) As soon as Guinea became independent, commissioned officers generously offered their services to the new state. But because the government's policy satisfied neither their hopes of promotion nor the desire for order inherent in the military ideology, the officers withdrew their support of the regime.

(5) Former civil servants of the colonial administration, who had quickly rallied to the PDG only to be disappointed in

their hopes for higher salaries which would enable them to keep pace with, or ahead of, the rising cost of living, either detached themselves from the regime or utilized the system solely for their personal advantage.

All basic contradictions must sooner or later break out into open conflicts. In the history of Guinea's nation-building, the times of major tension between the ruling elite and the groups opposed to them are clearly marked. These are the periods when Sékou Touré relied mainly upon pseudo plots as a pretext for ridding himself of his opponents.

An objective analysis of the causes of these plots indicates that, as a whole, they should not be attributed —as Touré has usually done for tactical reasons—to the covetousness of imperialism or to the subversive ambitions of the local valets of neocolonialism. To be sure, in most cases, except those of 1960 and 1970, it is difficult to know whether a *coup d'état* was actually attempted. Nor can any one determine what were the real aims of those who, supposedly hatching a plot, received support from outside the country, or exactly who, among those accused, were real plotters or were simply opposed to the regime but not to the point of ousting the head of state. In any case, the much-publicized trials and series of imprisonments that have marked Guinea's political evolution make clear what group was the main target, although no one group was exclusively purged, nor was any single element of a social class.

Without underestimating the value of a very precise historical analysis, one can safely disregard the circumstances surrounding the alleged plots that were merely catalysts and not the basic causes of dissensions. Moreover, in Africa, wherever there exists an illegal opposition within the single party, or simply party members eager to replace those in power, it is comparatively easy to discern a plot. As to why plots are discovered just at a certain moment, there are several answers. Sometimes there is a genuine attempt by the regime's opponents to resort to action. At other times, the government feels that it must revive fervor by proclaiming that the fatherland is in danger. The necessity for such reaffirmation derives from the permanent existence of a latent opposition to the regime, which can be displayed only by strikes and demonstrations that would be treated as political movements injurious to the security of the state. Even if the African population had an organization and an ideological leadership opposed to the PDG doctrine, the physical force represented by the militia, the police, and the army would prevent malcontents from taking action. Sékou Touré fears that the elite are becoming bourgeois far more than he fears opposition from the population, which can be suppressed.

The antigovernment "plots" that recur at crucial intervals can be viewed as historical-sociological sequences in the unrolling film of Guinea's political life: their interest lies in their context, and their efficacy depends on the moment when they occurred—that is, in the scenario and its implications. Each plot corresponds to political, economic, or social circumstances particularly difficult for the regime. Arrests always take place at just the right time to fend off demands, if not to counter protests created by the shortage of supplies or crises of a fundamentally political character. Thus the plot serves as a counterirritant, a diversionary tactic, and a means to circumvent economic and political difficulties. It is also a weapon employed chiefly to cut the Gordian knot of the government's rash policy in a manner favorable to the regime. In any case, it serves to intimidate the masses when the usual methods of so doing prove ineffective. At the same time, it functions as a preventive weapon useful in physically eliminating real or imaginary

The Perennial Plot

adversaries of the regime, who are invariably accused by the government of aiming to overthrow the head of state. The scenario seems to be always the same. During an interminable speech, the president announces that thanks to the Party's vigilance an "imperialist maneuver designed to overthrow the legal revolutionary government of the Republic of Guinea" has been discovered in the nick of time. Immediately, government agents, long practiced in the various techniques of preventive repression, move in everywhere to arrest by night men and women well known for their political nonconformism. It is at this moment that a selected group of the president's faithful companions set themselves up as a revolutionary tribunal. Its members carry out their own inquiries, conduct lightning interrogations, and pass sentences that are usually severe and in any case cannot be appealed. The accused is given no chance to defend himself. As a prisoner, he is kept on a starvation diet for a week and forbidden to communicate with his relatives, who have no idea what has happened to him or where he is incarcerated.

The foregoing description of the "plot" phenomenon is inadequate to provide an understanding of the impulses motivating the antigovernment reactions, the origin of the tensions behind an explosive situation, and the way in which the forces opposed to the regime pyramid. For this we need a more exhaustive and long-range explanation.

The Dynamics of Interelite Conflict

Our thesis is that Guinean society is corrupted from within by the incessant restlessness of the elite who are in the process of becoming middle class. The forces underlying the country's evolution are nipped in the bud whenever the amount of activity they unleash threatens to topple, sooner or later, the pedestal on which the leader of the regime has been placed. The analysis of these plots seems to bring us back to the dynamics of the social strata. A plot can be understood in terms of a barrier to the upward mobility of a segment of the elite who were trying to become bourgeois. This segment was composed of conservatives who belonged to the preindependence elite at the time of the plot perpetrated by "reactionary, feudal and decadent forces" (April 1960); it was made up of intellectuals who had been deprived of their share of jobs and who were infiltrating youth groups in order to orient their activities in a syndicalist and Marxist direction (November 1961); of merchants who, having acquired economic power by illicit trading deals, were trying to stabilize their position by taking over the key posts in the Party (November 1964) or by creating a counterparty (June 1965); of cadres of the state enterprises— BATIPORT, AGRIMA, ALIMAG, GUINEXPORT— who were living off public funds and wringing a livelihood from the nation (May 1967); and of military officers and high-ranking civil servants who were tired of a chaotic regime and its successive economic failures (March 1969, November 1970, and February 1971).

What is striking about the first so-called reactionary antigovernment plot is the imbalance between the meagerness of the deeds and the publicity given them. It has been interpreted as a kind of resurgence of the liberal spirit that prevailed among the favored social classes during the colonial period. This opposition arose in reaction to the following antiliberal measures taken by Sékou Touré during his first years in power:

(1) Suppression of the freedom of information by a decree (January 27, 1959) which forbade private individuals to own radio sets and another decree (March 1, 1959) forbidding publication of the French-controlled daily *Guinée-Matin*, thus making the Party daily, *Horoya*, the only authorized newspaper.

(2) Restriction of the right to exercise a profession: non-Guineans could no longer function as lawyers, law clerks, or notaries.

(3) The undermining of religious freedom by granting to the state (in September 1959) a monopoly of primary education, by suppressing Catholic youth movements, and by hindering any teaching of the catechism.

It was in the atmosphere created by such measures that the "plot" of April 1960 exploded. Three Frenchmen and one Swiss were accused of conspiring to assassinate the head of state. Sékou Touré declared in May, after the discovery of stores of firearms along the Guinea-Senegal frontier, that "the conspirators had been in correspondence with Gaullist organizations abroad." Even if the meeting attended by sixty thousand persons did not revitalize the masses as much as Touré had hoped, it at least succeeded in increasing their distrust of foreigners and in counteracting any liking they may have felt for the former colonial power. Among the hundred or so persons arrested, about ten died after being tortured, including the lawyer Ibrahima Diallo and the Imam of Coronthie, El Hadj Lamine Kaba.

In November 1961, a year and a half later, with the announced discovery of a new plot, the population was warned against the intellectuals who were threatening to overrun the regime from the left. On the twentieth of that month, before the High Court of Justice, the government prosecuted members of the teachers'-union executive committee, who were accused of subversive activities. Two sentences of ten years' imprisonment (Koumandian Kéita, Ray Autra) and three of five years (Djibril Niane, Ibrahima Bah, Ibrahima Seck) were the penalty for "editing and circulating both inside and outside Guinea a deceitful memorandum representing a new counterrevolutionary attempt."

In fact, the intelligentsia, envious of the benefits that accrued to the politicians by virtue of their positions, wanted to move against the dictatorial turn taken by the regime and expressed its dissatisfaction with the government's ideological orientation for not being more communistic. Yet the memorandum sent to the government by the officers of the national teachers' union was restricted to professional demands—a salary increase and the continued grant of free lodging. However, these demands were only the forerunner of a strategy designed to utilize union action in order to promote the Marxist-oriented PAI. By delving more deeply into the plot, the government—which had already charged the accused with having collaborated with anti-Guineans in Dakar and Paris—discovered documents that also involved an Eastern European embassy. A few days later, it was learned that Daniel Solod, the Soviet ambassador, had been recalled by his government. Even before this happened, however, any urge the intellectuals may have felt to take action had been repressed, for the solidarity strike by students and professors was severely put down by the army and the militia on November 25. And even now, the remembrance of the numerous arrests and the closing down of secondary schools at that time still paralyzes many of the intellectuals who disagree with the regime.

Although a sharp blow had been struck at the leadership of the teaching corps, those who had been successful in the economic sphere tried to form an organization. At the Labé conference of December 1961, where the intellectuals' activities were again censured, the opposition of the small merchants and truckers to economic planning, to the closing of the Guinea-Senegal frontier, and to the monetary troubles arising from nationalization of the wholesale trade made itself felt. In September 1963, those same merchants were accused of illicit dealings in currency and merchandise. On November 8, 1964, a return to the system of state control over wholesale trade was ceremoniously instituted after promulgation of the *loi-cadre* creating such controls and the confiscation of ill-gotten gains. A stringent ruling eliminated large- and small-scale merchants and also appreciably reduced the number of those halfway between the two. Under this law, it became illegal to both engage in private trade and hold an executive political job. It was as a reaction to this measure that the PUNG was created under the leadership of Mamadou Touré, a cousin of Sékou Touré nicknamed "Petit." After being dismissed from the management of the state textile-import firm of SONATEX, Petit Touré branded the PDG as bankrupt, demanded a return to the free-enterprise system, and was so deluded as to draft the regulations for his new party. Such temerity quickly led to the uncovering in September 1965 of a plot by "important merchants collaborating with the Party's traitors and ingrates, and supported by French imperialism." Thereupon *all* Petit Touré's friends were imprisoned. This crushing of troublesome elements was followed by suppression of the incipient *bourgeoisie* made up of private traders, principally from Kankan. Demolished inside Guinea, the opposition of this group was evidenced outside the country by the formation of the Front National de Libération de la Guinée (FNLG). Now what some called the bureaucratic *bourgeoisie* of the PDG, which comprised all the leading politicians and the cadres of the public sector of the economy, was left wholly in control.

Thanks to its privileged position, the group consisting of the political elite was actually trying to become middle class through the accumulation of considerable wealth from sinecures and the embezzlement of public funds. Creation of a national currency in 1960 notably strengthened their economic position because they then gained control of the country's foreign exchange. The establishing of an import-license system served as a means for exerting pressure on the big merchants, who were thereby forced to knuckle under to the high-ranking civil servants, buy the latter's favors, and become dependent upon their clientele. The nationalization of properties abandoned by the former colonizers, the state's creation and control of industries, the division of investments according to the three-year development plan, and the state's assumption of control over the wholesale-distribution network provided the channels used by the political elite to infiltrate the economic circuits. Beginning in 1964, incontrovertible proof of this phenomenon was provided by the emergence of an administrative and political *bourgeoisie*—if one can judge from the following measures directed against it that were taken on November 8:

(1) The setting up of two commissions—one to regulate and control rents (by establishing rental rates) and the other to check on the property acquired by Party leaders since independence and to confiscate what had been illegally obtained.

(2) The prohibition of any activity by directors, managers, and officials of state enterprises or companies that involved remuneration.

(3) The sentencing to fifteen to twenty years in prison of those trafficking in currency and fraudulently importing or exporting merchandise.

(4) The removal from Party executive posts of any individuals sentenced for theft, embezzlement, or subversion.

(5) The requirement that administrators and heads of government services and state enterprises participate in Party activities under pain of dismissal.

At the same time, many leaders were reprimanded for their egoism, individualism, avarice, cheating, corruption, and lying.

The attack on the bureaucracy, however, was overshadowed in this instance by the measures directed against trade, and in fact the bureaucracy strengthened its position to the extent that it was charged with carrying out the above measures.

The next year, nevertheless, some former members of the national politburo began to be cited by name as targets. To eliminate them, it was necessary only to implicate them in the Petit Touré affair. Thus Bengali Camara and Jean Farégué Tounkara were arrested for "divisive tactics and regionalism," and Daouda Camara for "mismanagement of the Office de la Banane." Not yet daring to attack incumbent ministers, Sékou Touré decided after the January 1967 CNR to cut himself loose from the clique of Ismaël Touré, Saidou Conté whom he transferred from the Education Ministry to Justice, and Fodéba Kéita whom he transferred from the National Defense Ministry to that of Agriculture. Following the example of those ministers who tried to defend themselves by banding together, some regional governors joined forces that same year to prevent having any one of their number singled out for punishment as a scapegoat. Disillusioned as to the loyalty of his cabinet, the head of state tried throughout 1967 to prevent any coalition from being formed by his opponents. He therefore continued to transfer such high-ranking civil servants as Moussa Diakité from the Ministry of Finance to the post of governor of Nzérékoré, which was widely viewed as a demotion. On the other hand, such promotions as those of Karim Fofana to the Ministry of Public Works and of Mamouna Touré to the national politburo seemed to indicate a rejuvenation of the Party at a high level.

Some exemplary punishments were meted out to the heads of national enterprises whose iniquities were the most flagrant at the time when the financial scandals were brought to light on May 1, 1967—60 million francs had been embezzled at BATIPORT and undetermined sums at AGRIMA, ALIMAG, and GUINEXPORT. Yet the head of state alone had the right to make public statements on such matters. Thus when, as minister, Moriba Magassouba took it upon himself to publicize to the nation in the August 23, 24, and 25 issues of *Horoya,* the misdemeanors of some responsible administrators, he drew a rebuke from the leader, who knew all about them but preferred to remain silent because they showed a certain weakness in his regime. In September 1967, when the eighth PDG congress met, the verbal strategy had been worked out and the way found to dissociate the regime from any representatives displaying bourgeois tendencies. In the report on Sékou Touré's doctrine and policy, the existence of social classes and the class struggle were formally recognized: "The interests of the toiling masses require that the working class, the peasantry, and the progressive elements lead and control all the vital sectors of the life of the nation, and that the reactionary elements of the *bourgeoisie,* bureaucracy, and capitalism even on the national level should be removed from the functions of orientation, policy-making, and control."[1] And a general resolution was adopted declaring that "no person can be a state or Party leader at any level who exploits his fellow man directly or indirectly for his personal advantage in an industry or commercial enterprise or if his behavior and attitude violate revolutionary morality and austerity."[2]

Whereas Sékou Touré had been able to subject the intellectuals and traders to political controls, neither these declarations nor the arrests later carried out succeeded in stopping the drift of the bureaucratic elite toward the *bourgeoisie,* and he

[1] *Horoya,* Sept. 26, 1967.
[2] *Ibid.,* Oct. 3, 1967.

had to adjust himself to the facts of this situation. Moreover, it was clear that among the delegates to the congress, civil servants—398 of a total of 724—were in the majority. Furthermore, those who purported to represent the peasantry were none other than former government agents or still-functioning civil servants and traders, who had benefited handsomely by grants for the development of their properties with modern equipment and agricultural labor.

According to *Horoya,* September 29, 1967, "there has occurred a real rush to agriculture even by residents of the big towns, from which retired civil servants and merchants have gone to the country to clear the land and till the soil." Although guidelines for the reconversion to agriculture had been laid down in the *loi-cadre,* the measures dealing with civil servants had not been applied, as noted in resolutions by the Party federations.[3] Indeed, it was the *contrôleurs* themselves who should have been supervised. At the eighth congress, those most insistent on building up socialism, such as Diéli Bakar Kouyaté, were the very ones who did not hesitate to advance their own fortunes at the people's expense. After Kouyaté had been shifted from the post of manager of the railroads to that of heading the Entreprise Nationale d'Acconage et de Transit (ENTRAT), he was relieved of his duties on the grounds of incompetence and dishonesty, then later placed in charge of the GUINEXPORT. In short, events in 1967 showed the government's determination to stifle the embryonic bureaucratic *bourgeoisie.* They also indicated that the very structure of the regime, combined with shortages at the time, helped to aggravate the grave malady inside the Party. Simply to attack certain contaminated elements did not suffice to eliminate the causes of opposition to the regime and of the growth in in-

[3] *Ibid.,* Oct. 1, 1967.

equities. Thenceforth, in the evolution of Guinea, the politico-administrative elite carried too much weight because of their power of decision at the local level, their role in diagnosing situations, and the example set by their behavior. Consequently, their secret ambitions would be achieved, although these were contrary to the utopian ethical code advocated by the head of state.

For those unwilling to be satisfied with the crumbs available to them under the regime, the quickest way of removing the barriers to their socioeconomic rise is to seize power. And the army is the sole organized and efficient body possibly capable of overthrowing the regime. That Sékou Touré was not unaware of this was shown in 1965 when he split up the armed forces into three elements, and offered his analysis of the military coups that had taken place in Africa between 1963 and 1966. Profoundly disturbed by the fall of Mali's Modibo Kéita, he instituted in 1969 a political supervision of the officer corps by setting up a political committee in each barracks with the most active Party militant in charge. (Since that militant might be only a simple corporal, one can easily imagine the possible conflict in authority.) The history of the plots of 1969, 1970, and 1971 clearly shows the power struggle between the head of state and the military.

At the outset, the "plot" of February 1969 appeared to be limited to the Labé region. At a social gathering there, two officers criticized the head of state. Sékou Touré, to whom his agents reported their remarks, ordered them immediately transferred to Conakry. During the helicopter flight they threw out their guard. Sékou Touré at once sent for the head of the camp (Cheikh Kéita), who was arrested the moment he reached Conakry to prevent the development of a solidarity movement among the military. The officers closest to him were also arrested—Colonel Kaman Diabi, deputy head of the general staff; Captains Tierno Diallo, the tank commander, and Abdoulaye Baldé, in charge of the paratroops; and Pierre Koïvogui, Sangban Kouyaté, and Oumar Alpha Diallo, members of the general staff. To describe the foregoing revolt as simply a local uprising would show too clearly the existence of internal foes operating on their own, so the government chose to announce it as a plot it had "discovered" that was "supported by imperialism" with the collusion of its "lackeys," Ivory Coast, Mali, and Senegal. To give substance to this thesis of a pro-French plot, a supposed liaison agent was found in the person of an employee of the foreign private company, Compagnie de Financement du Commerce Extérieur (COFICOMEX). He had formerly been on good terms with Fodéba Kéita and Karim Fofana, who were arrested and sentenced to death. The arrest also of Diawadou Barry (former deputy to the French National Assembly and minister under Sékou Touré), was part of a complex strategy that enabled the government to rid itself of a politically troublesome individual. During the following days, the government lost six of its members. In the whole country, more than a thousand persons were arrested.

The next year, Sékou Touré chose as his principal target the men who were organizing an army outside Guinea. On July 25, 1970, he denounced "the agitation stirred up by white mercenaries and Guinean traitors who are aiming to overthrow the revolutionary government in Guinea." He claimed that in Dakar former soldiers were being recruited at a cost of 10,000 CFA francs each, and that groups of twenty or so soldiers had been stationed along the frontier in Koundara, Nzérékoré, and Beyla. On July 28, the radio hinted that nine Guineans had been recruited to undergo a three-month training period in sabotage in Portuguese Guinea. Also broadcast were the names of eighteen Guineans described as "traveling salesmen of imperialism and subversion."

The Abortive Coup d'Etat of November 1970 and Later "Plots"

As a matter of fact, a coalition against the government had indeed been organized by some soldiers in Guinea-Bissau, who were furious with Sékou Touré for giving shelter and funds to their adversaries. At the end of the rainy season, on November 22, 1970, an invasion force disembarked at Conakry just at the time when Guinea least expected it to come. It consisted of soldiers from Guinea-Bissau, bent on freeing their imprisoned compatriots and on eliminating Amilcar Cabral, along with Guineans led by David Soumah and an army officer, who wanted to overthrow the Touré regime—for their own private reasons, no doubt. They seized control of two military camps but failed in their attempt to attack the president's palace and the radio station. This abortive *coup d'état* stirred up world opinion as well as Guinean opinion. Among its consequences were the closing of Guinea to newspapermen, the close supervision of, and directives issued to, Guinean delegates to the Organisation des Etats Riverains du Fleuve Sénégal (OERS) and the United Nations, and the charges that were made against Senegal.

Then, in February 1971, there followed the series of 159 convictions of which 91 were death sentences, the gruesome "carnival" of the hangings, and the expulsion of West Germany's diplomatic mission—all of which betrayed Sékou Touré's isolation and the hardening of opposition to his regime. The Revolutionary Court's verdict charged the accused indiscriminately with complicity in the November 22 attack, treason and espionage, harming the internal and external security of the state, large-scale contraband with the aim of undermining Guinea's economy, speculation in foreign exchange, incitement of the population to "dissolute debauchery," smuggling of ultramodern firearms into Guinea, consistently and ignobly attacking the honor and dignity of "our beloved leader," and organizing attempts to assassinate the head of state and his collaborators.

It was the collaboration of some military elements with the invaders that was surprising. Besides the death sentences passed on a number of the government's enemies whom it had decided to liquidate, similar sentences were dealt out to some forty military men—officers, NCOs, and simple soldiers—who had assumed specific tasks in the planned overthrow of the regime. In July 1971, the army, already paralyzed, was further deprived of its commanding officers by the death sentence passed on eight of them, including General Noumandian Kéita, chief of staff.

Beginning in 1971, repercussions from the recent abortive *coup d'état* and the real threat of an invasion compelled rethinking as to how the established authority could best be protected. During 1971—a year of agitation and of mobilization for national defense—the psychosis of aggression intensified progressively along with the mock trials that were being carried on. These were trials in which the accused were present only in the form of their photographs in *Horoya* and their voices recorded on tape. On August 3, a new charge was brought before the United Nations Security Council against Portugal, which Radio Conakry accused of planning grimly to attack Guinea again.

Since the November 1970 invasion, it appears that Sékou Touré had come to realize that his greatest danger of subversion came from the activities and armed elements of the *émigré* elite based abroad. Moreover, the opposition leaders had been forcibly eliminated inside Guinea, for those still at large were subject to police surveillance or had voluntarily gone into exile.

There is no doubt that the threat to Sékou Touré from outside the country was more verbal than real. Several factors support this contention: the exiled leaders' quarrels over the means of carrying out the *coup d'état* and the eventual division of the spoils; the spying done by Sékou Touré's agents; and the plotters' shortage of funds (in contrast to the sums collected during the past decade by the regime's passive opponents, who solicited money for the ostensible purpose of "bringing about a change" but who used it for their personal income). Yet it cannot be ruled out that among the alleged 1.5 million Guineans abroad there might be a certain number sufficiently dedicated and influential to enlist some foreign aid.

At different times during 1972 and 1973, Sékou Touré announced that the imperialists were planning new attacks against his country. In September 1972, he accused France of dispatching two ships to Bissau. On February 11, 1973, just when Guinea itself was retracting the foregoing allegation, Portuguese Guinea was said to be the base for a new aggression. Soon after, on March 2, Radio Conakry announced that a group of American veterans from Vietnam had embarked on the Spanish ship "Albatros" and were preparing to invade Guinea. Two days later it was asserted that "men dressed in military uniform and fraternizing with Guinean troops with a view to overthrowing the regime" had been arrested. (At the Samori and Alfa Yaya military camps, full attendance was required at morning roll call.) From a broadcast on March 31, it was learned that a clandestine movement aiming to restore freedom in Guinea—a movement which had the support of Dr. Roger Accar, former Minister of Health now a refugee in France, and which was kept informed of developments by two

The Perennial Plot

incumbent ministers—planned to overthrow the Guinean government in May. Responsibility for organizing this plot was laid at the doors of France and Ivory Coast, but then or later, and to varying degrees, Belgium, Great Britain, South Africa, Rhodesia, and Israel were charged with helping the conspirators.

In late August and early September 1973, when fifty-nine enemies "trained in Ivory Coast and infiltrated into Guinea" were arrested, they included one Alain Cantara. He was said to own a "special camera equipped with a silent pistol," with which he planned to kill the head of state on October 20. According to letters written by a so-called Patricia Morley, of American origin, October 23 had been fixed as the date. The hounded president was terrified, and in Abidjan, *Fraternité-Matin,* the Ivorian party's organ, poked fun at this "new outbreak of plotitis" diagnosing it as a "rash of the explosive diatribe." Again in October 1973, charges of aggressive projects were lodged with the Security Council, after Presidents Senghor and Houphouët-Boigny had been castigated as criminals and two members of the Guinean delegation to Washington and the United Nations had chosen freedom through escape rather than the status of submissive citizens in Guinea.

In this writer's view, an important turning point was reached on November 22, 1970, with respect to the manner in which accusations were made and in the determination shown by those planning subversive activities. Prior to 1970, the main fear of the Guinean authorities was the upsurge of forces inside the country, and especially an awareness of the formation of social classes. After the abortive invasion of Guinea, the external forces seemed preponderant. The regime feared no violent confrontation from its internal enemies, for they either had been liquidated or had been cowed by the hangings. On the other hand, the bitterness of the elite who had fled the country and were further frustrated by being uprooted and organized only into tiny groups made the threat to the regime much graver. Sékou Touré began to show signs of a persecution mania, although it was accompanied by moments of brilliant lucidity. After so many years of tension, 1974 seemed a serene period, despite the farfetched accusations made in January that a French submarine had violated Guinea's territorial waters, and despite cabinet reshuffles and transfers of diplomats.

The frequency with which plots are announced and the methods of intimidation used create an atmosphere of repression. While the masses live in fear of informers should they display too much indifference to politics, the president dreads his ultimate overthrow and indeed fears his closest collaborators. Sensitive to public opinion, he reduces it to silence by the use of police methods and by stifling any expression of its views through a party that might compete with the PDG. But the elite are also intimidated. They fear dictatorship by the Party secretary, the loss of their jobs (because they must profit by their great luck in sharing the power while it lasts), the exposure of their shady actions by politicians more honest or zealous than they, and in some cases the influence of religious and occult forces. (Before Kaman Diabi was arrested, Sékou Touré had already blocked any possible move on his part by making a solemn pact with Diabi's family and the population of his native town, Faranah, in a ceremony involving the sharing and eating of a cola nut.) The elite class is quite aware of the growing opposition it faces, but its will to resist its opponents is offset by the persistence of a traditional fatalism. Its current concern is to ward off fear by somehow viewing the present reality as idealized. Toppling the throne can be done only when the elite have the strength to do so, and now there is no united and effective force except that outside the regime.

CHAPTER 5

Balanced Neutralism

By rejecting the colonial system on September 28, 1958, Guinea committed itself to creating new forms of social organization. In breaking away from the colonial power, Guinea was forced to seek friends and aid elsewhere. Guinea's negative vote in the referendum proposed by General de Gaulle distinguished it from all the other African territories that were dependencies of France. The rich nations, attracted by Guinea's potential, its temerity, and its ideological idealism, showed an interest in the country so obsequious as to be sometimes wearisome.

For the Eastern bloc, eager to gain a foothold in Africa, Guinea, judging by the terminology it used, appeared to be the most receptive to Marxist teachings and to represent a possible bridgehead for communism. In the capitalist countries, potential investors coveted Guinea's undeveloped resources. International capitalism could foresee a prosperous future for a country so rich as Guinea in resources of bauxite, iron, diamonds, and gold, and in unharnessed hydroelectric power from the waterfalls in rivers flowing down from the Fouta Djalon. Furthermore, agriculture in Guinea looked exceptionally promising, through its enormous potential for growing many tropical crops, such as bananas, pineapples, citrus fruit, oil palms, and coffee. To those assets were added a sufficiently numerous population and a long seacoast, which reduced the cost, respectively, of production and of transport.

Compared with some other African countries, Guinea offered the advantage of having modern administrative, political, and social institutions, thanks to the influence of a party that had achieved a dominant position under the *loi-cadre*. It was so structured as to assure freedom—the principal aspiration of all colonized peoples—and to heal a continent infected by the virus of ethnocentricity and bloated chieftaincies. As the first French-speaking African country to affirm its capacity for self-government by freeing itself from the colonial strait jacket, Guinea further enhanced its prestige as a bright self-taught pupil by becoming both a symbol for oral tradition and for demonstrating how a country can be transformed from a subjugated land to a sovereign state in the comity of nations. Finally, the underdeveloped tropical states, deeply troubled by their isolation, sought in African unity the means of restoring their impoverished and divided economies.

Apart from this dream of African unity, which Guinea continued to cherish without necessarily seeking the means of making it a reality, Sékou Touré's ideology has made positive neutralism the guideline of his foreign policy. The policy of positive neutralism, inspired by the Afro-Asian conference at Bandung in 1955 and dear to Nkrumah, aims to attain the goal of preserving world peace through respect for the rights of man and for national sovereignty. Thus it can be defined as both an attitude of nonalignment in relation to the big Western and Eastern blocs and as one of resolute opposition to any attempt to force the acceptance of an ideology. Taking the equality of all states as its basis, the policy of positive neutralism requires refusing to follow the behests of the former colonial powers. In practice it has given birth to a truly African diplomacy that allows any and all relations to be formed or broken off between countries at will. But neutralism, if it is to be regarded as positive, also implies taking into account, and eventually taking a stand on, major international problems that relate to the guiding principles of peace and freedom and the rejection of domination. Those principles, in effect, imply condemnation of an atomic weaponry, the wars in Vietnam and Algeria, Biafra's secession, Portuguese colonialism, apartheid, and neocolonialism.

In part, the strategy used by a country to preserve its independence derives from this ideological choice. To some, such a strategy appears to be a sophisticated balancing act between the two blocs, between Moscow and Peking and between the different Western governments. To others, it reflects the dependency on both East and West. And to still others, it is a sequence of incomprehensible whims. Alternating concessions with firmness, zigzagging between a theoretical ideal and a pragmatic response to changing circumstances, sharing certain benefits or using them as bargaining counters—these are part and parcel of a policy of deliberate unpredictability in governmental action.

As if to escape the grasp of capitalism just at the time when American investments were expanding, Guinea in 1969 stepped up the exchange of official visits and agreements of many kinds with all the socialist countries. The conceding of the Boké bauxite deposits to the U.S. was matched by that of analogous deposits in Kindia to the U.S.S.R., which was anxious for repayment of the debts contracted by the Guineans in the course of more than ten years.

Sometimes the presence in Guinea of one country led to the temporary eviction of another. For example, in February 1971, West Germany was accused by Sékou Touré of having participated in a plot. Many observers related this to the establishment, six years earlier, of diplomatic relations with East

Germany, which until then had had only relations of trade and cooperation with Guinea. At Conakry some hinted that this about-face was the result of mutual accusations made by the two Germanys to the Guinean government, while others believed that Sékou Touré was availing himself of an alibi so as to avoid for the time being paying his debt to one of his biggest creditors.

In other cases, some tentative steps toward a rapprochement were seriously compromised or at least delayed by external or internal events that fanned the flames of old hostilities. For example, no sooner had Sékou Touré been reconciled with President Houphouët-Boigny in 1970 than he categorically denounced any dialogue between Ivory Coast and South Africa and stated that students who had been expelled from Abidjan University would be welcome in Conakry. And after congratulating Georges Pompidou on his election as president of the French Republic and establishing contacts with the Bank of France in 1969, Sékou Touré violently attacked the former colonial power's military intervention in Chad.

From time to time in its political evolution, Guinea has changed course: at first it favored the East, but beginning in 1961 it turned to the West. In 1965, it veered back again to the East, only to change again in September 1967, when it began to cooperate with both blocs. In certain cases such fluctuations could be traced to external forces, for obviously each bloc tried to check Guinea's drift to the opposing camp.

No matter what pressures were exerted, they were ineffective unless sanctioned by Sékou Touré. Indeed, all foreign-policy decisions were made by one man and not by a group, and were determined by the impulsiveness of the Guinean leader and by his desire to serve as an example of revolutionary behavior. His obsession with persecution, as much as his feeling of insecurity, caused him to develop a network of police informers, who could furnish him at any time with more or less trumped-up charges against some foreign power, charges of spying or of plotting an attack against the Guinean regime. Sékou Touré closed one eye to the cross-frontier smuggling but kept the other trained on the outlying regions of the country. He paid special attention to the seacoast, where ships were occasionally seized, but his vigilance proved unavailing there on November 22, 1970. He also kept under close observation those areas along the Senegal and Ivory Coast borders where troop movements took place and was alert to the restiveness in neighboring countries that had brought about the downfall of Nkrumah and Modibo Kéita.

If one considers the ideological, strategic, and psychological factors as a whole, Guinea's foreign policy is more comprehensible and in part explicable. But to grasp fully the nature of that policy, it must be viewed in its historical context and in relation to the internal evolution of Guinea—that is, in the light of the loyalty inspired by the regime on the one hand and of the economic situation on the other. One clue, in particular, indicates how Guinea's foreign policy was the extension of its domestic policy: each announcement of a "plot," prompted by worsening economic conditions and social unrest, has coincided with charges against an imperialist power. That power is accused of instigating or being involved in the plot, and if diplomatic relations have not already been severed they are immediately broken off.

Over and above these conflicts, their profound economic causes, in which internal and external problems are intertwined, must be comprehended. Take, for example, the cause-and-effect relationship among the following sets of facts: monetary independence—the shortage of merchandise, which would promote production so as to increase local purchasing power—the collapse of agriculture—the rise in the public debt, due notably to the clearing agreements with the U.S.S.R.— and Guinea's inability to meet its obligations on time. After recognizing the failure of the small processing industries financed and launched by a wide range of donors and investors; after endeavoring to survive by expedients such as American grants, and after trying to revive the population's flagging spirits by a Chinese-style cultural revolution, the solution finally attempted was the gamble on mining development. Because farming had declined disastrously, both for export and for domestic subsistence needs, its revival and reorganization would take too long and, moreover, offered no assurance of success. Each year, therefore, the government sought to revive the economy by raising capital in the easiest and least socialistic manner possible, and this was also the safest and least burdensome way, because it involved neither a gift nor a loan. That capital came from royalties on the ores that were produced.

Furthermore, mining by foreign companies was the surest guarantee to the countries making investments that they would remain in Guinea. In return, Guinea acquired most of its foreign exchange thanks to mining operations. Even in instances when diplomatic relations had been broken off, informal contacts could be maintained through the agency of companies established in Guinea, as was the case of Fria-Péchiney for France. In an economy where the wholesale trade and processing industries have been largely nationalized, mining activity paradoxically confirms the grip of large-scale international finance on the country. At the same time, it helps Guinea appreciably to balance its foreign trade, and perhaps in time it may enable the country to emerge from its economic tunnel. But the length of this tunnel is unknown because we lack data

Balanced Neutralism

on Guinea's current foreign trade—the real barometer of the economic and political development of the country. Without such a yardstick, we must simply study some of the most stable factors, as well as those that fluctuate most widely.

Viewed from the angle of motivation, two categories of attitude seem predominant. First, attitudes toward the rich nations of the East and West are determined mainly by economic considerations. However, the rejection of any commitment curtailing the exercise of national sovereignty, and the rupture of relations with a creditor when the debt falls due and becomes too flagrant (as with West Germany in 1971), can modify the policy of smiles and the welcoming hand which are the forerunners to soliciting funds. Second, attitudes toward Third World countries are generally inspired by ideological and political concepts—such as African unity, rejection of racism, struggle against Portuguese bastions of colonialism, extolling of revolutionary countries—and by psychological motivation. The latter could explain the personal ties of the Guinean head of state with the Osagyefo Kwame Nkrumah until his eclipse; with the one-time leader of the Arab world, Gamal Abdel Nasser; and with the nostalgic spokesman of an idealistic African tradition, Julius Nyerere. This is true also of the still lively resentments between Sékou Touré, who had only an elementary vocational education, and two other leaders of French-speaking Black Africa—Senghor, who had a distinguished university career, and Houphouët-Boigny, the president of the RDA, from which the Guinean president had seceded. Furthermore, in regard to Senegal and Ivory Coast, Guinea's relations are inevitably influenced by questions of political choice, of monetary zones, and of the protection offered to voluntary emigrants.

Perforce the Guinean head of state recognizes the reality of internal conflicts in Africa, and moreover he intensively contributes to them. But to evidence how little influence his policy has had on the course of African events, it suffices to list his main disillusionments, which began with the PDG's split from the RDA and then from the French Community. These are:

—Collapse of the Guinea-Ghana-Mali Union.

—Disintegration of the Casablanca group after it was unable to attain its goals.

—Failure of attempts, after the Monrovia summit conference, to create a free-trade zone between Ivory Coast, Liberia, Sierra Leone, and Guinea.

—Aspirations rather than achievements within the framework of the OAU, in particular the dream of an African bank in which Guinea's currency would be revalued upward.

—Disappointments and rebuffs in dealing with the Organisation de la Coopération Africaine et Malgache (OCAM) countries, and the strong terms used to denounce African *"francophonie."*

—Hesitations concerning the agreements between the countries bordering on the Senegal River.

The climate of the relations between Guinea and the African states (except for the so-called revolutionary governments, especially those of Mauritania and Tanzania) has been alternately stormy and clear. Following ruptures after some *coups d'état,* relations with them were resumed. This was the course followed with Houari Boumédienne of Algeria in 1966; with Dr. Kofi Busia of Ghana in 1969, three years after asylum had been offered to Nkrumah; and with Lieutenant Moussa Traoré, president of Mali, at the February 3, 1970, meeting of the OERS.

The Guinean president has no special liking for his English-speaking neighbors except when they agree to help him. Those who have done so were Gambia, which handed over political exiles to him in 1970, and Sierra Leone under Siaka Stevens. In June 1970, Sékou Touré unsuccessfully proposed to the latter a union for the purpose of getting rid of British influence and of lending their armed forces to each other in case of need.

As for his French-speaking neighbors in the former French West Africa, their relations with Guinea were influenced by Franco-Guinean relations, which were a mixed bag of personal relationships, principles, and concerns.

The events of late 1958 and early 1959 have often been recounted. The clash between de Gaulle and Touré, and the latter's refusal to accept the former as a father figure explain in part the developments that followed—the search for other fraternal ties, the haste and radicalism of the decisions taken, the attempt to decolonize completely, and the breaking of currency ties that marked the onset of Guinea's stagnation. Yet it must be admitted that the status of Franco-Guinean relations did not vitally alter the character of Guinea's regime. Between 1962 and 1965, the steady improvement in relations between the French and Guinean governments served chiefly to lay bare the points at issue between them. These concerned mainly financial transactions, such as the payment into French banks of Guinean veterans' pensions against which Guinea drew especially for transferring the savings of experts and technicians and for the purchase of French matériel and products—motor vehicles for the administration, school books, etc. Since the rupture of November 1965, there has been a vacuum, marked from the Guinean side by discreet overtures voiced at the eighth PDG congress in 1967, by frequent denunciations of French imperialism, and, for about six months in 1970, by a semireconciliation whose purpose was to settle in Guinea's favor a financial dispute involving some 10 billion CFA francs at the time (the veterans' pensions that had been frozen since 1965).

While General de Gaulle continued in power, relations between Guinea and France could never be wholly serene. Yet the presence of Guinea's delegation at de Gaulle's funeral suggested either a silent admiration for the famous French statesman on the part of Sékou Touré and the Guinean people or the wish to normalize relations, as had already been tacitly implied by the congratulations sent to Georges Pompidou upon his election as president of the French Republic. In Paris, the establishment of an *entente cordiale* with Guinea is seen as difficult, so long as its leaders cultivate close friendships with the Socialist[1] and Communist members of the French government's opposition. Since the surprise attack of November 22, 1970, which was followed by charges against France and the sentencing of French nationals to death, Franco-Guinean relations have remained tense, although the election of Valéry Giscard d'Estaing as president of France led to a change of attitude beginning in 1974. On the other hand, the Soviet Union, China, and the United States have preserved their favored position.

Despite temporary disagreements, Sékou Touré, who was awarded the Lenin Peace Prize, has for many years received considerable technical and economic aid from the East for widely diverse sectors of Guinea's economy. Aid supplied by the U.S.S.R. includes mineral prospecting, agricultural improvements, national education, administrative advisers, and the building of certain public works and processing industries,

[1] On Nov. 22, 1972, François Mitterrand, leader of the French left, was at Conakry at the very time that President Pompidou was completing his third official tour of the French Community states.

including canneries, sawmills, a stadium, a polytechnic institute, and a radio station. Eastern European countries have contributed a furniture factory, fisheries, urbanization assistance, a printing press, a brick factory, a generating plant, and other facilities. The Chinese have built a combined cigarette and match factory, a hydroelectric dam and plant, a people's assembly hall, cinemas, a tea plantation and factory, and other structures.

Nevertheless, counterbalancing the above-mentioned aid, the following assistance from Western countries should be cited: Great Britain sponsored the building of a textile complex; Italy, a fruit-juice factory and oil mill; the German Federal Republic, an abattoir, a tannery, and a shoe factory; and the United States, investments through the Harvey Aluminum Company at Boké, and a plant for making household utensils (American aid projects are fewer but more valuable).

Yet relations with countries of the Eastern bloc continue to be favored, as shown by the frequency of visits by their ministers, civil servants, labor leaders, and party militants; the exchange of youth delegations; the sending of students (200 in 1959, 860 in 1962, 450 in 1965); the sojourns of experts; the organizing of trade exhibitions; the free distribution of news by Tass and the New China News Agency; and work carried out under the three-year and seven-year plans.

The ties binding Guinea to the socialist countries are also apparent in the sphere of technical and financial aid. Clearing agreements have dealt with the loans received from those countries, which were for long terms and at low interest rates (the first loans from China were interest-free). The grant of loans on a government-to-government basis, thus by-passing the underwriter companies, the speed with which decisions were made, and the low cost of technical assistance have all been advantageous to Guinea. However, they are accompanied by certain drawbacks, such as an overrapid turnover of technical-aid personnel (who risk losing their Marxist zeal in Guinea), the psychological gap between the Soviets and the Guineans, the mediocre quality of the merchandise supplied, and an insufficient knowledge of the French language among many teachers. Given technical and even administrative responsibilities, the Eastern-bloc counselors, whose advice has certainly influenced prominent politicians, have nevertheless not been decisive factors in Guinean policy-making. The differences in viewpoint among the Guinean leaders and Sékou Touré's determination to pursue a neutralist course have lessened the possibility that communist propaganda by means of the press and cinema might exert an undue influence. Thanks to this control mechanism, the massive aid received from the Eastern bloc has never, in the eyes of the Guineans, constituted a danger to their independence. The fact that the chief of state, in 1973, entrusted the piloting of Guinea's planes and its navy to Soviet technicians even conferred a certain security.

Although psychological influences are hard to evaluate, it must be admitted that the U.S.S.R. and China have the ear of those leaders of the national politburo who have undergone Marxist training. The population, on the other hand, does not relish the moralistic zeal of the Chinese workers, the discourtesy (in the light of familiar French standards of behavior) of the proselytizers of development from the backward Eastern-bloc region, nor the Cuban bodyguards of Sékou Touré. But the Yugoslavs, Rumanians, Hungarians, and East Germans are oblivious to these Guinean reactions and do not suffer from any lack of self-confidence.

Chinese and Soviet nationals coexist peaceably in Guinea, though without contacts aside from the exchange of formalities at official receptions. The same could be said of relations of those nationals with the Cubans and Vietnamese. Conakry's policy of balancing Moscow against Peking, like its policy between East and West, is sometimes slightly askew. This imbalance can be seen by studying the list of trade agreements, cultural delegations, and diplomats' visits. Such an analysis discloses clearly that the main thrust of Guinea's policy does not reflect the slavish imitation of some foreign model. Chinese technical aid (involving between 2,500 and 4,000 persons in 1972, depending on the source of the figures and on the scale of the work being done) for rice-culture improvement, industrial construction, and agricultural experiments and education, is appreciated by the rulers of Guinea pretty much at its true worth for its scope, efficiency, and discretion. At the same time, however, steps are taken to keep watch on the judicious mixture of economic advertising and political propaganda (pamphlets and sayings of Mao, and Chinese films) that are the stock in trade of China's strategy in Africa.

Despite its liking for "scientific socialism," is Guinea likely to become, in the words of Alpha Condé, "the valet of American imperialism?" To find the answer, one must study the American tactics.

Immediately after Guinea's independence, the Republican administration of President Dwight D. Eisenhower adopted a temporizing policy toward that country, even though a United States mission[2] had defined the precise objectives of access to raw materials, of trade development, and of American moral leadership. Following the Democratic Party's victory in 1960, a change of policy took place under President John Kennedy. In February 1961, only a month after Sékou Touré had ac-

[2] See Alpha Condé, *Guinée: L'Albanie de l'Afrique ou néo-colonie américaine?* (Paris: Git-le-Coeur, 1972), p. 173.

cused the United States of involvement in the assassination of Patrice Lumumba, William Attwood was sent to Guinea as ambassador.[3] He became the first architect of the operation of "salvaging" Guinea, by gradually persuading the Guinean president to join the International Monetary Fund, facilitate and guarantee private investments, and accept the services of the Peace Corps, at least in the fields of education and health. The visit to Guinea by Peace Corps director R. Sargent Shriver preceded a visit by Sékou Touré in October 1962 to the White House. One writer commented that "Touré was won over by Kennedy's charm, which is a mixture of attentiveness, humor, frankness and grace."[4] Economic and aid agreements concerning the delivery of food products, the sending of rice-farming specialists, the electrification of nineteen towns, and so on had already been signed. In the ensuing years, the United States Agency for International Development (AID) program expanded.

It has often been stressed that American aid, with Sékou Touré's consent, was aimed at offsetting the influence of the Eastern-bloc countries. Moreover, it is quite possible that sometimes certain stands taken by the Guineans sharpened the rivalry between Paris and Washington. It can be said with some certainty that the waves of pro- and anti-Americanism in Guinea were colored by the factor of aluminum.

In 1964, the American ascendancy began to be more marked. Olin Mathieson Chemical Corp. became a majority stockholder (48 per cent) in Fria; Harvey Aluminum Co. re-

[3] William Attwood, *The Red and the Blacks* (New York: Harper & Row, 1967). This is the ambassador's own account of his mission at Conakry.

[4] John Henry Morrow, *First American Ambassador to Guinea* (New Brunswick, N.J.: Rutgers University Press, 1968), p. 106.

vived its plan to extract ores at Tamara and Boké; the Mack Truck Company built an assembly plant for trucks and utility vehicles; and Pan American Airways and American oil companies were more firmly established in the country, inasmuch as the former reorganized Air-Guinée and Texaco planned to build a refinery. United States AID to some degree controlled the money in circulation, through the assistance provided by its "food for peace" program and by the financing of some industrial installations. In 1965, the United States became Guinea's ranking supplier and its second most important customer. The next year, the detention of a Guinean delegation at Accra, as described below, gave Sékou Touré a pretext to find out how far he could go in detaching himself from this "imperialism." But the hopes of finding another Fria near Boké created new links of self-interest between the United States and Guinea (through Aluminium Ltd. of Canada, Aluminum Company of America, and Harvey Aluminum Company). Consequently, no amount of anti-imperialistic fulminations could thenceforth be strong enough to destroy the web of mutual obligations, political complicity, and common interests.

The Chronological Periods

With these general clues in mind, it may now be easier to interpret the meaning of the periodic fluctuations in Guinea's foreign policy.

Initial Hopes and Trends (September 28, 1958–February 1960)

The conditions under which Guinea obtained its independence in September 1958, aside from the temporary restrictions caused by the suspension of FIDES aid, led to a rapid deterioration in its relations with the French government. As a result of the negative vote in the referendum, France sternly ordered the immediate withdrawal of all technical, administrative, military, and economic aid. Right after the September referendum, five hundred French civil servants were repatriated. The unambiguous offers of association made by Sékou Touré to the former Metropole in the months following Guinea's secession did not suffice to heal the breach. On the contrary, they intensified the former administrators' itch for revenge. Three preliminary draft agreements between Guinea and France were signed in January 1959, and several French missions were sent to Conakry in June and August of that year. But relations could scarcely improve in the atmosphere created by Guinea's radio campaign against the Algerian war and the Community and by the haste with which Guinea solicited—and received in March 1959—from the Eastern bloc in general and Czechoslovakia in particular the arms which it had vainly sought to obtain from Eisenhower. Moreover, Guinea resented the implicit decision of the French trading companies, banks, and planters to cause financial difficulties for the country that they foresaw they must abandon, and it therefore decided to create the Guinean franc.

This quarrel with the former Metropole necessitated an adjustment of Guinea's economic and political relations with the rest of the world. During the first years of independence, the bilateral agreements concluded by Guinea reflected quite clearly the orientation of the new state—as indicated in Table 2—despite a very few omissions, which do not invalidate the over-all picture.

After the rupture that followed the referendum, so many misunderstandings, grievances, and petty rancors accumulated that Guinea, now divorced without alimony, had to turn to the Eastern bloc. It did so in order to counteract the French blockade and France's persuasion of its allies to delay their recogni-

Table 2. Summary of Guinea's foreign agreements, 1958–1963[5]

Signatories	Number of agreements					
	1958	1959	1960	1961	1962	1963 (3 months)	Total
Western-bloc states	—	8	5	3	11	6	33
Eastern-bloc states	8	14	26	27	19	14	108
African states	1	1	5	9	17	1	34
Other	—	—	2	—	5	—	7

tion of the new state. By October, however, such official recognition was granted out of fear that Guinea would join the rival camp, and then missions and delegations began to arrive.[6] The United States moved to match the gift shipment of five thousand tons of rice from China. Neutralism and nonalignment were emphasized during Sékou Touré's trip in October and November 1959 to the United States, Great Britain, West Germany, the U.S.S.R., and Czechoslovakia. The aim of the trip was to procure material advantages for Guinea, as well as to assert the personality of that country and, even more, that of its president.

Nevertheless, the 1960–1961 agreements show clearly that the scales were tipping in favor of Eastern Europe. This was due in part to the pressure successfully exerted by the advisers who had come to place their services at the disposal of the new state and in part to Guinea's eagerness to demonstrate its independence of Western imperialism.

[5] Based on Bernard Charles, "La Guinée," in André Mabileau and Jean Meyriat, *Décolonisation et régimes politiques en Afrique noire* (Paris: A. Colin, 1967), pp. 159–204.

[6] Fernand Gigon, *Guinée: Etat-pilote* (Paris: Plon, 1959), pp. 67–75.

Revolutionary Radicalism (March 1960–November 1961)

The withdrawal of the Guinean franc from the franc zone on March 1, 1960, because of the prevailing economic and financial situation in Guinea, was followed the next month by the discovery of a "plot" implicating three Frenchmen and one Swiss. (Forewarned of Sékou Touré's intention to arrest them, two of the men took flight in a small plane stolen from the Aero Club.) These developments aggravated the deterioration in relations between Guinea and France, which was accused of wanting to reconquer its former colony.

At the same time that Guinea's policy became violently anti-French and was moving toward the nationalization of French properties, its links with the Eastern bloc were strengthened. This is clearly shown by the country's financial balance sheet during its early years. From November 1958 to October 1963, Guinea received the equivalent of about 44 billion Guinean francs, or three times the total of its annual budget at that time. Of those 44 billion, 18 came from the U.S.S.R., 6 from China, and 7 from Eastern European countries. Early in 1959, Ghana had loaned Guinea the sterling equivalent of 6 billion Guinean francs. As for the United States, its massive aid in dollars (a total of 39 million dollars as of October 1963) did not begin until 1962. Bernard Charles wrote, with discernment, that

it is not easy to assess the importance and the repercussions of the aid given. In some cases the grant and the acceptance of aid seem to have been principally political gestures, with little attention being paid to their utilization. By the end of 1962, a considerable portion of the credits, such as those from China and Egypt, had not yet been put to use, or to only a slight degree. Another deduction that can be made is that Guinea, unlike some other states such as Egypt, seems not to have played the East against the West during the 1959–1962 period, or in any case not to have earned dividends therefrom. The 3 billion Guinean francs received from West Germany did not match what Guinea had received from the Eastern-bloc countries.[7]

Profiting by the welcome accorded its financial and technical assistance, the Eastern countries believed that it was necessary at the same time to help the Guineans with their thinking. The speeches of Khrushchev, Mao's *Thoughts*, the works of Lenin, and Marxist economic treatises arrived in such profusion and were so widely distributed among the young people that the toxic effects of this intensive propaganda were denounced by Sékou Touré himself. On December 14, 1961, he actually reproached the U.S.S.R. for continuing to disseminate its propaganda widely (despite the warning issued to the foreign embassies the preceding month) without official Guinean approval, and also for making direct contacts with Guinean youth. These accusations of ideological infiltration, which coincided with the teachers' plot, the recall of Ambassador Daniel Solod, and the icy reception given to Anastas Mikoyan, the Soviet foreign minister, contrasted with the warmth of the meeting between Sékou Touré and Heinrich Lübke, president of the German Federal Republic. Mikoyan realized that the wind was now blowing from a different direction when Sékou Touré told him that "revolutions can be neither imported nor exported."

The Ebbing of the Revolutionary Wave
(November 1961–November 1965)

By warning the overzealous supporters of communism in this way, eight months after he had closed down the American cultural center, Sékou Touré reaffirmed his insistence on neu-

[7] Charles, *op. cit.*, p. 197.

tralism and independence so as to preserve at all costs his freedom of maneuver. His refusal to accept a dependent role or binding ties, and his determination to remain master in his own house, seemed to be Sékou Touré's guiding principles in the event that the United States should decide that the time was opportune to support the Guinean economy with abundant and multiform aid. Such aid was to include tractors, motor vehicles, fishing nets, textiles, fuel, asphalt, the restoration of rice fields, projects to increase the production of paddy, corn, and palm oil, the electrification of towns, the improvement of civil aviation, the training of middle-category technical cadres, scholarships to American educational institutions, a language institute, and a visit by the hospital ship "Hope." In 1963, American aid in the form of agricultural surpluses alone (rice, flour, powdered milk, soybean oil, etc.) amounted to 3 million dollars. In June 1964, a new Guinean-American agreement, involving 8.57 million dollars' worth of foodstuffs, was signed. This raised the total American imports under the Food-for-Peace program through the fiscal year, October 1, 1964–September 30, 1965, to 14 million dollars, or 3.5 billion Guinean francs. The government of the Republic of Guinea paid this sum into a special fund, most of which was available for financing its plan for economic development.[8]

All the Western and pro-Western nations benefited by the change in Guinea's policy that had taken place since November 1961, because it had been marked by a definite rapprochement between Guinea and the other former French West African partners, notably Ivory Coast and Senegal. In the meetings between Sékou Touré and Houphouët-Boigny at Bouaké (April 1964) and at Nzérékoré (early 1965), it looked as if the former solidarity of the RDA might be revived. As for

[8] *Marchés tropicaux et méditerranéens,* No. 972 (June 27, 1964).

Senegal, President Senghor, in his encounters with Sékou Touré at Labé and Dalaba during January 1965, tried to reach an understanding on fourteen agreements for economic cooperation in the framework provided by the new Inter-State Committee for Improvement of the Senegal River (which became the OERS).

Similarly, beginning with the agreement of May 22, 1963, between France and Guinea, the annual conferences (especially the one May 1965) of the mixed Franco-Guinean commission took place in a serene atmosphere. Each side saw to it that the annual debt payments were made regularly, and the French companies which had stayed on in Guinea resumed their transfers of capital abroad. These companies had not given up hope of another improvement in relations, even if the *loi-cadre* of November 1964 was creating some temporary economic difficulties, particularly in trade. Their optimism disregarded the possibility that a new "plot" would be uncovered and another marked change in policy would occur.[9]

The Regime's Isolation (November 1965–September 1967)

From the time it was founded in February 1965, the OCAM, which represented the group of moderate African states, was deemed by Sékou Touré to be incompatible with the new Organization of African Unity (OAU). *"Francophonie"* and the activities of the OCAM and its leaders (especially Maurice Yaméogo) were regularly and vehemently denounced in colorful language by the irascible Guinean leader. This was the state of affairs at the time Conakry claimed to

---

[9] To follow these events in detail, especially those that occurred between 1963 and 1966, read the eight excellent studies on Guinea by Victor DuBois, *American Universities Field Staff Reports*, West Africa Series, 8, Nos. 7–9 (1965), and 9, Nos. 1–5 (1966).

have discovered a new plot, which allegedly was hatched by the Ivory Coast leaders and their friends, including two French ministers, Pierre Jacquinot and Raymond Triboulet. Diplomatic relations with France were broken off forthwith, and eight years later Italy was still representing French interests in Guinea.

The country's isolation became more pronounced in 1966. In February, with the overthrow of Nkrumah, Guinea lost one of its strongest ideological allies (while shortly afterward also assuming responsibility for him). In March, Touré accused the Ivory Coast president of organizing subversive activities in Guinea and mobilized his troops along the Ivorian frontier, as much by way of a challenge as to restore the Osagyefo to power in Accra. As a result, there was a brief clash in the Beyla region, along with a continued war of insults. On the Ivorian side, Guinean refugees were encouraged to organize a National Front for the Liberation of Guinea. Pressure was exerted by Ivory Coast on the great powers, especially the United States and the German Federal Republic, to make them stop providing assistance to Guinea.

In September, the Ivorian appeal seemed to elicit a response. It was then learned that—among the general steps taken, it must be admitted, with regard to all the African countries—American aid (AID and Food-for-Peace) to Guinea during that fiscal year (October 1, 1966–September 30, 1967) would be reduced by three-fourths—that is, from 24.6 million dollars in 1965–1966 to 6.8 million. (Nevertheless, total American aid to Guinea during the years 1962 to 1967 amounted to 105 million dollars.) At the end of October, American-Guinean relations were further strained. The Guinean delegation on its way to attend the OAU congress at Addis Ababa was arrested at Accra, and because the delegates were traveling in a Pan American Airways plane, the United States was held responsible for the incident. Mass protest meetings and denunciations of imperialism, the placing under house arrest of 408 American nationals, the expulsion of the Peace Corps, and the cancellation of Pan American's operating permit followed. The sequence of such immediate reprisals showed no signs of abating until Emperor Haile Selassie and Presidents Nasser and Tubman intervened. After a few days, the Ghanaian military officers, who had tried simply to deflate the Nkrumah myth in their own country and to divert popular attention from the economic difficulties at home, agreed to free their captives. When contacts with Washington were resumed at the end of the year, it was not forgotten that in a radio broadcast on November 8 Sékou Touré had told the United States to "give us no more aid because Guinea needs only its freedom and dignity." Among the big Western powers, only the German Federal Republic still maintained good relations with Conakry at the end of 1966.

Deprived of funds from the West, Guinea cultivated relations with the Eastern-bloc countries and multiplied its trade agreements, as well as its cultural and diplomatic exchanges with them. At the same time, it vainly tried to bring revolutionary African states together in a new group reminiscent of the Casablanca bloc.

Throughout 1967, there was a hardening of Guinea's attitude toward Senegal and Ivory Coast, which were friendly to France. Evidences of this were the suspension of Guinea's participation in the inter-State committee for the Senegal River (January), Senegal's closing of its embassy at Conakry for "reasons of economy" (March), and the seizure of an Ivorian trawler, the "Ker Isper," which had been forced into Guinean territorial waters by rough seas. Early in July, Ivory Coast retaliated by arresting certain Guinean passengers of a plane that had been forced by mechanical difficulties to land at Abidjan airport. The arrested passengers were members of the Guinean delegation to the United Nations, headed by Louis Lansana Béavogui, Guinea's foreign minister. Abidjan let it be known that they would be held until Guinea freed the crew of the "Ker Isper" as well as François Kamano, manager of the Ivory Coast Family Allowance Fund, who had been imprisoned at Conakry since the "plot" of October 1965. The Guinean government promptly placed the blame for the arrests on the United Nations and even more on KLM, whose plane had carried Béavogui and his colleagues, and the KLM staff in Conakry were put under house arrest. Air Afrique and UTA, fearing reprisals, suspended their flights to Conakry, as Pan American had done the previous year. As a result, Guinea found itself extremely isolated.

The Resumption of Cooperation
(September 1967–November 1970)

Public opinion in Guinea was critically affected by the misunderstandings with France in 1965, the United States in 1966, and Ivory Coast and Senegal in 1967. It was also perturbed by the difficulties with the U.S.S.R., which began in 1967 to ration its gasoline shipments to Guinea because of Guinea's failure to repay its debts, as well as by the spectacular defection of Nabi Youla, the Guinean ambassador to West Germany, in 1967. Disagreement in the country about future policy grew apace during the rainy season of 1967. Some maintained that the revolution should be given a fresh start on a new basis and with new men, whereas others favored closer ties with neighboring countries, as well as France, the Soviet Union, and the United States, so as to obtain from them the material aid that China was unable to supply. The pro-Chinese supporters of the former policy, who controlled Radio Conakry and the daily, *Horoya,* seemed to have the upper hand at the end of August. The inauguration of the People's Hall (Maison du Peuple) in September, when the eighth PDG congress would be in session, should, they believed, mark the revolution's revival and demonstrate China's favored position as an ally. But the more realistic group, including Saifoulaye Diallo, Ismaël Touré, and Fodéba Kéita, and also Moriba Magassouba, whose writings had clearly diagnosed what was wrong with Guinea's economy, eventually won out. It became obvious that their view had prevailed when, on September 5, Radio Conakry announced the imminent departure for the United States of a delegation led by Ismaël Touré, and of a delegation to the U.S.S.R. headed by Saifoulaye Diallo. Delegates to the PDG Congress favored the resumption of relations with Guinea's neighbors in Africa, and even with France and Great Britain.

Under the influence of President Moktar Ould Daddah of Mauritania and of Dakar's offers to renew the dialogue, the inter-State committee for the Senegal River was reactivated at Bamako on November 6, 1967. Furthermore, at the end of September, the liberation of the Ivorians held prisoners in Guinea, as well as mediation by the Liberian president, served to draw Guinea and Ivory Coast together again. France and Great Britain, for their part, remained cautious. Past experience and the fear of an adverse reaction among pro-Chinese Guineans were factors weighed by the French foreign-affairs ministry in the discreet contacts that were being renewed with Guinea. The U.S.S.R., now cheek by jowl with the Americans and West Germans in Conakry, would not be displeased by the return of a French diplomatic mission to Guinea. As for the

British Foreign Office, it seemed anxious to avoid vexing the new government of Ghana.

Economic considerations were mainly responsible for this turnabout at the end of 1967, which persisted in 1968. National revenues were estimated at 180 billion Guinean francs in 1967, whereas the official public debt stood at 240 billion. In other words, the need for additional capital once again justified a policy of cooperation, more with Europe and the United States than with the socialist countries. The following chronology shows the pro-Western trend of events during 1968:

—Resumption of diplomatic relations with Great Britain in February.

—Renewal of the military-aid agreement with the German Federal Republic in April.

—The welcome extended to the American Assistant Secretary of State for African Affairs in Conakry in June.

—Successful negotiation in September of a loan of about 100 million dollars for the mining of bauxite at Boké. Of this total, 75 million was supplied by Kuhn, Loeb and Co. and 25 million by the Export-Import Bank of the United States, on condition that equipment material would be purchased in the United States.

—Business trips by Ismaël Touré to Italy, West Germany, and Belgium in October.

—Fria's decision to increase its production capacity from 500,000 to 700,000 tons between 1968 and 1970, if it could obtain 10 million dollars in investments. Mining operations were to be expanded in the ensuing years.

Nevertheless, Franco-Guinean relations did not move off dead center. France, although remaining silent, could not lightly dismiss the rapprochement between Guinea and Senegal. That was given concrete form in March 1968 by the commitment to economic regional integration implicit in the transformation of the Inter-State Committee of the Senegal River into the Organization of the Senegal River Border States (OERS). Guinea's reconciliation with Ivory Coast, on the other hand, was viewed by France with smiling approval. However, the exchange of visits by soccer teams in 1970 was not enough to erase the remembrance of past disagreements, which could easily revive should the Ivorian president make the slightest move of which the president of Guinea disapproved.

From 1968 to 1971, the socialist countries continued to maintain close and varied relations with Guinea. In 1968, two military and commercial delegations were exchanged with China on a capital-to-capital basis, the first series in April and May and the second in August and September. Concurrently, exchanges with the U.S.S.R., consisting of a cultural mission (at Conakry in March), a trade mission (at Moscow in April), and a military and parliamentary mission (at Moscow in August), served to keep that country in the foreground. The Communist world's ideological influence continued to be predominant in 1969. That year was marked by the sending of two Guinean missions to Peking, in February and October, and by the visit to Conakry of a Soviet delegation, which signed an agreement to mine bauxite at Kindia. Soviet investment in that enterprise amounted to 83 million rubles, or 22 billion Guinean francs. But there was apparently no further talk of the Konkouré dam, which had been proposed to the U.S.S.R. in 1965. Obviously that project would arouse no Soviet enthusiasm if it were to serve, as originally intended, to supply energy to the American-Guinean plant at Boké.

Throughout most of 1970, Guinea's political life was

marked by calm on the domestic front and by continued cooperation with the East and with the West. Until November, there was general approval of the attempts to renew ties with Guinea's French-speaking neighbors on the one hand and with France on the other.

The Period of Panic (November 1970–February 1972)

Suddenly, once again, a chain of revolutionary events was set in motion—this time by a surprise landing during the night of November 22 by soldiers from Guinea-Bissau and Guinean émigrés. The former aimed to free the prisoners held by the PAIGC, based in Conakry, and the latter's objectives was to seize power. This attempt was foiled by disagreements among those in charge of the raid and by the protection given to the Guinean president by his armed militiamen. Those accused of participation in the raid were tried in two stages. The trial of the "mercenaries" ended in late January with the sentencing of 159 persons, including some West German nationals; the related trial of the so-called Fifth Column lasted from August to December and dealt with those charged with lack of zeal in defending the regime. For almost a year after the danger was over, the overexcited Guinean public was kept mobilized so that it could pass judgment on the accused and carry out some of the death sentences by hanging. The delegations sent to Conakry by the United Nations learned only what the president wanted to tell them, and the staff of the German Federal embassy was expelled because a former SS officer was accused of having been in collusion with the invaders by correspondence. Violent verbal attacks were made against France and Portugal, some of whose nationals were involved in the trials, and also against Senegal, which was accused of sheltering Guinean exiles. The OERS broke up and Sierra Leone signed a mutual-defense treaty with Guinea. But the sympathy of the whole world for Guinea at the time of the attack was considerably weakened when it learned of the bloodthirsty rage of the Guinean president and his use of fake trials and summary executions as a means of getting rid of his opponents. Nevertheless, on February 2, 1972, 34 of those accused were released.

The Return to Calm (February 1972–June 1976)

With the restoration of a degree of calm in 1972, the government was eager to put a rapid end to its isolation. At first it tried to normalize relations with the neighboring countries. A meeting with President Senghor took place in Monrovia under the aegis of the OAU on May 29, and one with the Ivorian president in Faranah on July 24. (Later these relations were broken off because of new Guinean charges on September 7, 1973, "against those traitors and puppets, Houphouët and Senghor.") Nkrumah's body was returned to Ghana, and diplomatic missions were exchanged with that country in March 1973. This was followed by a vigorous and wide-ranging diplomatic offensive. The presidents of Cameroun, Algeria, and Zaïre honored Sékou Touré by visits in 1972, and they concluded agreements with him. Of these, one of the most important was that with Zaïre, which provided for the processing of Guinea's bauxite in that country. Good relations already established with Liberia were further strengthened, as were those with Nigeria and Sudan, as a result of the visits to Conakry made by Generals Yakubu Gowon (March 1972) and Gaafar al-Nimeiry (August 1973).

Relations with the socialist countries and the United States continued to be important and fruitful. All of those countries are assured of liens on Guinea's mining economy, which serve as collateral for their loans to Guinea. Thus they are protected against any attempt to oust them from the country in the event of political upheavals there. Japanese, Yugoslav, Swiss, and Spanish companies have only business dealings with Guinea, for they want simply to acquire markets and raw materials (especially bauxite and iron ores).

A visit to Guinea by Nicolas Ceausescu, head of the Rumanian state, March 9–11, 1974, culminated in an important agreement concerning the processing on the spot of Boké's bauxite, an operation for which Rumania provided credits amounting to 80 million dollars.

The suddenly acquired power of the oil-producing countries prompted a not disinterested trip by the Guinean premier, Louis Lansana Béavogui, to Lebanon, Kuwait, Qatar, Abou Dhabi, Egypt, Syria, Iraq, Saudi Arabia, and Libya. But it is with Algeria, above all, that economic cooperation in the fields of health, electronic communications, meteorology, youth, sports, and the training of cadres is genuinely developing.

As for the new French government of Valéry Giscard d'Estaing, its desire to normalize relations was clearly shown by the sending to Guinea of the former minister André Bettencourt and then the visit of André Lewin, member of the French mission to the United Nations. In the final months of 1975, the points at issue were finally settled by negotiation. In exchange for liberating about twenty French nationals imprisoned in Guinea, the French government agreed to pay the pensions due to the Guinean veterans who had served in the French army. Jean Lecanuet, the French Minister of Justice, was given a hearty welcome at Conakry, where he was embraced by President Sékou Touré. And André Lewin, appointed ambassador to Guinea, arrived at his new post early in January 1976.

What is the future likely to hold for Guinea? No more than

common sense is needed to understand that the country, in the post-Touré period, will not turn to the Eastern bloc. To be sure, some Marxist intellectuals, unaware of Guinean realities, dream of a genuine socialism that Sékou Touré has never achieved. But the significant fact is that the population associates socialism with Sékou Touré, and that henceforth no one will be carried away by an oratory like his that has provided the background music for bitterness, fear, torture, and shortages. Among the Guinean elite there is scarcely a single family that has not had a brother, cousin, or friend who has suffered maltreatment by the militia, the wrath of a politically fanatical informer, imprisonment, or purges that recall the worst periods of Stalinism. Guinea's future leaders probably realize that America, albeit distrusting of Sékou Touré, has had its eye on Guinea's bauxite, while adroitly playing the role of dispenser of generous gifts. To the degree to which the influence of the Soviet Union and China is offset and the whims of Guinean rulers are moderated by tacit pressures, the presence of the United States in Guinea is not without its usefulness. As for France, the attitude of its government and public opinion toward Guinea and the rest of Africa since the referendum of 1958 precludes the eventuality of any attempt at reconquest. But it seems obvious that the regime runs the risk of extinction at the hands of the Guineans themselves who fled from the country and have endeavored to form an organization abroad. And it is not impossible that the military elements and the civilian population may find "understanding allies" in their teachers of former decades, in the friendships made during the 1950s, and in the relationships of the postindependence period. It will be up to Guinea to defend itself against predators at the crucial moment.

CHAPTER 6

National Resources and Individual Poverty

Benefiting by the enhanced prestige that resulted from the national unity created by the PDG, Guinea became the first country of Africa to adopt an economic policy of total decolonization, and to test the formula of state control over the commercial sector as a means of financing its first development plan. Within the framework of Sékou Touré's version of socialism, those steps met three fundamental needs: the acceleration of the formation of national capital, the stabilization of export revenues, and industrialization.

During the transition period from 1958 to 1961, when French interests in Guinea were radically affected, the aim was to reconcile the contradiction between an economic development based on the state's role and the socioeconomic habits inherited from the colonial structure. This coincided with the period in which politicians assumed control of the economy and small public works were undertaken amidst popular enthusiasm (called "human investment"). Subsequently, the arrival of foreign investors and the work they accomplished enabled the three-year plan to be carried out. In 1964, however, the difficulties encountered by all the state enterprises, the pessimistic reports submitted by experts, the waste of funds by a bureaucracy out of control, as well as negligence and theft, did not encourage the countries which had participated

National Resources and Individual Poverty 173

in those operations to persevere, unless they were committed by contracts made a few years earlier.

Consequently, the seven-year plan (1964–1971) could count on aid only from the United Nations, the United States, and the People's Republic of China. As mentioned in the preceding chapter, the U.S.S.R., for its part, had abandoned its project of building the Konkouré dam. Indeed, the lack of large-scale capital and of foresight has accentuated the trend toward economic drift.[1] That drift has been obvious in the partial paralysis of enterprises, the breakdown of the cooperative system, the stagnation of plantations and rice culture, and the embezzlement of public funds to the detriment of the accumulation of national capital and of productive activities.

We shall examine from different angles this economic drift under the seven-year plan,[2] as well as study the draft five-year plan and the investments in mining. Those investments launched a genuine economic recovery at the same time as they sacrificed some former socialistic goals.

Public Finances

The financial structure of the Guinean state comprises the Ministry of Finance, charged with executing the national budget, and a Ministry of Financial Control, created in March 1967 with a view to promoting economic recovery through

---

[1] Because enterprises have been installed where they would be most effective politically, their economic viability has often been undermined by the failure to take into account the dimensions of the market, transport costs, or the availability of sufficient amounts of raw materials.

[2] The author has in his possession unpublished statistics for the 1964–1972 period, which came from a confidential source in the office of the Presidency of the Republic of Guinea. Their accuracy has been confirmed by the documented information infrequently printed in *Horoya*, broadcast over the radio, or published in the *Revue RDA*.

Table 3. Public finances of Guinea, 1964–1973 (in millions of Guinean francs)

Budget headings	1964–1965	1965–1966	1966–1967	1967–1968	1968–1969	1969–1970	1970–1971	1971–1972	1972–1973
A. National budget Total expenditures	22,570	25,080	29,640	32,100	23,476	25,880	22,856	27,830	45,000
Revenues									
Tax receipts	15,340	15,860	15,930	16,600	17,276	17,580	17,356	18,430	18,500
Domestic loans	630	2,620	6,710	850	600	1,500	280	2,700	4,200
Foreign gifts	1,230	830	560	150	400	300	4,020	2,300	2,300
Foreign loans	5,370	5,770	6,440	6,650	5,200	6,500	1,200	4,400	20,000
B. Fiscal revenues	15,340	15,860	15,930	16,600	17,276	17,580	17,356	18,430	18,500
Direct taxes	2,640	3,150	3,350	3,500	3,260	3,490	3,520	3,610	3,700
Indirect taxes	6,460	6,700	6,700	6,700	6,800	6,990	7,170	7,260	7,530
Other fiscal taxes	1,480	1,410	1,070	1,230	1,410	1,640	1,270	1,480	1,520
Other nonfiscal taxes	4,760	3,600	4,740	5,100	5,806	5,460	5,396	6,080	5,750

C. Operating budget	12,530	14,680	15,270	15,500	16,600	17,150	17,260	17,900	18,200
Defense	2,590	3,190	3,430	3,500	3,630	3,720	6,480	7,210	7,470
Agriculture	110	110	120	120	105	110	90	120	130
Education	3,280	3,740	3,580	3,850	4,320	4,570	2,080	2,210	2,300
Public health	1,420	1,660	1,280	1,650	1,735	1,680	1,490	1,670	1,820
Miscellaneous	5,130	5,980	6,860	6,380	6,810	7,070	7,120	6,690	6,480
D. Investment budget	10,040	10,400	14,370	16,600	6,876	8,730	5,596	9,930	26,800
Agriculture	380	380	1,800	550	410	350	380	960	2,900
Education and housing	310	310	2,620	780	270	720	540	630	3,500
Public health	80	80	290	110	56	170	320	780	1,200
Transport and communications	4,420	4,420	5,290	6,320	1,460	2,680	1,990	3,190	7,600
Industry and energy	4,710	4,710	3,630	7,180	2,920	2,860	2,150	3,070	8,800
Miscellaneous	140	500	740	1,660	1,760	1,950	216	1,300	2,800

Note: Guinea's fiscal year runs from October 1 to September 30.
Source: *La Guinée libre*, No. 9 (Feb. 14, 1974).

strict supervision of the accounts of state enterprises, regional treasuries, and assets of individuals.[3] It also includes an Audit Office (Cour des Comptes), which audits the budget accounts (but without any real control over them), and a general treasury, which supervises the state's cash income and expenditures.

All these organizations have failed to prevent the mismanagement of public funds, colossal waste, and such disorder that Guinea changed its banknotes five times between 1960 and 1972. When, on October 2, 1972, the Guinean franc (FG) was replaced by the sily (worth 10 FG, and divided into 100 cowries), the amount of money in circulation totaled 38 billion FG, compared with 12,350 million at the time of the March 1963 reform.

A study of the national budget reveals some stagnation, not to say retrogression, in the economy, if the slight increase in the budget since 1964 is compared with the rate of world inflation. The spectacular increase in revenues for 1971–1972 was due simply to the 20 billion FG borrowed from external sources for mining investments. The table of public finances prompts the following brief comments:

(1) Under the heading of foreign donations the main entries are, first, the food surpluses given by the United States AID program, and second, the gifts in kind—rice, sugar, salt, and the like—furnished to the Guinean government by the People's Republic of China, which were sold to the population for the benefit of Guinea's treasury.

(2) The domestic loans take the form of official deductions from the funds of the state enterprises.

---

[3] This caused highly placed but insecure civil servants to denounce the minister, Ousmane Baldé, as a mercenary. In consequence, he was hanged in 1971.

(3) The meagerness of fiscal revenues is indicative of Guinea's poverty.

(4) Direct taxation consists of the head tax, whose rate is comparatively low. Furthermore, the mass exodus to Senegal, Ivory Coast, and France of nearly one-fifth of the population explains the slight growth in revenues from that source.

(5) Indirect taxes consist almost exclusively of customs duties. To offset the quantitative decline in exports and imports, customs duties have been increased, and their rates on certain items are exorbitant.

(6) Total operating expenditures remain fairly small. In this respect, it is noteworthy that the salaries of Guinea's civil servants are the lowest of any West African country.

(7) Whereas agriculture and the social services are neglected, the largest share of the budget is reserved for the forces repressing illegal activities, as can be seen from the amounts granted to the departments of defense and education. (The latter incorporates the people's militias and the youth movements—Jeunesse de la Révolution Démocratique Africaine (JRDA) and Pioneers.)

(8) The investment budget shown in the table reflects, until 1971, the seven-year plan, more than 60 per cent of whose projects could not be realized because of lack of money. The official figures shown are forecasts, which were not necessarily fulfilled in practice.

(9) Operating expenditures are roughly equal to the country's real revenue—that is to say, to its fiscal intake. One might therefore well ask what becomes of, and what is produced by, the foreign loans destined for development of the country. Elsewhere it can be seen that the foreign-trade balance is in deficit and that Guinea's foreign debt is large. As of June

1965, that debt totaled 204 million dollars;[4] in 1970, it was 328.7 million dollars; and in 1972, 410.8 million dollars.[5]

Foreign Trade

Foreign-trade statistics for the years 1964–1972 (those for earlier years were published in a *Bulletin Spécial de Statistiques*, the only such report issued by Conakry) show a relatively stable volume. That stability is more apparent than real,

Table 4. Guinea's foreign trade in selected years, 1964–1972 (in millions of Guinean francs)

	1964	1968	1972
Exports, F.O.B.	15,470	13,080	12,870
Imports, C.I.F.	12,380	15,150	17,520
Trade balance	+3,090	−2,070	−4,650
Exports	15,470	13,080	12,870
Alumina	7,250	8,400	9,100
Iron ore	1,380	—	—
Pineapples	—	750	980
Bananas	1,200	750	320
Coffee	900	1,480	550
Palm kernels	730	740	740
Imports	12,380	15,150	17,520
Textiles and clothing	1,520	500	1,520
Machinery and metals	1,850	740	2,150
Rice	980	740	2,450
Petroleum products	250	740	2,700

Source: *La Guinée libre,* No. 10 (Feb. 21, 1974).

for to compare the trade of those years would require taking into account several factors, such as currency devaluations and

[4] An OECD document. Details about this debt on a country-by-country basis were published in *Guinée: Perspectives nouvelles,* No. 30 (Aug. 1973), p. 13.

[5] *La Guinée libre,* No. 8 (Feb. 7, 1974).

Table 5. Trade with Guinea's major suppliers and customers (in millions of Guinean francs)

	1964	1965	1966	1967	1968	1969	1970	1971	1972
Imports from—	12,380	13,080	17,280	16,530	15,150	13,080	17,280	19,760	17,520
United States	2,890	4,630	2,960	1,730	1,480	830	900	1,280	1,450
Common Market	4,070	5,280	5,280	4,700	3,700	3,800	3,850	4,500	4,700
United Kingdom	1,360	910	670	250	490	180	70	150	120
Yugoslavia	70	350	760	550	680	590	650	530	610
Cameroun	20	440	370	210	250	250	300	350	340
U.S.S.R.	530	610	950	1,330	1,620	1,740	2,180	3,800	3,950
China	40	70	220	480	740	830	1,450	1,720	1,800
Other Eastern European countries	1,275	720	770	840	880	750	1,170	1,350	840
Exports to—	15,470	13,330	14,320	12,600	13,080	14,070	13,330	12,350	12,870
United States	1,780	2,960	2,960	1,240	1,480	530	1,200	470	350
Common Market	2,910	2,120	2,150	2,250	2,880	3,170	2,950	2,760	2,810
United Kingdom	520	520	520	110	10				
Yugoslavia	220	570	860	350	210	240	270	180	110
Cameroun	1,410	1,480	540	740	1,240	1,240	1,150	1,270	1,120
U.S.S.R.	310	530	620	950	980	1,110	1,130	1,470	1,420
China	20	40	90	250	410	520	510	650	590
Other Eastern European countries	890	670	850	780	750	620	940	1,050	1,060
Norway	1,750	1,880	1,980	2,470	2,470	2,520	2,320	2,120	2,070
Spain	540	890	1,110	420	220	170	50	20	20

Source: *La Guinée libre*, No. 10 (Feb. 21, 1974).

price increases. Although certain elements indispensable for such a comparison are unavailable, Julien Condé, an Organization for Economic Cooperation and Development (OECD) statistical expert, believes that in taking the year 1961 for the base index of 100, that of 1970 would fall between 40 and 50.[6] If world inflation is taken into consideration, it must be recognized that the volume of Guinea's trade is declining year by year and that the deficit in its trade balance is growing dangerously. This becomes even more apparent if the following adjustments are applied to the trade figures:

(1) The alumina exports of the international Fria Company (now called FRIGUIA) bring in to the Guinean government only what that government is entitled to as a shareholder. Moreover, the Fria Company imports petroleum products for its own use.

(2) The Compagnie de Financement du Commerce Extérieur (COFICOMEX), with headquarters in Geneva, has a twenty-five-year exclusive concession (which began in 1967) for the production and exportation of pineapples by its subsidiary, the Société Industrielle des Fruits Africains (SIFRA). This concession enables COFICOMEX to collect the debt owed it by the Guinean government. The company also imports fertilizer for its plantations.

(3) Not all the items imported under the development plan are incorporated in these statistics, but the exports which supply the funds to pay for those imports are included.

Heading the list of exports is alumina, whose production rose from 480,000 tons in 1964 to 700,000 in 1972. Between 1964 and 1972, the share of alumina in the country's exports grew from 46.8 per cent to 70.7 per cent. Pineapples hold second rank. It is curious, to say the least, that together those two products of capitalistic companies operating in a self-styled

[6] *Ibid.*, No. 10 (Feb. 21, 1974).

socialist state account for nearly 80 per cent of its exports, and they are the only ones to have made normal and steady progress. All Guinea's other exports have steadily declined. Iron ore, gold, and diamonds no longer appear among its listed exports.

The two biggest mining companies created under the colonial regime (the Bauxites de Kassa in 1952 and the Fer du Kaloum in 1953) have closed down. The former ceased operations in November 1966, following its nationalization in 1962 and the exhaustion of its deposits. The latter firm disappeared at the end of December 1966 for the following reasons: competition in the world market from Swedish and Mauritanian iron ores, which were purer and cheaper as well as nearer to Europe; deterioration of equipment and installations; and deficits in its operation for the six preceding years.

Gold production in the Siguiri region during the colonial period, although not worthwhile on an industrial scale, was carried on by individual workers, with a record output of 4,750 kilograms in 1936 but only 187 kilograms by 1947. To prevent smuggling and speculation, a stop was put to production after 1950. Gold production fell victim to the gold exchange standard and above all to the discovery of diamonds, whose extraction was less onerous and better paid than gold panning. As a result, the latter became simply a secondary seasonal occupation for a few gold miners of the region until March 1, 1961, when it was formally forbidden throughout all of Guinea.

In the foreign-trade figures, it should be noted that diamonds no longer figure among the exports after 1965. The high-quality alluvion deposits in the southwest region of Kérouané were first mined in 1934 by Société Guinéenne d'Exploitation du Diamant (SOGUINEX), which was joined for this operation by the Société de Beyla in 1950. The combined output of the two companies came to 48,200 carats in 1960.

However, in November 1960, a decree forbade all individual diamond-mining operations. On March 1, 1961, the whole diamond industry was nationalized, and only the Entreprise Guinéenne d'Exploitation was authorized to continue diamond mining, with the aid of a team of Soviet specialists. In 1963, 52,280 carats were extracted,[7] and by the end of that year the diamond exchange, which held the monopoly of sales, was transferred from Kankan to Conakry. According to reporters of *La Guinée libre,* receipts for the deliveries made to the head of the Mines de Diamant de Kérouané (for example, the delivery of 52,000 carats in 1972) were regularly transferred to the office of the Presidency of the Republic: "Diamonds mined in Guinean soil are the personal property of the head of state. The sale of diamonds brings in 3 billion CFA francs a year on the average."[8]

In Table 4, under the heading of imports in 1972, it should be noted that if petroleum products are omitted, of which two-thirds are imported by the Fria Company as fuel for its thermoelectric plant, rice heads the list, whereas before independence Guinea exported rice. Machinery and metals represent a comparatively small part of total imports. The remaining items are consumer goods, of which some are acquired with funds allotted to economic projects under all the plans—a procedure detrimental to the nation's development. Moreover, when stocks run short, goods are imported in such a disorderly way that some articles are bought in large quantities or perishable goods go to waste because they have been poorly stored. For example, pens rust, food is spoiled, and cement is ruined by rainfall, as it was in 1965. Finally, there is speculation on the

[7] Confidential report submitted to the Guinean government by a team of Soviet geologists.

[8] *La Guinée libre,* No. 12 (Mar. 7, 1974).

resale of such goods when they become scarce in the local market.

Table 5, which lists Guinea's major trading partners, shows that commerce with the Western nations has obviously declined to the benefit of countries of the Eastern bloc. Thanks to their clearing arrangements, and their long- and medium-term loans, the latter countries have enabled Guinea to obtain manufactured goods in exchange for locally produced merchandise, and this phenomenon is more apparent in imports than in exports. The trade balance with the Eastern-bloc countries is in deficit, but it is favorable with those of the West (thanks to Fria's alumina and COFICOMEX's pineapples). Despite Sékou Touré's many pleas for African political and economic unity, Guinea's trade with other African countries remains almost nil. Trading with Cameroun is restricted to the Fria company, which ships some alumina to its plant at Edéa, where, by means of the electricity generated by the dam there, it is transformed into aluminum.

Mineral Production

Despite the foregoing difficulties, it appears as of this writing that Guinea's economy has gotten its second wind after long years of paralysis. Business has won out over palaver. Fria's success has set the pace, but it has taken ten years or more for Guinea to realize how disastrous socialism has been for its economy, and how a cure of rejuvenation can be effected by "taking the waters" of capitalism.

The Boké project, taken over from the Bauxites du Midi by the Harvey Aluminum Company and by Aluminium Ltd. of Canada, represented one of the greatest hopes for Guinea's economy. From October 1, 1963, when the agreement was signed, it gave rise to malicious comments about the concessions made to American capitalism and Guinea's abandonment of its sovereign rights. Let us examine exactly what the agreement involved.

In the joint venture known as the Compagnie des Bauxites de Guinée, the Guinean government holds 49 per cent of the shares covered by the mining permit, and its partners who make up the Halco Mining Corporation hold 51 per cent of the capital. Of their shares, ALCAN owns 27 per cent, ALCOA 27 per cent, Harvey Aluminum 20 per cent, Péchiney-Ugine 10 per cent, Aluminium-Werke 10 per cent; and Montecatini-Edison 6 per cent. Guinea's Minister of Economic Development is chairman of its board of directors. The Société de Transports Maritimes (SOTRAMAR), a joint venture for sea shipping created in December 1971 by the Guinean government and the Intermaritime Bank, is the carrier for Boké's bauxite output. Guinea is entitled to 65 per cent of the profits from the combined Boké-SOTRAMAR operations, and the Halco Corporation has committed itself to buy 6 million tons of bauxite annually from Guinea over a twenty-year period.

Between 1969 and 1973, 339 million dollars was invested in this project, about half of which was earmarked for building the infrastructure. This consisted of the port of Kamsar on the estuary of Rio Nunez, a residential settlement at Sangarédi, and a 137-kilometer railroad which Guinea is to build. The guarantees of the United States AID and the World Bank for the investments date from June 1965. Yet it was not until October 3, 1969, that a token start was made on work for the Boké project, after prolonged negotiations and the grant of an initial 10-million-dollar loan by the Société Financière Européenne. On August 2, 1973, the first shipment of Boké's output left the port of Kamsar. The 900,000 tons exported in

1973 earned 6.5 million dollars,[9] and it is hoped that production will attain 5 million tons a year beginning in 1975. Ismaël Touré stated to an Algerian journalist in April 1974: "Annual exports will very soon reach the record figure of 10 million tons a year, and this will make Guinea the premier bauxite-exporting country, as regards both the volume and the quality of its output."[10] Assured of its future potential, Guinea has joined forces with the other bauxite-producing countries—Sierra Leone, Yugoslavia, Jamaica, Austria, and Surinam. On July 15, 1974, Guinea convened the representatives of those states in Conakry to sign the final document of the international agreement on bauxite.

Before the Boké project got under way, Guinea continued to export the bauxite mined from the Los Islands—at Tamara (by Harvey Aluminum) and at Kassa (by a joint Guinean-Polish company)—as well as from Fria, where not all the bauxite mined is locally processed into alumina.

As of 1974, the Fria mines, situated 150 kilometers from Conakry, still constituted Guinea's richest source of bauxite. They provided three-fourths of Guinea's foreign exchange and nearly half of its exports, especially those to countries where Fria's shareholders have their alumina plants: Norway, which took 22 per cent in 1966, and Cameroun. In 1970, a quota of about 10 per cent of Fria's production was allotted to Guinea for sale to its socialist clients in Europe—namely Poland, Czechoslovakia, and the Democratic Republic of Germany. As a result of the agreement of February 12, 1973, between the international company of Fria and the Guinean state, Fria's name and statutes have been changed. In the new

[9] *West Africa*, May 6, 1974.
[10] Interview given by Ismaël Touré to a journalist of *Révolution africaine*, Algiers, Apr. 19–25, 1974, p. 31.

joint venture, called the FRIGUIA company, Guinea has been assigned 49 per cent of its capital (in exchange for permits to develop new deposits) and 63 per cent of its profits. Among Guinea's partners, the American firm of Olin Mathieson heads the list, holding 48.5 per cent of the capital. Péchiney-Ugine is next, with 26.5 per cent, and it is responsible for managing the local operation. Total production rose from 480,000 tons of alumina in 1964 to 700,000 tons in 1972, when a new policy was adopted. At that time, the two parties associated in the FRIGUIA company announced their common "conviction that Fria's new orientation conforms to Guinea's economic policy, and they pledge to do everything possible to attain quickly the assigned objectives, notably an annual production of one million tons of alumina."[11] The policy of Africanizing the company's cadres has resulted in reducing the number of foreigners employed from three hundred to thirty. A similar employment policy is being actively pursued at Boké. Several other development projects are anticipated for the coming years. These also should make it possible to increase Guinea's revenues appreciably.

The decision to mine the deposits at Kindia was taken by Guinea and the U.S.S.R. in an agreement made in 1968. Subsequently, Guinea was granted a loan of 83 million rubles to finance the whole operation. This includes reconstructing the two ore-loading quays at Conakry port, including a 98-kilometer railroad to link Conakry with Débélé (near Kindia), making improvements at the mine, and constructing a hostel for mineworkers. When full operation is reached, in about 1978, the annual production of the Office des Bauxites de Kindia (OBK) is to be 2.5 million tons of bauxite for shipment to the

[11] *Le moniteur africain*, Aug. 30, 1973.

U.S.S.R. over a thirty-year period. Kindia's reserves are estimated at 42.8 million tons of bauxite, with a content of 48 per cent alumina and 1.7 per cent silica.

In still another development, the Alu-Suisse Company and the Yugoslav Energoprojekt Company agreed in April 1974 to accept the "suggestion of the Guinean government to merge the joint ventures, the SOMIGA and the Société des Bauxites de Dabola (SBD) to work the bauxite deposits of Tougué and Dabola in the context of a tripartite company in which the Guinean government is to participate. By common agreement, it has also been decided to create a consortium to build and operate an aluminum plant. Its initial capacity is to be one million tons, and the bauxite required will be supplied by the above-mentioned tripartite company. Engineering and other technical assistance is to be furnished by Alu-Suisse and the Société Anonyme pour le Développement de l'Industrie d'Aluminium de Tougué-Dabola (SADA)."[12]

Guinea holds nearly two-thirds of the world's known reserves of bauxite, which amount to more than 8 billion tons. It aims to increase its production to 25 million tons a year by about 1980, when it plans to share in the enormous profits yielded mainly by the transformation of alumina into aluminum. To that end, negotiations were begun with Rumania in 1974 for construction in the Boké region of an aluminum plant with a 75,000-ton capacity. In August 1973, an agreement was reached with Zaïre by which Guinean bauxite and alumina would be processed in plants built near the Inga dam in Zaïre. Furthermore, it was decided at a meeting of the PDG on September 16, 1974, to build a dam at Koutoutamba in north central Guinea. After completion of that project about 1980, the dam should supply the electric current then needed to

[12] *Révolution africaine, loc. cit.,* p. 30.

operate the bauxite mine and alumina plant of Tougué-Dabola. It should also provide energy for the cement factories of Siguiri and Mali, as well as the factory for the processing of aromatic plants, which Japan is modernizing.[13]

Already well endowed by its bauxite-mining operations, Guinea plans to add iron to its productive resources. Estimates of the iron-ore reserves in the Nimba and Simandou mountains in southeastern Guinea range from 300 to 600 million tons, with an average iron content of more than 56 per cent. The joint venture MIFERGUI-Nimba, a mining company created at Tokyo on April 6, 1973, comprises Guinea (holding 50 per cent of the shares), Nigeria, Algeria, Liberia, the Rudis and Energoprojekt companies (Yugoslavia), Bexa (Belgium), Alu-Suisse (Switzerland), Nichimen and Mitsubishi (Japan), Ini (Spain), and the Intermaritime Bank. At a time when many countries are denouncing multinational companies, Sékou Touré prides himself on forming one as a means of developing his country and in the hope of eventually playing off the divergent interests against each other.

When MIFERGUI starts operations, scheduled for 1978, it will produce 10 to 15 billion tons a year. For the transportation of Guinea's iron ore to the Liberian port of Buchanan, an agreement between Monrovia and Conakry was signed in 1973. However, Liberia's greediness in respect to royalties necessitated further negotiations in September 1974, between LAMCO and MIFERGUI-Nimba, to reach an agreement for the transportation of some 15 million tons a year. As for the remainder, the Transguinean railroad from Nzérékoré to Conakry (1,200 kilometers), with a freight-carrying capacity of 50 million tons, should be able to transport the ore from the Nimba and Simandou mountains, as well as the bauxite of

[13] *Marchés tropicaux et méditerranéens,* Sept. 27, 1974.

Dabola and Tougué and the agricultural and forest produce of the country. It is to be built under the direction of the Japanese company, Nipponkoei, and is expected to be completed in about 1982. That company is also involved in building a deep-water port at Conakry, able to handle ore-cargo ships of 100,000 to 300,000 tons. The railroad and port should enable Guinea to export annually mineral products worth 270 million dollars at present prices.[14]

All these various projects require considerable amounts of energy. Although Guinea possesses a great hydroelectric potential, it now has only two comparatively low-powered generating plants: the Grandes Chutes, 4 kilometers from Kindia, and the Kinkon dam in the region of Pita, which supplies electricity solely for domestic usage and craft enterprises. The thermal generator at Conakry, a gift from AID, supplies energy only to the capital city, and Fria consumes all of the 91,500 kilowatts of power produced by its thermal plant to transform bauxite into alumina by electrolysis. Dam construction has been among the projects included in the several three-, seven-, and five-year plans, but there has been no follow-through for lack of foreign investors interested in undertaking expensive enterprises from which they cannot repatriate profits. Thermal generating plants cannot solve the problem at a time when the price of petroleum is soaring. Between the crisis of 1973 and July 1974, for example, the cost of gasoline (which comes in niggardly amounts almost exclusively from the U.S.S.R.) rose 307 per cent, fuel oil 157 per cent, and petroleum 118 per cent.[15] Until the SOGUIP, a joint venture in partnership with the American company Buttes Resources In-

[14] *La Guinée libre,* No. 12 (Mar. 7, 1974); and *Marchés tropicaux et méditerranéens,* Sept. 13, 1974.
[15] *Marchés tropicaux et méditerranéens,* July 19, 1974.

ternational, strikes oil, the Guinean government (which nationalized gasoline filling stations in 1969) can count only on the eventual construction, with Algerian assistance, of an oil refinery at Conakry with a production capacity of about a million tons.

State Enterprises

Compared with the huge revenues that Guinea expects to receive in the 1980s, those now provided by the national enterprises appear ludicrously small. In 1968, they contributed no more than 2.6 per cent to the gross national product. Serious problems exist in obtaining raw-material supplies, in the repair of machinery, in the availability of technical skills, and in transportation and markets, as well as in respect to production costs and waste. To illustrate the foregoing statements, it will suffice to cite some significant examples without listing and analyzing all of Guinea's producing enterprises.

At the Mamou cannery, the high cost and uneven quality of its output and the lack of reliable markets are not enough to account for the fact that it has never operated at more than 20 per cent of capacity. Built during the three-year plan with aid from the U.S.S.R., it began functioning in 1963. Three years later, it was supplied by the peasants with only 308 tons of tomatoes instead of the 2,000 tons it was equipped to process. The peasants are paid 25 FG per kilogram by the cannery, but with a monthly income well below 10,000 FG they cannot afford to pay 350 FG for a 500-gram can. Similarly, the state meat-preserving and sales firm, OBETAIL, and the Conakry abattoir (built by the German Federal Republic in 1962) pay 15,000 FG for a bullock, whereas private butchers offer 40,000 FG. Furthermore, canned meat of any kind is regarded with suspicion by the predominantly Muslim population. It can therefore be readily understood how little the rural population has been inclined to participate wholeheartedly in this national enterprise, which has been able to function at all only thanks to the army's tomato plantations, the "production brigades," and the regional market gardens of the Collèges d'Enseignement Rural (CER).

The Sanoya textile complex, built with British aid and by Lebanese subcontractors and equipped with 20,000 spindles and 780 looms, has never functioned at more than a third of its capacity since 1966. Because of the great care it requires, cotton culture is not considered a paying proposition by the peasants. After Guinea's sobering experience with the cotton campaign of 1966, cotton had to be bought from Egypt and consequently stocks ran short. Furthermore, considering that the average age of its 1,045 workers in 1967 was between seventeen and eighteen years, and that its personnel was relatively unstable and unreliable, it is no wonder that the work done there was shoddy and that the equipment rapidly deteriorated.

At Wassa-Wassa, 24 kilometers from Conakry, the state tobacco and match factory built by the People's Republic of China in 1963–1964 is the only public enterprise on a national scale that might be termed a success, both technically and because of its large domestic market. Its construction cost 5 million dollars (or less than half the funds invested in the textile complex), and it can produce 24 million packs of cigarettes and 45 million boxes of matches a year. However, the tobacco supplied by the farmers of Beyla has never amounted to more than a scant third of the 500 to 1,000 tons required each year, so additional supplies have had to be imported from China and Malawi (and even from Rhodesia). The plantations of gmelina wood, cultivated for use in making matches, have been unable to supply more than half the amount needed, and some have been severely damaged by brush fires. The factory's successive managers (a government clerk, a school monitor, and a magistrate) were scarcely prepared by their former occupations to take charge of such a factory. Finally, it should be noted that the heaviest demand for cigarettes comes from the forest peoples who live near the frontier and who use the Guinean products as a medium of exchange for trading across the boundary.

In 1967, a sawmill and plywood factory built in the Nzérékoré region with Soviet aid and inaugurated in 1964 turned out only 16,000 of the 50,000 cubic meters it had the capacity to produce. Machinery not built for tropical use often broke down, and sometimes there were fuel shortages. Inevitably, forest regeneration is a slow process. As the output must be transported over 1,200 kilometers of rough trails to the Sonfonia furniture factory (built by the Yugoslavs near Conakry), it is very difficult to supply that factory. The sawmill's wood debris was supposed to go to a plant which had been constructed between 1965 and 1967, at Sérédou in the Macenta region, for the manufacture of panel boards of compressed sawdust. Some of the cinchona wood from Sérédou was to be shipped to Nzérékoré for processing and then returned to Sérédou. But the only connecting link between those two places is a very difficult mountain trail some 100 kilometers long. Furthermore, certain difficulties regarding policy and management arose with the Belgian construction firm, Omnium Chimique, that first delayed and then seriously hampered its operation.

The Kassa oil mill, completed by an Italian firm in 1968, was designed to process, alternately, peanuts, palm kernels, and copra. Soon the peasants of lower Guinea realized that the prices paid for their palm kernels and coconuts were too low. Then, because the mill had been built on an island, the cost of bringing raw materials there was high, given the small size of the boats carrying them. Finally, Senegal, the source of the mill's peanut supplies, stopped shipping them, not only because Guinea was insolvent but also because its leader used any pretext at hand to insult his neighbor at Dakar. The factory is therefore even more inactive than the peanut mill built at Dabola by the People's Republic of China. The same inactivity—along with damage to equipment by weather—characterizes the fruit-juice plant at Kankan and the tea factory at Macenta. In 1974, the quinine factory at Sérédou was paralyzed because the agricultural monitor who managed it had not renewed the cinchona plantations at the proper time.

At Dubréka, Conakry, and Foulaya there are junk yards of machinery, whole factories, and equipment that have never been installed. Here one finds the makings of a soft-drink plant and of a dairy, and there the machines for a palm-oil mill given by AID. To supply the sugar mill at Koba, which began operating in November 1973, 211 hectares of cane are being cultivated instead of the 2,000 hectares' worth the mill is equipped to process. To be sure, that mill's requirements in fuel come to 350,000 liters of gasoline and 545,000 of oil . . . and it does not earn the foreign exchange needed to buy them. Nevertheless, Guinea must reimburse the countries that loaned it the funds to set up these insufficiently productive installations.

The Economic Strangulation of the Private Sector

Since independence, the steadily dwindling private sector has survived only in the hope of a change in the regime. It could hardly be satisfied with an economic setup that brought it more losses than profits (except in mining enterprises).

Had Guinea moved directly to eliminate private companies by nationalizing them, the nation would have had to pay damage claims and would have been weighed down by lawsuits. Furthermore, Guinea after independence had neither the native entrepreneurs nor the technical cadres able to render the same services as the Europeans. Consequently, by pursuing an economic and monetary policy that gave it control over the capital of the private companies, the state retained the option of getting rid of those companies, if need be, at a time of its own choosing. To this writer, it seems that the economic strangulation of the private companies was deliberately planned by the Guinean state, which wanted to manage its own economy, and that, at the same time, it stemmed indirectly from the economy's widespread difficulties, inasmuch as in the long run even the national enterprises were adversely affected.

Several factors successively played a part in the process of eliminating the private companies. Profit margins were reduced by a two-stage control. In the first place, a monopoly for the importation of raw materials and manufactured goods was granted to state enterprises which realized profits of about 30 per cent. In the second place, the private companies were compelled to resell their merchandise at a fixed price that restricted their profits to 10 per cent. The state, lacking hard currency especially after 1964, reduced to a minimum the number of import licenses issued. Consequently, the enterprises had to cut back on production and sometimes even suspend it altogether. Thus the Société des Brasseries de Guinée had to stop delivering beer several times a year because administrative red tape had delayed the delivery of bottle caps, hops, and spare parts for its machinery, or because the state financial services had reduced the quantity of imports requested by that company. Delays in getting supplies, reductions in their quantity, and the state's refusal to grant more licenses could not fail to diminish seriously the earnings of all the enterprises.

Compounding these difficulties was the shrinkage in the private companies' European staff following two further developments: the cancellation in 1965 of permission for the European cadres to repatriate their savings (which thenceforth became the responsibility of the foreign company, whose branch in Guinea was simply a subsidiary) and the nonrenewal by the Guinean state of a European's contract whenever it decided, rightly or wrongly, that a Guinean could perform the same task. With the departure of most of the European cadres of an enterprise, its productivity declined, its poorly guarded equipment and tools disappeared, and its managers became the target for accusations by their politically zealous accountants. As a result, the enterprise might decide to close down its money-losing Guinean branch. Then the next step often was the taking over of the factory by the Guinean government, which carried it on with its former workers, under the management either of other foreigners working under the state's control or of Guinean technicians. There ensued a progressive deterioration caused by negligence, theft, and waste.

Fully aware of this chain of events, the private companies decided to make their enterprises yield profits as long as possible by offering their employees monetary inducements to work and, at the same time, by sidestepping any control whatsoever on the part of their subordinate Guinean cadres or laborers. In this way, the private sector's employment policy and its wage strategy grew out of the working conditions imposed upon it. As a matter of fact, the private sector was overpaying its workers so as to retain their services and, at the same time, to avoid certain pitfalls, such as changing job classifications or even promoting Guineans to the rank of foreman.

One manager told the writer, "Promotion to a higher job category means that a Guinean would become more demanding and work less. . . . [If he were made a foreman,] he would want simply to give orders and no longer work. . . . They haven't the training needed . . . and they would interfere in their boss's affairs, accounts, and decisions."

Except for the Fria Company, which has its own training school, none of the private enterprises has tried to train its apprentices. Their workers learn on the job, merely receiving from their overworked European overseers instructions on how to carry out a given piece of work. Under the present program, an apprentice must attend night school, taking courses both in his own specialty and in political ideology. At the end of two years of such instruction, he automatically receives a "certificate of professional aptitude," regardless of his actual qualifications. The company is then obliged to keep him on, give him the job classification as determined by the Ministry of Labor, and assign him a foreman's position after two or three more years. Such a procedure leads to the dismissal of a European and an increase in the cost of services because an African foreman does not work productively himself (he confines his activity to supervising operations). Furthermore, it introduces a disturbing element into the enterprise's business should the anti-imperialist ideology of the Guinean foreman impel him to scrutinize his European superior's words and actions and possibly denounce him.

To sum up the situation: The private sector, which accounted for virtually every industry in 1958, represented only 57 per cent of the total by June 1966. Wage earners in private industry had become fewer than those in the public sector. Excluding the large group of 1,379 workers employed by the Fria Company, only 1,719 were employed in small private industries, whereas there were 4,069 in the public sector.

Several private enterprises went out of business in 1971, either because their European manager had been imprisoned at the time of the November 22, 1970, invasion or because they were unable to obtain supplies. Among those companies were the Société des Plastiques de Guinée, Construction Métallique de Dixinn, the Société de Préparation de Peintures, the Société de Montage de Camions Mack Trucks, and FRUITA-GUINEE (carbonated fruit beverages).

No foreign private enterprise was founded during the three-year plan. This is the more significant in that in 1962 a new investment code was promulgated which, *inter alia,* protected foreign investments against nationalization, granted them a favorable tax status, shielded them against competition from alien companies, and guaranteed their right to repatriate a certain percentage of their earnings in cash. Only the Harvey Aluminum Company in 1967—that is, during the seven-year plan—took the risk of mining Tamara's bauxite under economically mediocre conditions, in the hope of sharing in the future development of the Boké deposits.

From a global socioeconomic viewpoint, Guinea offers private capital no guarantee that it can enjoy full scope, and, moreover, discourages the potential investor in other respects. These include Guinea's cyclical changes in foreign policy, intervention in and financial control of the economy, and harassment by a politically oriented administration. Even for the private sector, the state restricts and controls production, sets prices, imposes its distribution network, and regulates the labor market. Lacking the power to negotiate with the state, a foreign enterprise can survive only if its manager or director cultivates personal relations with some minister or high-ranking civil servant. Even then, such protection is jeopardized if the official is dismissed from his post. Excepting the Swiss company COFICOMEX, which has ties with the most stable ministers (among them Ismaël Touré) by means of bribes and commissions paid into their Swiss bank accounts, foreign businessmen have no real economic power. Constant intervention by the public authorities, the always latent threat of nationalization, and the extreme difficulty of repatriating profits—all these add up to genuine economic strangulation (except for enterprises like those of public works, which are agencies of the state). FRUITAGUINEE, the only private Guinean firm employing more than ten persons, closed down in 1971 after its director was put in jail.

Agricultural Production

Whereas the food industries, like those of manufacturing and equipment, either stagnate or retrogress, agriculture is sinking back to the subsistence level. This has taken place despite the emphasis placed at four 1964 conferences upon developing complementary regional economies. The major regions' specializations, as determined by climate and soil, are as follows:

Lower Guinea: bananas, pineapples, palm kernels, rice, manioc, cereals.

Middle Guinea: stock raising, fruits, vegetables.

Upper Guinea: rice, cotton, tobacco, peanuts, textile fibers.

Forest zone: coffee, oil palms, rice, woods, tea, tobacco.

According to a government estimate in 1959, 90 per cent of the active population (almost entirely peasants) furnished only 56 per cent of the total national revenues, as contrasted with 44 per cent produced by the 10 per cent of the population then working in other sectors. At that time, agricultural productivity was seven times less than that of the other sectors.

Despite persistent official efforts to change attitudes in the rural world, it has remained strongly traditionalist, and rudimentary means of production continue to be used. Moreover, the peasants' meager cash income and lack of technical knowledge are barriers to modernizing their equipment. Other factors that contribute to maintaining the *status quo* are the retarded growth of the transportation infrastructure, a declining commercial sector (where the colonial trading system still largely prevails), the fall in world prices for tropical produce, and the quantitative and qualitative inadequacy of wage earners and of their supervisors.

Guinea's agriculture is unsatisfactory on three counts: in supplying the population with enough good-quality foodstuffs, in providing the processing plants with agricultural raw materials, and in delivering large quantities of products for export.

A reporter for *Horoya hebdo* pointed out very clearly some of the technical faults from which his country's agriculture is suffering. The thrust of his articles may be briefly summarized as follows: insufficient water control, because of only small-scale improvements; problems created by the cost and scarcity of chemical fertilizers; the virtual nonexistence of manure and of crop protection; and an excessive infatuation for tractors, which are uneconomic for use on small areas and on poorly cleared fields. Other harmful factors are brush fires and over-deep plowing, which sterilize some flat surfaces, the lack of fuel and spare parts, and the incompetence of many farm-machinery operators. Much of the machinery imported to help the peasantry is owned by urban merchants, by political leaders and administrators, or by rich peasants, who either rent it out at high rates to the PRL or CER or transform the tractors into rural taxis by putting platforms on them.

The large-scale importation of farm machinery has only a small impact upon the national production of salable commodities. . . . In 1969, family cooperatives replaced other cooperatives that had proved unworkable. These are family consortiums made up of wealthy persons who band together to buy a tractor, or they are special-interest associations artificially organized for the purpose of obtaining grants of matériel and seed. . . . Expansion of the PRL has been hampered in many [party] federations by a restrictive interpretation of the brigade principle. This had led to assigning projects on a permanent basis to a small group of individuals who, in the long run, feel that they are being exploited.[16]

In 1973, the PRL strove to correct that formula by organizing work brigades of fifteen peasant volunteers. They were issued plows, draft animals, cloth, food, and seeds as short-term loans, for which repayment fell due after the harvest. By this means, members of a brigade were to become owners of the means of production. Their leaders, however, are afraid that a conflict of interests may develop inside the PRL; the alternative base for rural development is the "socialist cooperative societies which should emerge from our schools located in rural centers. Indeed, after a course lasting twelve to thirteen years, most students at our Centers for Rural Education should form socialist cooperatives."[17] The addition in 1973 of a thirteenth year of study in 200 schools should make available 6,000 to 7,000 more young graduates for setting up cooperatives. The People's Republic of China has been asked to send 150 experts to guide those graduates in their early stages.

What results should be expected when, for the nth time in Guinea's more than fifteen years of independence, the head of state, in July 1974, felt impelled to advocate once again a "true agricultural revolution" based on production brigades

[16] *Horoya hebdo,* Mar. 7–13, 1970.
[17] *Horoya,* June 14, 1973.

and on increasing output and productivity? He also sounded this warning:[18] Guinea, which had spent about 3 billion FG between 1970 and 1972 for the 60,000 tons of imports it needed to cover its food shortages, had to spend 7 billion FG more in the 1973–1974 fiscal year, because of soaring prices and the shortfall in crops in an exceptionally dry year. The holder of a food card was entitled to a maximum of 8 kilograms of rice per month, but in April 1974 that ration was cut to 3 kilograms. Periodically, oil, soap, sugar, milk, salt, and tomato concentrate disappear temporarily from the market. In September 1970, the shortage of rice,[19] Guinea's staple food, was already so serious that the government had to send out a real S O S. Thanks to help from Senegal, Egypt, and United States AID, Guinea was able in one way or another to bridge the difficult period until the next harvest.

Nevertheless, many rice-growing projects had been undertaken on the basis of the local improvements that had been planned and started by the French before independence. In the Fié valley, near the Niger in upper Guinea, the Soviets invested, under the three-year plan, 3 billion FG in matériel and hydraulic construction before they abandoned the project "for financial and perhaps political reasons."[20] Programs sponsored by the UN and AID in Kaback and Koba ended abruptly as a result of the deterioration of Guinean-American relations in 1967. Later, a mission from the modestly endowed UN Special Fund tried without visible success to revive farming on the arable areas of those same regions and also in the Kapatchez,

---

[18] *Marchés tropicaux et méditerranéens,* July 19, 1974.

[19] Increasingly, the population prefers rice to *fonio* (a not very nutritious cereal), manioc, and yams. Guineans eat little corn.

[20] Jean Suret-Canale, *La Republique de Guinée* (Paris: Editions Sociales, 1970), p. 240.

where they encountered tremendous technical difficulties and a shortage of experienced laborers. The Vietnamese and the Chinese, especially after 1968, worked with the very limited means at their disposal to improve here and there the fields cultivated by the CER.

As for the goals set for industrial crops, most of the manufacturing enterprises which they were to supply operated at a slow pace or only periodically for lack of raw materials to process, as has already been explained. The new five-year plan, launched in September 1973, offers little hope for improvement, inasmuch as agriculture has been allotted only 9 per cent of the total estimated expenditures, compared with 10.8 per cent and 12.9 per cent in the preceding plans. Under such conditions it would be surprising if the agricultural situation were saved by the "production brigades" or even by the "socialist cooperatives" which the tenth PDG congress held in Conakry in September 1973 decided to create.

The remembrance of many past failures weighs too heavily. Coercion and the grip of the administration explain why the decline of the colonial power brought down with it the Sociétés Indigènes de Prévoyance (SIP). The disappearance of the Sociétés Mutuelles de Développement Rural (SMDR) was due to the embezzlement of their funds. Even the government recognized the faults in the management of the Coopératives Agricoles de Production (CAP), created after independence, and in the Coopératives de Production Agricole et de Consommation (COPAC), which reactivated the moribund CAP by replacing them. Most of the time, their executive committees were held in check by a chairman who, in making the decisions himself, violated the principle of collective responsibility. (This was notably the case of the Bangtama cooperative, which was chaired in 1967 by the secretary of the local PDG section, and also that of the Gbaia cooperative in 1968, when it was headed by a former regional governor.)[21] Many cooperative groups continued to be formed for the sole purpose of getting loans, of which 80 per cent had not been repaid by the end of the three-year plan. The dissolution of a cooperative did not bring about the restitution of funds that had been wasted or misappropriated by those responsible for its management.

On the whole, it might be argued that the mechanization introduced by the pilot centers was simply a simulated modernization, and that the individuals holding political and economic power found in the cooperative society a very malleable agrarian structure.

If rice cultivation was the chief food-crop production to be hindered by the successive reorganizations of the cooperatives and by modernization, it was not the only one to suffer a setback. The cultivation of manioc, millet and sorghum, corn, and sweet potatoes followed a similar course.

This distinct decline in food-crop production can be explained in large part by the massive exodus of peasants to foreign countries (notably Senegal and Ivory Coast) and of young people holding some kind of school diploma to the capital, and by the permanent mobilization of the peasants for unproductive tasks, such as political meetings, receiving traveling officials, and recruiting young persons into the militias. It was further aggravated by the population's indifference to increasing cultivation, because the people were aware of the

[21] Tierno Nabika Diallo, "Bilan et perspectives de la coopération dans le développement de l'agriculture guinéenne" (mimeographed; Conakry: Institut Polytechnique, 1967). Henri de Decker, *Nation et développement communautaire en Guinée et au Sénégal* (Paris: Mouton, 1958).

draining off of rural assets by urban centers and the failure of local tradesmen to offer wanted goods in exchange for the sale of surpluses. Still another factor in food-crop shortages is the lack of a nourishing diet, which adds to the vicious circle of underdevelopment. The peasant exodus explains also the decrease in the livestock population, which declined from one cow to two inhabitants in 1964 to one to three in 1974. Whereas Guinea's population is growing at an annual rate of 2.7 per cent, the over-all production of paddy declined from 360,000 tons in 1964 to 200,000 in 1972.[22]

Export crops suffer from the same regressive tendency. At the time Guinea became independent, bananas and coffee made up nearly 60 per cent of its exports in terms of value, the balance being supplied mainly by bauxite and iron ores. As of 1966, bananas, pineapples, and coffee represented no more than 27 per cent of total shipments. Among the agricultural exports, coffee accounted for 33 per cent, bananas 26 per cent, palm kernels 17 per cent, and pineapples 16 per cent. In the meantime, to be sure, Fria's alumina plant had entered into production, providing the Guinean state with 70 per cent of its foreign exchange. Clearing agreements had been made with the U.S.S.R., but these were not particularly helpful to foreign planters, who accounted for 70 per cent in value of the banana exports, grown on 51 per cent of the areas devoted to that crop. Only from time to time did the government fulfill its promise to planters in 1973 to recompense them for bananas and pineapples exported to the extent of 3 FG and 5 FG in currency per kilogram, respectively. One must also take into account the damage to coffee and bananas by plant diseases and nematodes, as well as the high cost of combating them.

[22] *La Guinée libre,* No. 13 (Mar. 14, 1974).

The discouraged native planter who lets such plant diseases ravage his 2 or 3 hectares of fields indirectly facilitates their spread to neighboring areas. Even worse, about one-fifth of the French plantations that were abandoned during the three years following independence came into the possession of politicians, who were content simply to profit from their production without making any outlays for their upkeep or expansion.

The total production of bananas—for local consumption as well as export—declined steadily from 1955 to 1971, which was the year of the Fifth Column trials. The volume increased slightly to about 30,000 tons in both 1972 and 1973. The most prosperous planters either turned to growing pineapples, which were more remunerative, or to trucking, while the small-scale planters reverted to food crops.

The land best suited to banana culture is in lower Guinea, which has favorable climatic conditions: intense sunlight, a constant temperature of 25 to 30 degrees Centigrade, high humidity, and a dense network of rivers. Most of the coffee is grown in the forest zone. Plantations of this semiwild crop are family-owned and require only small investment. Nevertheless, by 1964, a virulent plant disease had destroyed half the plants that had existed in 1958, and the proximity of the plantations to Guinea's frontiers facilitated illegal sales in Sierra Leone and Liberia. The result was that exports shrank from 15,662 tons in the record year of 1959 to 8,700 tons in 1963.[23] For recent years, only figures of total production are available. In 1971, the total came to 9,000 tons as against the 43,000-ton goal set by the seven-year plan. In 1972, it declined to 7,000 tons,[24] which suggests that some 5,000 tons were exported that year.

[23] Source: Direction Générale de la Statistique de la République de Guinée.
[24] *La Guinée libre,* No. 13 (Mar. 14, 1974).

Of all Guinea's industrial crops, only pineapples have followed an upward curve. After a fast take-off (2,900 tons in 1958 and 7,800 in 1960), they fell back (to 3,600 tons in 1961 and 1,600 in 1962) before progress was resumed (8,000 tons in 1966 and 11,000 in 1968). For the following years, one must subtract from the figures for total production—the only data available—4,000 to 5,000 tons of pineapples that were consumed locally as fresh fruit, juice, or preserves. Over-all production was reported as 25,000 tons in 1969, 27,000 in 1970, 30,000 in 1971, and 32,000 in 1972.[25]

Other agricultural exports—such as palm kernels (20,000 to 25,000 tons), citrus (about 4,000 tons of orange essence) and some mangoes and avocados—have stagnated for the past ten years. Almost all of the 25,000 tons of peanuts that Guinea produces are consumed by its increasing population.

From the foregoing information, it is easy to see whether the goals of the seven-year plan were attained. Without giving precise figures, that plan aimed to consolidate Guinea's economic independence between 1964 and 1972 in three respects: by meeting basic food needs without recourse to imports; by providing factories to the greatest extent possible with local raw materials; and by promoting exports. To the surprise of no one, no accounting of that plan has been published. Moreover, it is certain that the three-year plan was far more successful than the 1964–1971 plan.

The Five-Year Plan

A five-year development plan for the 1973–1978 period was whipped into shape and launched at the tenth PDG congress on September 28–29, 1973. It comprised the following three sections:

[25] *Ibid.*

(1) A plan for each PRL (of which there were 7,790 at that time in Guinea) based on its known or estimated resources in manpower, matériel, and funds. The execution of this plan depended essentially on the group's own efforts and especially on its capacity for work.

(2) The point of departure for the regional development plan was the region's development budget, which determined the objectives assigned to the community involved (such as collective fields and plantations and the building of roads, schools, bridges, and the like). "Before the five-year plan is completed, each region should be able to feed itself properly without requiring supplementary external aid."[26] No figures are specified in this part of the plan, and there is little doubt that the drafting of this and the preceding section caused difficulties.

(3) The national plan was drawn up jointly by several ministries, including that of the plan, and also by the planning commission of the Central Committee of the Party. It anticipated investments amounting to 58,680 million sylis (or 586,800 million CFA francs) by 1978. In the portion dealing with rural development, priorities were given to food crops, hydroagricultural improvement of the great plains, industrial and export crops, research centers, the development of animal husbandry, reforestation, and an increase in the potential of Guinea's fisheries (currently negligible). In other words, the priorities assigned were the same as those of previous plans. Most of the industrial investments were earmarked for a sawmill, an oil refinery, cement plants, a paper mill, a tin plate factory, and a saltworks. For the sector of mining development, the "socialist" regime of Sékou Touré relies almost wholly upon investments by private capitalists in the so-called im-

[26] Sékou Touré, speech made Sept. 29, 1973, rebroadcast by Radio Conakry and monitored at Dakar.

perialist countries. Investments in that sector totaled 34,330 million sylis, constituting 58.5 per cent of the plan budget, not including the 12.8 per cent allotted to energy. To anyone familiar with the dilapidated state of Guinea's houses and highways, it is astonishing that only 10.8 per cent was allocated to public works, urbanization, housing, and roads. It simply comes down to a question of choice. It is hard to see how the public-health service could modernize its equipment, as it is expected to do, with only 752 million silys, or 1.3 per cent of the budget. One must wait and see. Nor is the banking and trading sector of the economy (allotted 1.2 per cent of the budget) likely to become self-supporting when it has been chronically in deficit. The head of state himself has attributed that deficit to embezzlement. Perhaps the answer lies simply in turning out more banknotes.

In the light of these data, what judgment can be reached as to Guinea's economy? Doubtless a fairly pessimistic one, if consideration is given to the meagerness of the local financial resources, the debts owed to foreign creditors, and the chaotic state of the processing industries and the commercial sector. It is necessary to take into account also the inadequacy of the infrastructure for generating energy and for roads and towns—all indispensable for an economic take-off—and the relapse of agriculture to the subsistence level. For the very long run, however, one might hazard a more optimistic appraisal, considering the many varieties of Guinea's climate and soil favorable to agriculture, and especially its huge mineral resources now in process of development. In a medium-term perspective, the comparative wealth of the debt-burdened state will continue to coexist with the poverty of its individual inhabitants.

Viewing Guinea's comparative failure over a period of more

National Resources and Individual Poverty

than fifteen years from a certain angle, it appears to have been caused by an unduly hasty identification of political awareness with social capital. Guinea has been suffering from an illusion as to its wealth even more than from the delay in developing its productive strength (which is characteristic of underdevelopment everywhere). A political structure is not in itself a valuable asset, and it can become one only to the extent that it effectively changes human beings and exploits existing resources. Those resources can become a source of wealth only to the degree that the state can dispose of the human, technical, and financial capital needed to turn its economic potential to its own advantage.

Fortunate in the aid it receives from all quarters, Guinea has been richer in material assets than in entrepreneurs, and better endowed with resources than with incentives. It is regrettable that the Guineans' extraordinary capacity for mobilizing their potential should have been used mainly for tilting at windmills. But a technical civilization cannot be generated spontaneously. The gestation period for a politician is shorter than that for an entrepreneur, and bureaucracies proliferate faster than technicians. Moreover, it is those bureaucrats and politicians who are trying to monopolize the national revenues, while sometimes ignoring the basic principles, who determine the functioning of the economy.

For the time being, every Guinean, living in the shadows of underdevelopment, is experiencing an alarming rise in living costs, shortages of imported consumer goods, a depletion of the nation's foreign-exchange assets, and a decline in job opportunities. Yet at least the light that he sees on the horizon now comes from the glow of aluminum rather than from the glittering mirage of revolutionary oratory.

CHAPTER 7

The Strategies of National Integration

All African countries, once independent, are prey to internal conflicts, and they seek in different ways to bring about social integration. The major forces hindering attainment of the unity needed by every developing nation are the disparities between tribes, in the inferior status of women, in the tradition of rule by the elderly, and in religious differences. How can antagonisms based on tribe, sex generation, and religion be overcome? What attitude should the government and citizenry adopt toward the traditional or mystical forces (which might well hamper the search for bold and up-to-date solutions to the problems of development)? Such questions immediately confront an observer, especially in a country like Guinea, which boasts of being the standard-bearer of the "African Democratic Revolution."

It should be emphasized that the PDG's strategy in dealing with tribal dissensions has been to serve as conduit for their many diverse forces toward a single objective. As regards the gaps between men and women and between young and old, the PDG has attempted to strike an even balance, but in matters of religion it has insisted on submission to its authority even when that required using force against refractory elements. Undeniably, in each of those sectors of the society, a profound evolution has taken place. However, when one considers the trend of those forces and of the pace and scope of change, it seems more suitable to speak of social modifications or mutations than of evolution. If "social mutation" is taken to mean a sudden change in the basic structure of an entire social organism, following an upheaval caused by accumulated antagonisms, that term may well be applied to the radical changes of direction that have occurred in Guinean society.

Tribal Integration

The metamorphoses that have marked newly independent countries have often demonstrated the frailty of unity built upon a collection of heterogeneous tribes. In Guinea, the conflicts between ethnocentrism and nationalism have been surmounted, on the whole, to the latter's benefit. This can be attributed to the mingling of its tribes since the beginning of the twentieth century, but even more to the policy effectively applied by a political party.

Even during the colonial regime there had developed an awareness of African realities and a sense of black brotherhood in territorial federations, such as those of French West Africa and French Equatorial Africa. Those developments had several causes: the rotation of the elite, as represented by primary-school teachers and civil servants, among the different territories (often for the purpose of strengthening the colonial power's security, especially after World War II); military service, which served as a melting pot and exposed not only the recruit but also his family and village to the values of other civilizations; and the migrations of laborers because of the economic development and the growth of towns. As for the movements of labor, the decisive cause was economic upheavals.

The widespread application of the colonial trading system (*économie de traite*) forced a number of tribes to participate in the same economic circuit, as was the case with rubber around 1900.¹ Half a century later, the Kissi, Toma, and Guerzé coffee planters realized that they had common interests and identical problems. In lower and upper Guinea, the introduction of a new crop (bananas) and new farming techniques (the plow) disrupted the existing ethnocentric social structures. Those structures had isolated villagers to the point of making them almost inbred, encouraged abusive demands based on blood relationships, assigned excessive importance to old men and to the masters of the land, and encouraged local myths and customs. By breaking these down, the peoples of Rio Pongo came to share the same historical development. Some crops even required a large-scale regrouping of the tribes. The cultivation of rice and cotton along the Niger River attracted as many as 22,000 Malinké, Bambara, and Senoufo tribesmen. Peanut farming created annual contacts between Guineans and Senegalese through the migrants known as *navétanes,* of whom there were some 50,000 each year in Mali and Guinea. Migrant communities, sharing a common way of life, sprang up near the banana groves of lower Guinea² and the gold placers and diamond mines of upper Guinea.³

After the outbreak of World War II, the founding of towns (if not urbanization in the proper sense of the term) brought diverse tribes into close contact.⁴ They were taught European farming and other techniques so that they could assist the colonists as scribes, doctors, schoolteachers, government clerks,

[1] Jean Suret-Canale, "La Guinée dans le système colonial," *Présence africaine,* 29 (Dec. 1959–Jan. 1960).

[2] Jacques Richard-Molard, *Problèmes humains en Afrique occidentale* (Paris: Présence africaine, 1946), Ch. 5, "La Banane en Guinée."

[3] Claude Rivière, "L'Or fabuleux du Bouré," *L'Afrique littéraire et artistique,* No. 23 (1972), pp. 41–46.

[4] Claude Rivière, "La Toponymie de Conakry et du Kaloum," *Bulletin de l'IFAN,* 28, B.3–4 (1966), pp. 1009–18.

The Strategies of National Integration

soldiers, foremen, and the like. The resulting acculturation of individuals belonging to various local ethnic groups automatically tended to obliterate tribal differences.

The role played by the PDG in moderating these differences is clearly evidenced by the manner in which a formerly divided population came together to join a single political party. It would not be inaccurate to say that the PDG succeeded in effecting tribal integration by using the people's economic interests as the Party's base. An analysis of the progress of the PDG's militant activities shows that the mobilization of the population into the Party was accomplished first among communities that were already acculturated; then in regions that were the most heterogeneous and where the tribal structures were most loosely knit, hence most accessible to a unifying ideology; and finally in direct relationship to the population's involvement in a trading economy, to such a degree that one might argue that it was the very opposition of economic interests that promoted Guinean unity.

Lower Guinea was the region where the Party first gained members. In that region the modern economy was most developed, the possibilities for organizing trade unions and political groups were greatest, especially around the capital city, and education and acculturation had already broken down some ethnic barriers. Next to be mobilized was the forest region, whose many small tribes were far less strongly structured than was Peul or Manding society. As Sékou Touré himself noted:

These groups, formerly lacking any connections, thenceforth found their common denominator in the PDG's platform and in the struggle against the chieftaincy. Although economic activities in the forest region had become commercial in type, the situation was quite different in upper Guinea and in the Fouta Djalon, where a subsistence economy prevailed. The inhabitants of the forest zone traded in coffee, palm kernels, and colas. Consequently, the commercial relations there between producers and capitalists were characterized by a conflict of interests. Having become aware of this situation, the producers' major demand was for an increase in the prices paid for their output. Indeed, only the PDG could organize a campaign against their exploitation by merchants—a struggle which transcended ethnic, tribal, or religious antagonisms. Only an organized political party could give a modern form to this common factor, which dominated the struggle on the economic level. The economic development and the social problems arising from this regional conflict helped the Parti Démocratique de Guinée to take root and to organize there.[5]

In upper Guinea, it was not until 1954 that the Malinké farmers began to join the Party; this was the time of the struggles against the Sociétés Indigènes de Prévoyance and for higher pay and a change in the relations between men and women. Sékou Touré, a Malinké tribesman, had just been elected as one of the tribe's members to the territorial assembly from Beyla. At the same time, the few bourgeois merchants of Kankan took a stand against his party, the PDG, for they had made money under the colonial regime and did not support a party that criticized traders for making profits at the expense of rural producers.

The last element to adopt the cause of the PDG as its own was the feudal, pastoral, and seminomadic milieu of the Fouta Djalon, which was thoroughly Islamized and almost without business interests. Its extreme conservatism made Peul society almost impenetrable, yet there, almost more than anywhere else, the PDG's activities apparently had truly far-reaching repercussions. This was because the populations of

[5] Sékou Touré, *L'Afrique et la révolution* (Switzerland, 1966), p. 74.

Fouta benefited most from such social changes as the suppression of the chieftaincies, the granting of property rights to serfs, the sale of livestock, and a partial liberation from family domination. By eliminating the chieftaincy in 1957, the PDG pleased the inhabitants of *cercles* where the chiefs had become unpopular and also neutralized the popular chiefs who had opposed the Party's rise to power. In the process of losing faith in the religious character of the established order, the population's outlook was enlarged to the point where it could accept a nation-wide organization.

Once political independence had been won, education became one of the most effective means of integrating ethnic groups into the nation. The Party was conscious of this and invested heavily in education, imposing in this way a single mold upon the rising generation. Quite as much as by education, literacy campaigns, and radio broadcasts, the policy of promoting ethnic integration was pursued through national administrative, civic, and judicial institutions. Existing customs, the constitution, law codes, and the decrees applying legal regulations throughout the nation were replaced by a single party, a unicameral legislature, and one executive authority, along with new penal and civil-law procedures.[6] Furthermore, speeches, meetings, slogans, emblems, a national anthem and flag, and propaganda orchestrated by the mass media, served as institutions or as the means of promoting national unity above and beyond particularisms.

Whatever simple means were used to effect tribal integration, they were incomparably less effective than was the Party's deliberate policy, which consisted of presenting as poles

[6] See Seydou-Madani Sy, *Recherches sur l'exercice du pouvoir politique en Afrique noire: Côte d'Ivoire, Guinée, Mali* (Paris: Pedone, 1965).

of attraction a common ideal and a man venerated as the victor over colonization. It was hoped that this man, Touré, a Malinké fluent in Susu, could rescue his people from underdevelopment and rally the nation to his leadership. For a long time his close aides were a Peul, Saifoulaye Diallo, and a Toma, Louis Lansana Béavogui, and he placed as much confidence in Coniagui as in Guerzé civil servants.

In the hope of uniting the tribes, Sékou Touré pretended to deny the reality of ethnic groups. His policy was built upon certain unifying factors—speeches designed to restore prestige to a country exhausted by economic restrictions: the promotion of Samori, Alfa Yaya, Thierno Ibrahima N'Dama, and the wali of Goumba as national heroes who resisted the colonial conquest; the leadership of a single party victorious over colonial wickedness and assumed to be capable of bringing happiness to the nation; the adherence to a socialist ideology based on the comforting myth of equality between races, sexes, and occupations; the emphasis on colonialism (which he equated with imperialism) as a scapegoat and on himself as ordained practitioner of the national psychoanalysis. His propaganda was carried out by slogans and by easily grasped stereotypes, consisting of concrete, powerful, and unifying symbols, such as the elephant Sily, to represent both the party and its leader, and a flag whose colors of green, yellow, and red became the basis for all Guinean pictorial art.

It is not evident that this policy was altogether successful. Certainly, some tribal disparities have been blunted and the prospect of a civil war based on ethnic hostilities can probably be ruled out. Yet the periodic reappearance of vestiges of ethnocentrism was attested to by Sékou Touré in a speech of January 15, 1968,[7] in which he attacked Guinean racism.

[7] *Horoya,* Jan. 17, 1968.

Despite the strongly integrationist policy of the PDG, some taint of tribalism remains. The explanation seems to lie partly in the class differences that were generated after independence by the national administration and by economic penury, combined with the ingenuity and brashness of some individuals and groups in dividing the country's few national resources among themselves. Another factor has been the reinforcement of tribal and family ties, which are the best guarantees of survival for the poor and of a politician's ability to keep his post. Favoritism and patronage create a clientele. Those eager to seize the crumbs falling from the state banquet table have a fair chance of success if they use tribal relationships as the channel in begging a "brother" for favors.

The comparative balance in tribal representation that was reached among the cadres tends now to be upset by Malinké predominance and Peul underrepresentation in the policy-making decisions. Between 1958 and 1966, Malinkés formed 33 per cent of the total population and represented 40 per cent of the administrative staff and 36 per cent of the political personnel.[8] Among the governors, regional secretaries, heads of central *arrondissements,* and *arrondissement* commandants, that tribe accounted for 43 to 51 per cent. The Peul, on the other hand, constituted only 23 per cent of the administrative personnel, although they accounted for 30 per cent of Guinea's total population. Nevertheless, despite the difficulties in altering the population's outlook in a country that is 85 per cent rural—difficulties related to the ecological isolation of its regions, its varied life styles and consumer habits, and the inertia

---

[8] Bernard Charles, "Cadres guinéens et appartenances ethniques" (Paris, doctoral thesis, mimeographed, University of Paris, 1968), and Claude Rivière, *Mutations sociales en Guinée* (Paris: Marcel Rivière, 1971), pp. 57–74.

of collective and stereotyped attitudes—intertribal contacts have increased. This is the result not only of an antisegregationist policy but also, even more directly, of the economic resources of each region and the weakness of its sociocultural structures.

The Emancipation of Women

The political revival, combined with the PDG's struggle to acquire power, especially after 1953, provided women with the unforeseen opportunity to satisfy their hopes for emancipation. Since then, Guinea's women and its Party have been bound together by reciprocal activities. Women have supported the Party, and the Party has emancipated women.

The most radical measures changing the status of women were those put into effect shortly after independence. To strengthen the institution of marriage and to assure that it be freely contracted, the state took control over marriages by the ordinance of April 15, 1959. A civil ceremony performed in the presence of a registrar of vital statistics became the prerequisite for any religious marriage. In accordance with the resolutions passed by the PDG national conference, which met August 14–18, 1961, in Conakry, the law of April 14, 1962 (No.54/AN/62) laid down the conditions required for a marriage contract and the respective duties of husbands and wives. The legal marriageable age for girls became seventeen years (Art. 1), whereas formerly it was the custom for some girls to be affianced at twelve to fourteen years of age, or even before their birth. Another clause (Art. 2) required the consent of both parties for a valid marriage, although this did not eliminate the factor of family pressures. The amount of the bride price was restricted (5,000 FG for single persons and 2,500 for divorcées or widows), and it became the property of the wife, to whom it was delivered by the husband in the presence of the registrar of vital statistics. This gesture had a symbolic value, and the wife was no longer required to return the sum in case of divorce (Arts. 3 and 4). A woman was also given the right to prevent her husband from taking a second wife if she could prove that he did not have the means to provide a decent livelihood for them both (Art. 9). Finally, women were now legally entitled to control their personal property (Art. 13).

The law of April 14, 1962, also specified the conditions under which a marriage could be dissolved. Its outstanding stipulations were that a divorce must be pronounced before a law court (Art. 2)—a radical step in that it ran counter to the practice of repudiation that had been widespread in this predominantly Muslim country; and the court was empowered to grant damages to the spouse in whose favor the divorce had been granted (Art. 3), a provision aimed at providing a defense against capricious divorce suits, although in practice it failed to do so. It should also be noted that under the civil code, a widow could no longer be left destitute, for Art. 328 stipulated that a surviving spouse was a legatee, inheriting one-eighth of the estate if there were living parents or offspring, and as much as one-quarter if there were no such coheirs. Finally, a general resolution passed at the end of the first women's congress, on January 31, 1968, favoring the institution of monogamy was gradually spelled out in decrees. Polygamy was abolished "except in cases of *force majeure.*" Polygamous households already functioning when the resolution passed were not affected by these decrees, but in those cases the husband had no right to wed still another woman.[9]

[9] *Horoya,* Feb. 3, 1968.

To help women find their identity in modern society, a whole series of institutions was created with a view to integrating them into public life. The most important steps taken to supplement the marriage legislation concerned the education of women, their training in matters of health, their protection, and their participation in the national economy and political life. Consequently, the proportion of educated girls rose from one for every four boys in 1959 to one for every three by 1966. The first six years of independence brought an enrollment increase of 215 per cent for boys and 397 per cent for girls in primary and secondary schools. During that same period, the over-all school attendance by girls jumped from 4 per cent to 20 per cent.

Beginning in the primary grades, theoretical and practical training in hygiene is given, along with general education. In the Centres d'Enseignement Révolutionnaire (CER, the acronym that was used for Collèges d'Enseignement Rural until 1967), whose aim is to relate formal education to daily life, girls receive training in domestic science and in the activities of their rural local communities. Services for the care of mothers and children (of which the first was founded in July 1958) function in all of Guinea's thirty-eight medical circumscriptions under the guidance of a national center in Conakry. Legislation supplements the progress made in women's education. Legal protection is given to working women, pregnant women, and those who have recently given birth, and women wage earners are shielded against abusive dismissals for absenteeism because of pregnancy or childbirth. The law also forbids employers to assign heavy physical work to women and curbs their tendency to pay women wages lower than those earned by men doing equivalent work and having similar responsibilities. By a decree of April 26, 1962 (160/

PRG), women are reimbursed for any expenditures arising from the medical care and hospitalization for pregnancy provided in dispensaries, rural infirmaries, and maternal and child-welfare centers. The cost to women of prescription drugs is also repaid to them in full.

Thanks to the Party's policy of guaranteeing work to everyone and improving living standards, women no longer feel subservient to their husbands. They share in the national economy through wage earning and trading, and this trend is promoted by the efforts made to further urbanization, industrialization, and education. Nurses, social-welfare workers, midwives, primary- and secondary-school teachers, secretaries, gendarmes, and air stewardesses have been trained in specialized schools since the early years of independence. The census of May 1967 indicated that there were then 5,019 women working in the government. Of the employees of the national tobacco and match company and the fruit-canning plant of Mamou, 30 per cent were women. In 1967, two-thirds of the women wage earners in the former enterprises were under twenty-five years of age. This phenomenon can be attributed to the recent emancipation of women, which first of all affected the younger and more dynamic elements, and to the family responsibilities that keep women with children at home. Market gardening near the towns and small-scale trading offer women additional means of attaining economic independence. But above all it is the role played by women in Guinea's political life that is their most outstanding hallmark.

The women's branches of the Party supplement the traditional associations that have promoted solidarity in the village among members of the sex which has been oppressed emotionally and ritualistically. They concentrate on developing a political consciousness that eventually should help to build a nation in which women will have no cause to envy the status of men. Through their organizations, women already have a voice in the government. In his speech opening the first congress of the women of Guinea on January 27, 1968, President Sékou Touré pointed out his party's commitment to women's emancipation:

> In the PDG, 8,000 special committees composed solely of women are functioning at the village and city-ward levels. Every year each of those committees democratically elects 13 members to form its executive bureau. Next, in each of the Party's 204 sections (220 by 1974) and 30 federations, there function a sectional and a regional committee, respectively, composed of women. Each of the sectional and regional committees is governed by a bureau of 13. Thus there is a grand total of 3,042 women elected to fill responsible posts.[10]

Simply to cite the proportion of women deputies (27 per cent) or committees of women militants really conveys little information about the life of the nation. For some of the women, political power feeds their vanity, especially since alongside the educated young women (some of whom have only recently become town dwellers) there is an illiterate majority whose members are eager to overcome their feelings of inferiority in relation to their husbands and children by entering politics, an activity that has become synonymous with liberation and a means of acquiring prestige. It is therefore not surprising that the deterioration of the traditional system should have led to social imbalance, excessive individualism, and moral laxity. Rapid changes in the status of women have created certain psychological and sociological problems, such as struggles for power, bourgeois ambitions, a distaste for so-

[10] *Ibid.,* Jan. 29, 1968.

called women's work, sexual freedom, and aberrations in interpreting emancipation.

In short, the freedom movement, born of the aspiration for equality before the law and equality of opportunity, has moved in the direction of increasing women's power, under the influence of a money economy and urban acculturation. It has done so by providing women with the elements required to exercise that power—education, health, jobs, and government employment—a move that also guarantees stability to the established regime. The unifying process has given strength to the women's movement through marital institutions and the organization of women into pressure groups. In so doing, however, the process has given rise to deviations in morality that are harmful to family unity and has encouraged the formation of some groups based on class interests—such as women merchants, wives of bureaucrats, and the like. It has also led to glib talk, prostitution, or trickery as means of achieving upward mobility.

The Political Mobilization of Youth

Because the views of young people have been decisive in changing women's status and attitudes toward economic development, in creating a secularity that made possible the eviction of religious authorities deemed to be competitive, and in providing dynamism for a revolutionary party, the PDG has always regarded the problems of youth as among the most important to be solved. That they were crucial was underscored by the census of May 1967, which showed that 55 per cent of the total population were under twenty years of age and 69 per cent were under thirty. This demographic situation, combined with certain psychological and social attitudes of the young (such as an awareness of their strength, reformist tendencies, and an aggressive attitude toward marriage and religious customs), induced political leaders to exploit youth by making it the vanguard of the revolution.

From the time of its creation on March 29, 1958, the Jeunesse de la Révolution Démocratique Africaine (JRDA) waxed in strength as the sole national youth movement, especially after similar movements based on ethnic or religious affiliations were abolished. The JRDA, composed of young Guineans between the ages of seven and twenty-five, was ideologically and politically dependent on the PDG. Despite some conflicts in authority during its first two years, between its youthful members and those technically or politically responsible for their activities—some of whom were incompetent or incapable of enforcing discipline—the JRDA succeeded in developing a more closely knit organization. Committees of ten boys and girls operated at the level of the city ward and village. These were subordinate to ten-member sectional committees, which, in turn, were under the supervision of regional committees. Capping this organizational pyramid was the JRDA's national council, which consisted of four delegates chosen by each regional committee, and which met once a year. Every two years a national congress was held under the chairmanship of the Secretary of State for Youth and Culture, who was responsible to the national politburo.

The movement's basic purpose was to give its members political training and a militant spirit, and this was to be achieved through activities placed under various ministerial departments. Groups were formed for sports, young women's interests, economics, art and culture, and social welfare. JRDA associations were started in schools and in the university, and Young Pioneers and People's Militias were also organized. At the age of seven, the child in primary school was absorbed into the Pioneer movement, which was integrated with the JRDA. That movement tried to supplement the education given by the family and the school by organizing activities stressing teamwork, emulation, and self-discipline. By means of informal talks, meetings, parades, and market gardening, it also sought to give a revolutionary content to its political, ethical, and civic training.

The indoctrination of youth was prolonged beyond primary school at the same time as the child's awareness of, and active participation in, projects for the nation's revival was cultivated. Children helped draft slogans and execute projects. Convinced of the PDG's monopoly of righteousness, the young RDA members took it upon themselves to denounce the bourgeois youth of other African countries, and outdid Sékou Touré in his flights of eloquence against this or that imperialism or plots that might threaten the regime. They made statements favoring the abolition of polygamy and speculation on the bride price, denounced certain feminine styles as indecent or extravagant, took part in campaigns to promote farming and literacy, and organized athletic and cultural activities for their leisure time.

Sports, especially soccer, were viewed as means for promoting mutual understanding, honesty, and militant fraternity, because they served to mobilize and unite society. They also satisfied the African admiration for physical prowess, exemplified in the prestige of a charismatic champion. Next in order of importance after sports came artistic and cultural performances—theater, dance, instrumental music, and singing—as leisure pastimes. Such performances undoubtedly lent themselves to exhibitionism, but by the choice of themes for plays and songs, they were also useful as propaganda and as vehicles for inculcating morality and conformity. Although there were some very mediocre works, in which revolutionary ranting took the place of art, some of the reinterpretations of traditional melodies and dances were excellent. They served to heighten appreciation of the country's folklore, especially when combined with a degree of inventive genius. This could be seen each year in the "artistic fortnight," geared to the high standards of performance set by Fodéba Kéita's Ballets Africains.

Even more than such spare-time diversions, the activities of the People's Militias served as training for civic mobilization, and were also a means of self-defense and a bulwark against possible political plotters. Organized in villages and city wards, the Militias aimed to exercise control over youth in each locality, and thus to nip potential aberrations in the bud. Until the National Congress of the Revolution met in Labé, July 28–30, 1966, service in the Militia was directed toward reviving the rural economy and giving political training to young people of both sexes between the ages of twenty and thirty. Beginning in 1966, the paramilitary and repressive aspect of the Militia was intensified in consequence of the October 1965 "plot" of Petit Touré, the overthrow of Nkrumah on February 24, 1966, and the example provided by the Chinese Red Guards in August 1966 and thereafter. The Militia, often recruited from among the urban unemployed, served to back up the security forces, thus competing with the army and restricting its power, and it also acted as a Praetorian Guard. In the latter capacity, there was no assurance that the Militia would carry out its duties when the time came, for its braggarts would probably run for cover. Destructive in their zeal, militiamen would sometimes force their way into privately owned places and compel anyone they encountered to attend a meeting or a parade. They were immoderate and inopportune in their reactions, inexperienced, garrulous, and only recently indoctrinated. It is no wonder, therefore, that from time to time clashes occurred between these auxiliary police and the population or the army.

To the question of how such activism and such political practices could become and remain productive and constructive only temporary answers were given. These included voluntary work in building roads, dispensaries, and maternity hospitals, and in collective farming, but such activities were no longer mentioned four years after independence. Next came the "workshops of the revolution," which lasted only a brief time, to be succeeded by civic brigades. Those brigades still exist, but only sporadically and for some agricultural tasks or certain public works. Except when carried out under the CER's supervision, such assignments were of short duration. The mediocre accomplishments of what the PDG pompously called youth's economic role can be attributed to the following causes: impracticality, improvidence, fitful enthusiasm, lack of technical means, insufficient motivation because of poor and irregular pay, embezzlement by responsible leaders of any profits that had been made, the inability to learn from failure, and a persistent self-delusion regarding aims.

Yet one should not overlook the results of the economic and technical orientation given to the educational system. Recognizing with disdain the meagerness of its educational heritage from the colonial period, independent Guinea built up a school system that marked a radical break with the past. The goal it set for its educational program was nothing less than to make the school an integrated and integrating force for development and modernization.

The classic Western style of teaching, under which the ruling elite had been trained, was replaced by another system, based on the following principles:[11]

[11] *Revue de l'éducation nationale,* No. 2 (Conakry, Oct. 1963), pp. 7–9.

(1) Revision of curricula with the aim of inculcating authentic African values.

(2) Giving free instruction at all levels.

(3) Lengthening the period of compulsory schooling to nine years—six in the first cycle for children, beginning at age seven, and three years in the second cycle, to be spent in the agricultural or technical CER.

(4) The extension of third- and fourth-cycle schools, which in April 1973 had 28,224 students in the *lycées,* and 5,050 in the national vocational schools (these together constituting the third cycle), and 3,995 in the university and 1,381 state-scholarship grantees living abroad (the fourth cycle).[12]

(5) Assigning precedence to scientific humanism and technical education over classical European humanism, all the classical and modern *lycées* having been transformed into technical *lycées* or national professional schools.

(6) The linking of education with social and economic realities, national policy, and Party ideology.

Beginning in the academic year of 1969, the last-mentioned objective was most evident in the type of education given exclusively—according to the region—in one of the eight national languages (vernaculars) in the first and second years of the first cycle. The same objective was furthered by organizing the CER into producing cooperatives made up of brigades, sections, and teams for agricultural or technical work. Still more effective was the importance given to ideological indoctrination at all levels of education.

Even a summary stocktaking[13] of the educational system

[12] *Horoya,* Apr. 28, 1974.

[13] For more details, see Claude Rivière, "Les Investissements éducatifs en République de Guinée," *Cahiers d'études africaines,* 5, No. 20 (Oct.–Dec. 1965), pp. 618–34, and Bernadette Lacroix, "L'Enseignement en République de Guinée," *Etudes africaines,* Nos. 116–17 (Brussels, Nov. 10, 1970).

The Strategies of National Integration

gives food for thought. In 1958, the primary and secondary schools of Guinea were attended by 45,090 pupils. By 1973, the school system as a whole, including the university, had 285,340 registered students. Nevertheless, taking into account the growth of the population, the prolongation of compulsory schooling, and the dispersal of pupils among the various institutions, one can clearly see that the percentage of children between the ages of seven and thirteen who were attending school, compared with the total school-age population, had increased from 9 per cent in 1958 to only 33 per cent in 1964 and 36 per cent in 1973. The scope of the major effort made between 1960 and 1965 can be measured by the allocation to education of between one-fifth and one-fourth of the national revenues during that period.

Since 1964, however, a ceiling has been reached in primary-school attendance (one child out of every three). The reasons for this are multiple: the traditional attitudes of illiterate parents, a reluctance to send daughters as well as sons to school, the utilization of children for minor agricultural tasks, the geographical location of schools, dissatisfaction caused by the incoherence of school reforms, and the overcrowding of one-class schools, where children barely learn to read after four or five years.

Few teachers in Guinea would deny that the diagnosis by the head of state in 1961 is still true today:

A noticeable decline in the quality of instruction has been caused by the shortage of qualified teachers, partial changes in the curricula, a lack of homogeneity in the teaching corps, overcrowding of classes and courses, a relaxation of school discipline, the irrelevancy of textbooks, the inadequacy of educational reform, and a faulty system of promotion from grade to grade. This failure to weed out the unqualified means that classes are cluttered up with a considerable number of mediocre pupils, so that the execution of our educational program is slowed down, sometimes to a serious extent.[14]

As of 1973, the Higher Council of Education still regarded as crucial the problems of equipping schools with furniture and books and of training teachers. Aside from the quality of the instruction given, however, the remarkable effort made by the Guinean government to educate both young people and adults should be recognized.

In this writer's view, it is the school system that best reflects the socialistic commitment of the regime. The "cultural revolution," as defined by the PDG at its sixth national congress in September 1967, could be interpreted as an effort to establish socialism by creating a proletariat, with youth playing the role of substitute proletarians in exercising control over the revolutionary process. China's cultural revolution raised a barrier against the bureaucratization of the administrative-political apparatus, and it took place after the political and economic revolutions. In Guinea, the cultural revolution tended to be a reaction against the further progress of an already well-developed *bourgeoisie*. It was concurrently political, economic, and cultural, and it preceded the advent of socialism. Leaving aside all the theoretical speeches made to justify it, which could be applied at any time to any revolution, we shall examine Guinea's cultural revolution as a phenomenon produced by a combination of circumstances.

By stressing the "cultural revolution," the head of state has implicitly tried to provide Guinean youth with a substitute for aggressive action, which might also serve to intimidate persons tempted to carry out a *coup d'état*. In practice, his strategy has worked out in this way:

[14] Sékou Touré, *L'Action politique du PDG pour l'émancipation de la jeunesse guinéenne* (Conakry: Imprimerie Nationale, 1962), p. 101.

The Strategies of National Integration

(1) Verbal pleas were made to revive zeal for farming under the leadership of youth. This followed failure of the cotton crop in 1966–1967 and recognition of an over-all decline in agricultural production. Pressure for a revival of farming was applied principally through the College of Rural Education, which was renamed the Center for Revolutionary Education. By 1972, some twenty CER ostentatiously termed themselves "socialist citadels."

(2) An opportunity for the strengthening of ideological indoctrination was offered to a population beginning to lose interest in politics.

(3) The groundwork was done for a literacy campaign in the national languages; during the summer of 1968, the theme for this campaign was supplied by the solemn return of the ashes of Samori Touré and Alfa Yaya, figures symbolic of the struggle against colonialism and consequently against cultural alienation.

(4) The emotions thus stirred up created an atmosphere propitious to launching the Local Revolutionary Power (PRL), a new organization at the village level in which the fieriest militants could supervise the activities of the basic party cells.

In the writer's opinion, the marked loss of momentum in 1971 (after it had been revived by the Fifth Column trials as noted in Chapter 4) was the result of several developments. One was the opposition between those holding political or administrative posts and their critics among the newly educated Guineans. The other was the contrast between the progress made by education and the meager development of productive forces. Indeed, the hyperpoliticized youth of Guinea, like the women's movement, acted far more as a pressure group than as an instrument of economic progress.

Socioreligious Mutations

The overpoliticization of Guinea's national life in a socialistic direction is quite as apparent in the attitude of the ruling elite toward religion. They have shown their firm intention to paralyze all religious institutions that do not become instruments of the single party's decisions. Illustrative of this determination was the arrest in January 1971 of the great Muslim imam of Conakry and of Monseigneur Raymond-Marie Tchidimbo, the Catholic archbishop. Formerly, the competition among Islam, Christianity, and indigenous religions[15] hampered national development less than the conflicts among the institutions set up and sanctified by religion and those promoted by the new society. Each religion had its own manner of reacting to political developments. The widespread influence exercised by sorcerers and healers in an animist society militated against the activities of the Party and the administration. The aristocratic structure of Muslim society was incompatible with the introduction of political democracy and economic reforms. Christianity, despite its slight influence, could hamper experimentation with bold and anti-French policies. Hence, the national politburo decided to launch campaigns aimed at "demystifying" animism, eliminating "maraboutism" from Islamic practices, and suppressing Christianity, with the aim of secularizing the country's institutions.

In the forest zone (inhabited by Kissi, Toma, Guerzé, Manon, and Kono tribesmen), the demystification campaign of 1959–1960 was as shattering as an earthquake, but its impact was much weaker in the coastal area (populated by the Nalou, Baga, and Landouman tribes). Strengthened by the

[15] A Catholic monthly, *Pentecôte,* in its April 1959 issue, estimated that when Guinea became independent there were in that country 1,625,200 Muslims, 729,600 animists, and 43,400 Catholics.

prestige that it had acquired immediately after independence, the PDG profited by the favorable mood of the country's youth, and by the over-all decline in religious faith after 1954, displaying a remarkable tactical sense in undermining animism by blending pressure with persuasion. Its campaign was waged simultaneously on several levels, with the result that its targets had no time to rally their forces. The press and radio, using the vernacular languages as their medium, strove to give religious beliefs a rational basis. The PDG ordered each of its federations to lay bare to everyone the so-called secrets of cult-initiates and to stigmatize the abusive practices of magicians and fetishers. Initiation rites that involved prolonged periods of seclusion and physical ordeals,[16] as well as the celebration of major tribal ceremonies, were forbidden. The public authorities collected masks and fetishes, sometimes confiscating them. The gendarmes and police were ordered to quell those who resisted. Well-publicized trials and the general opprobrium cast upon human sacrifice mobilized public opinion against fetishism. Theatrical performances produced by all the Party sections continued to discredit fetishism by ridicule. The population of Guinea was deeply impressed by the burning of fetishes, the revelation of the so-called secrets of male society to women and children, and the publicly demonstrated fraudulence of the cries and gestures of the traditional masks.

Eventually, the tension died down. The PDG took over the role played by fetishism in sustaining the ancient moral barriers, and those who had theretofore benefited by the "sacred character of the forest" were left with only nostalgia for the past. Even if the Party's campaign was not wholly

[16] Claude Rivière, "Circoncision et excision dans la Guinée nouvelle," *L'Afrique littéraire et artistique*, No. 15 (1971), pp. 44–51.

successful, it must be recognized that, on the whole, it weakened animism and relegated its ceremonies and rites to the realm of superstition and folklore.

Islam is professed by three-fourths of the Guinean population. Beginning in the thirteenth century, its spread was linked to the expansion of the empire of Mali, and then in the eighteenth century to that of the Peul almamis of the Fouta Djalon. Islam, too, was attacked by the state. The government tried to undermine that faith as a competitive power and to attenuate its conservatism more than it sought to reach some compromise whereby it might share in Islam's widespread influence. Between 1954 and 1957, the PDG in seeking power had solicited support from some of the religious chiefs and important Muslim merchants. Nevertheless, once in the saddle, the Party leaders—many of whom had attended Koranic schools —took the line of attacking the purveyors of Islam although not its doctrines. They denounced the marabouts' addiction to worldly pleasures and their exploitation of the people's credulity so that they might cling to their jealously guarded prestige and their revenue from alms.[17]

The principal steps taken against Islam coincided with the campaign to demystify animism. These consisted of the removal of imams from communal and magisterial posts (despite resistance to this in Fouta and Kankan): suppression of the Union Culturelle Musulmane (which had been founded at Dakar in 1953 by Cheikh Touré), until it was later reconstituted with leaders chosen or approved by the PDG; reduction in the number of daily prayers to two, so as not to interfere with working hours; orders sometimes requiring imams to preach their Friday sermons on themes provided by the Party:

[17] Circular No. 81/BPN (Oct. 16, 1959), signed by El Hadj Saifoulaye Diallo and Daouda Camara.

a ban on the tours made by marabouts to solicit alms; and a limitation of the number of pilgrims journeying to Mecca. After suppression of the mission schools in 1961, the Koranic schools (which had been closed temporarily) revived gradually, in much the same way as instruction in the catechism by the Christian missions. To be sure, such centers of Muslim study and prayer, as Touba, Kankan, Dinguiraye, and Labé were sometimes out of tune with the country's political evolution. This presented no serious problem, however, because of the strict control exercised by the political elite and some conciliatory gestures on the part of Sékou Touré—such as the supply of free electric current to mosques after 1971 and the donation of sheep to imams for the purpose of inducing Allah's blessing on the eve of the PDG's ninth congress. In brief, Islam was disciplined in the interests of a unified national development.

To understand the attitude of Guinea toward the Catholic Church, one must consider that church's relevance to the Party's claim to a monopoly of ideology and of "African authenticity," and to the concentration of power at the political level. The following chronology lists the successive steps taken by the government against that religion:[18]

March 26, 1959—Suppression of the movements of Catholic youth and sports associations, and the like to the benefit of the JRDA.

August 17, 1961—Decision of the national conference of the PDG to suppress mission schools and to nationalize education, beginning with the academic year in October.

August 26, 1961—Expulsion of the archbishop of Conakry, Monseigneur Gérard de Milleville, who had protested against the previous measure.

[18] For a detailed study of this problem and others taken up in this chapter, see Claude Rivière, *Mutations sociales en Guinée*.

May 31, 1962—Consecration at Conakry of a Guinean priest, Monseigneur Tchidimbo, as successor to Monseigneur de Milleville.

May 1, 1967—Decision to Africanize all the Christian clergy within a month, and to expel the 154 white missionaries (priests, nuns, friars, and their lay assistants) as well as the non-African Protestant ministers.

January 24, 1971—Sentencing of Monseigneur Tchidimbo to forced labor for life, on charges of treason and complicity in the plot and invasion of November 22, 1970; the real reason for this punishment was that he had become a critic of the regime after having been one of its supporters.

The points at issue between religious creeds and the state were thus not resolved by compromise but through the complete triumph of one of the parties to the dispute. The victor was the political power, which aspired not only to keep under its control all aspects of the life of the nation but, by preventing freedom of expression, to exclude or suppress even hints of ideological deviation. The net result was that most religions were devitalized.

Unquestionably, social mutations are occurring in Guinea. Albeit irreversible in its orientation, the outcome of these changes is open to question. Tribal integration gives rise to the problem of adapting the individual to social, ethical, and economic situations in society as a whole, whereas until now he has had to conform only with those of a restricted group. The emancipation of women leads one to speculate on the consequences of the disintegration of the extended family, as well as on how the monogamous family will be structured. The political mobilization of youth causes concern about how young people will approach adulthood: Will they choose the path of reason or of violence, of solid qualifications or of empty pretensions, of progress or of animosity? How will they react to the viruses injected by the ideologies of affluent societies and of those that practice revolution?

The demystification and weakening of religious faith raises questions about the population's sense of security and about what will be found to replace it. Will syncretism harden into a doctrine and a cult? Will Islam and Christianity further their conquests through a process of adaptation? To what degree can nationalism satisfy Guineans who want material advantages? Will it play the role of long-established religions in meeting the need for happiness and prosperity, which was formerly satisfied by the existence of myths of the supernatural?

Forecasting the future is inevitably hazardous, inasmuch as revolutionary pride, a form of bourgeois consciousness, is making its appearance among the younger generation, which is moving toward the acquisition of high posts. Among other elements, however, the zeal to insure the triumph of socialism has been transmuted into concern for the restoration of social equilibrium, along lines closer to individual profit than to the generous disinterestedness inherent as a principle in radical ideologies.

Conclusion

After a study from different angles of the evolution of Guinea since the time when the native Guineans made their collective appearance on the political scene, it seems possible to characterize the regime of Sékou Touré as a mobilization system, in which socialist, but not Marxist, goals only partially disguise the development of social inequality.

First of all, one must ask what has been the impact of the political and economic policy of the Guinean government on the stratification of society. In order to answer such a question, it is necessary to evaluate the real extent of integration and of internal conflict in that society by defining, at least in broad terms, the way in which the situation has evolved.

At the end of the colonial period, national integration was effected through the conflicts related to a domination/subordination situation, and by the ensuing elimination of the most brutal forms of oppression. At the same time that colonization engendered a sense of solidarity among the oppressed, it offered examples of social differentiation. Thanks to the impact of three major factors—a party, an ideology, and a leader—national solidarity developed. Nevertheless, the politicization or, rather, the hyperpoliticization of national life undermined the consensus. It did this to the degree to which inequalities in the sharing of power were accentuated by the existence of a hierarchy of partisans. The ritualization of the community's life and the stifling of adverse opinions by jailing the regime's opponents simply drove the conflicts underground.

Conclusion

Despite the muzzling of the opposition, the series of "plots" reveals a progressive emergence of certain social forces present in a new, or at least embryonic, stratification. Although a scarcity economy has leveled most incomes downward, it has at the same time favored the rise of those fishing in troubled waters.

Doubtless the political stalemate, the slow pace of economic development and modernization, the residual structure and compartmentalization of traditional society, and social instability and mobility have slowed down class stratification. Yet other factors have had the contrary effect of promoting the development of a *bourgeoisie*. In this respect, foreign aid and investments were used in part for the benefit of those running the state. The expansion of education has increased differences in cultural and consumption levels that follow bourgeois models. Moreover the stabilization of power among the ruling elements has tended to make a privileged group more conspicuous.

Admission to that elite group is determined by political militancy, and those who compose it are required to identify themselves very closely with a system in whose management they share. Considering the means of its recruitment, management, self-enrichment, and solving of disputes, the group can be described as a state *bourgeoisie*. By gaining control over surplus labor and contraband, they are the first class to be formed, in conjunction with the big merchants who also benefit from the high profits of trading and commercial and monetary speculation. The cooperative societies and opportunities offered by the state sector of the economy also serve to contribute to their advancement.

In other words, a social restratification is taking place, thanks to the primacy accorded to politics, the main driving force of this managerial element. But the corpulence of the group results principally from the place it occupies in an underdeveloped economy—that is to say, by determining the course of development, the group's members have become the main beneficiaries. Its profits are further increased because the economic machinery has not yet been broken in and is poorly controlled, and because the state has taken over a good share in the country's industrialization, so that the ruling group is in a strong position to exercise legitimate authority. Its members' tactical alliances and client relationship to the army commanders, the influential intellectuals, and the big merchants and planters foster the emergence of a class that predominates politically, economically, and culturally. In the present restratification, control over the means of production through political power carries more weight than does the actual ownership of the means of production. Guinea being a country where both agricultural and industrial output is small, the hierarchical scale of privileges can be assessed above all in terms of consumption. Those who are dominated by the privileged hierarchy—the only visibly dominant class—are not aware of themselves as a class, either as a whole or in their respective sectors (employees, laborers, and peasants). This is because the hegemony wielded by the supporters of the state system prevents any political confrontation by groups that are, as these tend to be, composed of barely literate individuals.

Independence has also caused the labor movement to lose momentum, because its leaders have joined the political elite. The minority of partly trained or wholly unskilled laborers still employed has served the purposes of this budding *bourgeoisie,* which, by assuring them of a wage, has given them a status somewhat superior to that of the farmers. Perforce submissive to the regime by their need for survival, the laborers have been unable to develop aggressiveness in relation to their principal employer, which is the state. The peasantry, even though numerically far more important, is inhibited from undertaking coordinated action on its own behalf because of the diversification of its subsistence agriculture—such as animal husbandry and rice culture—and by its dispersal on large and small plantations, as well as the disparity of its interests and revenues.

Most of the country's craftsmen are to be found within the rural world. They form a marginal category characterized by a caste system, especially among Peul and Manding, the meagerness of their earnings, and the irregularity of their work.[1] The modernization of Guinea's crafts has been hampered by the poor functioning of the cooperative societies. Even though the craftsmen have survived in a scarcity economy, they seem doomed by their inadaptability. For the time being, the artisans' status remains fairly ambiguous, for the government's policy oscillates between, on the one hand, its goal of eliminating castes because they perpetuate inequalities among the craftsmen and, on the other, its desire to preserve certain traditional values, techniques, and means of production, which were formerly inseparable because they formed a substratum of the system.

These few reflections on Guinea's social stratification obviously prompt the question as to how the existing inequalities can be reconciled with an emotional type of socialism. However, this problem of compatibility gives rise to still another question: to what degree can Guinea qualify as a socialist

[1] Claude Rivière, *Dynamique de la stratification sociale en Guinée* (Paris: Librairi Honoré Champion, 1975), pp. 569–615; "La Difficile Emergence d'un artisanat casté," *Cahiers d'études africaines,* 9, No. 36 (1969), 600–25.

country when, above all, it hands over its most remunerative assets—its mineral resources—to the international "imperialism" of the Western and Eastern blocs?

Socialism's impact certainly can be recognized in the predilection shown by Sékou Touré for the Groups of Communist Studies, the CGT, the French Communist Party (with which the RDA was temporarily affiliated), and, in the years following independence, the communist powers. It is also evident in the terms used by Sékou Touré, such as "progressive aspirations," "the revolutionary party," "dialectical analysis," "mobilization of the services of the toiling masses," "revolutionary awareness," "loyalty to the Party," "self-criticism," and "dictatorship of the people." But his additions to, and the elimination or special interpretations of, basic socialist themes suggest an ideological independence rather than filiation or orthodoxy. The phraseology remains the same but its significance varies. His ideological attempts to build a socialist state might operate at the level of oratory, both in syntax and in symbols, but that does not mean that they were applied in day-to-day living.

Nevertheless, in Guinea's organizational plan, it appears that the single party—at least in its early stages—was modeled after that of socialist countries. Its principles of democratic centralism, the proclaimed participation of the whole population in public life, the tasks assigned to the base committees, the role given to the unions, the system of people's militias, the elimination of individual liberties, and the purges and tortures bring to mind the operating mechanism of the U.S.S.R. Yet even so, they are less the phenomena of a socialist regime than the constant factors in the organization and operations of any mobilization system, whether it be that of a conservative or a radical totalitarianism. If one considers solely the organizational level, it cannot be determined whether a society is simply disciplined or is actually socialistic.

An examination of the economic structures whose aim was to suppress the exploitive relationships that prevail under neocolonial regimes makes more obvious Guinea's choice of a socialist system. This can be seen in the government's taking over the wholesale trade, including the setting up of distribution centers, state stores, and consumers' cooperatives, the nationalization of enterprises, the creation of state companies, the establishment of agricultural and craft cooperative societies, and the collective management of the apparatus of production. However, we know who benefited from those measures. Finally, by its strategy of alternating advances with retreats, *de facto* tolerance with the over-all control of policy, verbal propaganda and the indoctrination of youth, along with the interlude of a "cultural revolution," the government of Guinea has aligned itself with socialistic modes of action.

Yet one cannot affirm that Guinea is a model of Marxist socialism if such a judgment is based simply on certain resemblances in its organization of the masses and the style of its planning. Analogy is not tantamount to identity. The perseverance shown by the ruling group in building what they call socialism (albeit a socialism not based on any particular dogma) simply expresses their determination to remain independent in relation to capitalism. The very nature of the PDG as a mass party and not a vanguard party, and the pragmatic flexibility of its policies as well as its concrete actions, preclude excessive assimilation. Even though Sékou Touré truly desires to reduce social inequality, those who share power with him find that the ideology they proclaim serves— either unwittingly or deliberately—as a cloak for their growing transformation into a *bourgeoisie*. That transformation is facilitated by the fact that the ruling group itself represents the state, and the state is the authority which has the greatest influence on the distribution of social revenues. Everyone makes the maximum effort to gain the greatest advantages that may be derived from the disparity between the regime's ideological declarations and its practices.

The trend toward a form of authoritarian government is the most obvious threat to the system of mobilization of the kind portrayed by David Apter.[2] In that system, the government intervenes actively in effecting social changes and economic development. Moreover, one vital aspect of its activities is the establishment and maintenance of a strong, highly hierarchized organization capable of overseeing the execution of the policy decisions made by the government. The fact that such controls can be exercised over the organization itself leads to both conservatism on the part of the public organism and to a reinforcement of the constraints required to reach the goals set. The use of such constraints necessitates an ideological justification, but as the ideology proposes objectives as ambitious as they are sacrosanct, these goals are always formulated in terms of future but not of present satisfaction. The strengthening of coercive methods to bring about the desired changes results in a diminution in the freedom of information flowing from the base toward the decision-making centers of power and lessens the validity of such information. To offset the unsettling atmosphere of uncertainty, the government imposes obedience to its policy, and the price it pays for using coercion is a steady rise in the cost of government and in the mobilization process. The necessity for increased governmental supervision and the effort required to eliminate the major opposition forces have

[2] David E. Apter, *The Politics of Modernization* (Chicago: University of Chicago Press, 1965).

Conclusion

so reduced the valid information available that the policymaking centers are encountering growing difficulty in accurately assessing the popular support they enjoy as well as in gauging the disparities between their economic goals and the people's aspirations. Consequently, stress is placed on ideological conformity and on loyalty to the groups that protect the regime, such as the militia, the army, and the bureaucracy.

To conclude, the mobilization system is foundering in a totalitarian type of government and is leading to a misconception of the country's real needs. Because of growing constraints, consensus is lost. This loss of consensus between the people and the elite is due mainly to the latter's mistakes in management. The loss of consensus between the leader and the population, though less perceptible, results from the burden of constraints and the rigorous measures imposed by a disguised dictatorship.

Bibliography

Books

Adamolekun, Ladipo. *Sékou Touré's Guinea*. London: Methuen, 1976.

Ameillon, B. *La Guinée: Bilan d'une indépendance*. Paris: Maspero, 1964.

Amin, Samir. *Trois expériences africaines de développement: Le Mali, la Guinée, le Ghana*. Paris: Presses Universitaires de France, 1965.

Apter, David E. *The Politics of Modernization*. Chicago: University of Chicago Press, 1965.

Arcin, André. *La Guinée française*. Paris: Challamel, 1907.

——. *Histoire de la Guinée française*. Paris: Challamel, 1911.

Attwood, William. *The Red and the Blacks*. New York: Harper & Row, 1967.

Bénot, Yves. *Idéologies des indépendances africaines*. Paris: Maspero, 1969.

Camara, Sylvain. "Le Conflit franco-guinéen." Unpublished doctoral thesis, University of Paris, 1968 (mimeo.).

Carter, Gwendolen (ed.). *African One-Party States*. Ithaca, N.Y.: Cornell University Press, 1962.

Chaffard, Georges. *Les Carnets secrets de la décolonisation*. Paris: Calmann-Levy, 1967.

Charles, Bernard. *Guinée*. Lausanne: Rencontres, 1963.

——. *La République de Guinée*. Paris: Berger-Levrault, 1972.

——. "Cadres guinéens et appartenances ethniques." Unpublished doctoral thesis, University of Paris, 1968 (mimeo.).

Condé, Alpha. *Guinée: L'Albanie de l'Afrique ou néo-colonie américaine?* Paris: Git-le-Coeur, 1972.

Cournanel, Alain. "Planification et investissements privés en République de Guinée." Unpublished doctoral thesis, University of Paris, 1968 (mimeo.).

de Decker, Henri. *Nation et développement communautaire en Guinée et au Sénégal.* Paris: Mouton, 1968.

Diallo, Tierno Nabika. "Bilan et perspectives de la coopération dans le développement de l'agriculture guinéenne." Unpublished thesis, Institut Polytechnique, Conakry, 1967 (mimeo.).

Diawara, Alpha. *Guinée: La marche du peuple.* Dakar: CERDA, 1968.

DuBois, Victor. "The Independence Movement in Guinea: A Study of African Nationalism." Unpublished doctoral dissertation, Princeton University, 1966.

Dumont, René. *Reconversion de l'économie agricole: Guinée, Côte d'Ivoire, Mali.* Paris: Presses Universitaires de France, 1961.

Dupire, Marguerite. *Organisation sociale des Peul.* Paris: Plon, 1970.

Favrod, Charles-Henri. *L'Afrique seule.* Paris: Seuil, 1961.

Gigon, Fernand. *Guinée: Etat-pilote.* Paris: Plon, 1959.

Houis, Maurice. *La Guinée française.* Paris: Editions Maritimes et Coloniales, 1953.

Lestrange, Monique de. *Les Coniagui et les Bassari.* Paris: Presses Universitaires de France, 1955.

Lombard, Jacques. *Autorités traditionnelles et pouvoirs politiques en Afrique noire.* Paris: Armand Colin, 1967.

Marty, Paul. *L'Islam en Guinée.* Paris: Leroux, 1921.

Meynaud, Jean and Salah-Bey, Anisse. *Le Syndicalisme africain.* Paris: Payot, 1963.

Milcent, Ernest. *L'A.O.F. entre en scène.* Paris: Editions Témoignage chrétien, 1958.

Morgenthau, Ruth Schachter. *Political Parties in French-Speaking West Africa.* Oxford: Clarendon Press, 1964.

Morrow, John Henry. *First American Ambassador to Guinea.* New Brunswick, N.J.: Rutgers University Press, 1968.

Niane, Djibril Tamsir. *Recherches sur l'empire du Mali au moyen-âge.* Conakry: Institut National de Recherches et de Documentation, 1962.

———. *Soundjata ou l'épopée mandingue.* Paris: Présence africaine, 1960.

Paulme, Denise. *Les Gens du riz: Kissi de la Haute Guinée française.* Paris: Plon, 1954.

Person, Yves. *Samori: Une révolution dyula.* 2 vols. Dakar: IFAN, 1970.

Richard-Molard, Jacques. *Problèmes humains en Afrique occidentale.* Paris: Présence africaine, 1946.
Rivière, Claude. *Dynamique de la stratification sociale en Guinée.* Paris: Librairie Honoré Champion, 1975.
——. *Mutations sociales en Guinée.* Paris: Marcel Rivière, 1971.
Suret-Canale, Jean. *La République de Guinée.* Paris: Editions Sociales, 1970.
Sy, Seydou-Madani. *Recherches sur l'exercice du pouvoir politique en Afrique noire: Côte d'Ivoire, Guinée, Mali.* Paris: Pedone, 1965.
Touré, Ahmed Sékou. *L'Action politique du Parti Démocratique de Guinée.* 20 vols. 1958 to 1975:
> *Expérience guinéenne et unité africaine.* Vols. I and II combined. Paris: Présence africaine, 1962.
> *L'Action politique du Parti démocratique de Guinée pour l'émancipation de la jeunesse guinéenne.* Vol. VIII. Conakry: Imprimerie Nationale, 1962.
> *La Révolution guinéenne et le progrès social.* Vol. X. Conakry: Imprimerie Nationale, 1967 (4th edition.)
> *L'Afrique et la révolution.* XIII. Switzerland: 1966.
> *Plan septennal, 1964–1971.* Vol. XIV. Conakry: Imprimerie Nationale, 1967.
> *Défendre la révolution.* Vol. XV. Conakry: Imprimerie Nationale, 1969 (2d edition).
> *La Négritude et la cinquième colonne.* Vol. XIX. Conakry: Imprimerie Nationale, 1972.

Articles

Adamolekun, Ladipo. "Politics and Administration in West Africa: The Guinean Model," *Journal of African Administration,* Oct. 8, 1969.
"Bauxites: Sept producteurs à Conakry," *Le Moniteur africain,* 72 (Mar.–Apr. 1974).
Beaujeu-Garnier, Jacqueline. "Essai de géographie électorale guinéenne," *Cahiers d'outre-mer,* 44 (Oct.–Dec. 1958).
Césaire, Aimé. "La Pensée politique de Sékou Touré," *Présence africaine,* 29 (Dec. 1959).
Charbonneaux, Jean. "Les bauxites de Guinée," *Industries et travaux d'Outre-Mer,* 22 June 1974.

Charles, Bernard. "La Guinée." In *Décolonisation et régimes politiques en Afrique noire*, edited by André Mabileau and Jean Meyriat. (Paris: Armand Colin, 1967).

———. "Un parti politique africain, Le Parti Démocratique de Guinée," *Revue française de science politique*, 12, No. 2 (1962).

Chauleur, Pierre. "La Guinée après trois ans d'indépendance," *Etudes*, Nov. 1961.

———. "Un dictateur aux abois: Sékou Touré," *ibid.*, May 1971.

Cournanel, Alain. "Situation de la classe ouvrière en République de Guinée," *Partisans*, 61 (1971).

Decraene, Philippe. "La Guinée seule avec elle-même," *Preuves*, 133 (Mar. 1962).

Diallo, Ahmed Alfa. "Introduction à l'étude de la constitution guinéenne," *Recherches africaines*, 2 (Apr.–June 1962).

"Dossier Guinée," *Remarques africaines*, 13 (Nov. 10, 1971).

DuBois, Victor. "The Decline of the Guinean Revolution," *American Universities Field Staff Reports*, West African Series, 8, Nos. 7–9 (1965).

———. "The Rise of an Opposition to Sékou Touré," *ibid.*, 9, Nos. 1–9 (1966).

Fischer, Georges. "L'Indépendance de la Guinée et les accords franco-guinéens," *Annuaire français de droit international*, 4 (1958).

———. "Quelques aspects de la doctrine politique guinéenne," *Civilisations*, 9, No. 4 (1959).

"Guinea after Five Years," *World To-day*, 20 (Mar. 1964).

"Guinée: Le code des investissements," *Journal officiel de la République de Guinée*, Apr. 7, 1962.

"La Guinée six ans après," *Croissance des Jeunes Nations*, 46 (July–Aug. 1965).

"L'Industrie minière en Guinée," *Industries et travaux d'Outre-Mer*, 87 (Feb. 1961).

Kéita, N'Famara. "Le Plan triennal de Guinée," *Afrique-Documents*, 55 (1961).

Lacroix, Bernadette. "L'Enseignement en République de Guinée," *Etudes africaines* (Brussels), Nos. 116–17, Nov. 10, 1970.

Leunda, Xavier. "La Réforme de l'enseignement et son incidence sur l'évolution rurale en Guinée," *Civilisations*, 22, No. 2 (1972).

———. "Nouvelles institutions rurales en Guinée," *ibid.,* 23–24, 1–2 (1973–1974).
Perroux, François. "Une nation en voie de se faire, la République de Guinée," *Revue d'action populaire,* 129 (June 1959).
Poli, François. "La Guinée, un an après l'aggression," *Jeune Afrique,* 570 (Dec. 11, 1971).
"La Politique d'infiltration des pays du bloc soviétique en Afrique occidentale," *Témoignages,* 39 (July–Aug. 1964).
Portères, Roland. "Caféiers de la République de Guinée," *Café, cacao, thé,* I (Mar. 1962).
Rivière, Claude. "Comportements ostentatoires et style de vie des élites guinéennes," *Cultures et développement,* 3, No. 3 (1971).
———. "Dynamique des systèmes fonciers et inégalités sociales: Le cas guinéen," *Cahiers internationaux de sociologie,* 54 (1973).
———. "Lutte ouvrière et phénomène syndical en Guinée," *Cultures et développement,* 7, No. 1 (1975).
"Les Statuts du Parti Démocratique de Guinée," *Recherches africaines,* 4 (Oct.–Dec. 1963).
Suret-Canale, Jean. "Fria, un exemple d'industrialisation africaine," *Annales de géographie,* 73 (Mar.–Apr. 1964).
———. "La Guinée dans le système colonial," *Présence africaine,* 29 (Dec. 1959–Jan. 1960).
———. "La Guinée face à son avenir," *Nouvelle revue internationale,* 9 (Feb. 1966).
———. "La Fin de la chefferie en Guinée," *Journal of African History,* 7, No. 3 (1966).
"Tableau économique de la Guinée," *Bulletin d'Afrique noire,* 12 (Jan. 10, 1968).
Wallerstein, Immanuel. "L'Idéologie du Parti Démocratique de Guinée," *Présence africaine,* 40 (Jan.–Mar. 1962).

Newspapers and Periodicals

Afrique-Documents, Dakar.
L'Afrique littéraire et artistique, Paris.
Afrique nouvelle, Dakar.
American Universities Field Staff Reports, New York.
Bulletin de l'IFAN, Dakar.

Cahiers d'études africaines, Paris.
Cahiers internationaux de sociologie, Paris.
Cahiers d'Outre-Mer, Bordeaux.
Coup de bambou, Conakry.
Cultures et développement, Louvain.
Etudes africaines, Brussels.
Le Figaro, Paris.
Fraternité-matin, Abidjan.
La Guinée libre, Paris.
Horoya, Conakry.
Horoya hebdo, Conakry.
Journal officiel de la République de Guinée, Conakry.
La Liberté, Conakry.
Marchés tropicaux et méditerranéens, Paris.
Le Monde, Paris.
Le Moniteur africain, Dakar.
Pentecôte, Paris.
Présence africaine, Paris.
La Presse de Guinée, Conakry.
Le Progrés africain, Conakry.
Révolution africaine, Algiers.
Revue de l'éducation nationale, Conakry.
Revue française d'études politiques africaines, Paris.
Revue R.D.A., Conakry.
La Voix de la Guinée, Conakry.
West Africa, London.

Index

Accar, Roger, 138
Administration: post-independence, 30, 89-91, 94, 96-102; pre-independence, 42-44, 51, 64-68, 70, 71, 74, 76-79, 102; *see also* Civil service
Africanization, 101, 186, 195, 196, 236
Agency for International Development (AID), 154, 155, 162, 176, 184, 189, 193, 201
Agricultural policy, 30, 104, 111, 115-118, 133, 146, 198-208, 231; *see also* Animal husbandry, Crops, *and individual crops*
Aid, foreign, 95, 101, 112, 119-120, 146, 150-155, 158-159, 160, 162, 176, 182, 189-193, 200, 201-202, 209, 239
Air transport, 111n, 155, 160, 163, 164
Alfa, Karamoko, 37, 38
Alfa Yaya, 40, 216, 231
Alfaya clan, 38, 40
Algeria, relations with, 148, 169, 170, 188, 190
Al-Nimeiry, Gaafar, 169
Aluminium of Canada, Ltd. (ALCAN), 155, 183, 184
Aluminum (alumina), 50, 84, 154-155, 166, 178, 180, 183, 185, 186, 187, 204; *see also* Bauxite, Boké project, *and* Fria Company
Aluminum Company of America (ALCOA), 155, 184

Amicale Gilbert Viellard, 62, 63, 64, 66, 69
Animal husbandry, 23, 27, 30, 34, 198, 204, 207, 215
Animism, 33, 35, 36, 37, 232-234
Archinard, Louis, 41
Army, role of, 94, 95, 122, 124, 126, 128, 134-137, 138, 171, 226, 240, 245
Artisanry, 34, 35, 36, 241, 243
Attwood, William, 154
Autra, Ray, 65, 66, 127

Baga tribe, 26, 31, 72, 232
Bah, Ibrahima, 127
Baldé, Ousmane, 176n
Ballay, Noël, 24, 42
Bamako conference, Oct. 18, 1946, 63
Bambara tribe, 25, 212
Bananas, 26, 48, 49, 105, 118, 141, 178, 198, 204, 205, 212
Bangoura, Karim, 69
Banking, 95, 104, 106, 114, 119, 144, 148, 156, 208
Barry, Ibrahima, 69, 70, 74, 75, 79
Bassari tribe, 24
Bauxite, 23, 27, 50, 56, 103, 110, 141, 143, 166, 167, 169, 170, 171, 181, 183-188, 197, 204; *see also* Aluminum (alumina), Fria Company, *and* Mining
Bayol-Noirot mission, 39
Béavogui, Louis Lansana, 164, 170, 216

Belgium, relations with, 139, 188; *see also* Western bloc, relations with
Bénin, *see* Dahomey, relations with
Bérété, Framoi, 69
Bloc Africain de Guinée (BAG), 69-76, 79, 80, 85
Boké project, 155, 166, 167, 183-185, 186, 197
Bouët-Villaumez, Louis-Edouard, 39
Boumédienne, Houari, 148
Brazzaville conference, Jan. 30–Feb. 8, 1944, 61, 62
Budgets, 46, 95, 96, 103, 113, 158, 173-177, 207, 208, 229
Bureau Politique National (BPN), 93, 96-99, 131, 224, 232
Busia, Kofi, 148

Cabral, Amilcar, 136
Caillé, René, 38
Camara, Bengali, 131
Camara, Daouda, 131
Cameroun, relations with, 169, 183
Ceausescu, Nicolas, 170
Census, 28-29, 31, 223
Chevence, Maurice, 62
Chieftaincy, 34, 36, 37, 39-45, 67, 69-73, 77, 78, 116, 117, 142, 215, 234
China, relations with, 8, 143, 150-153, 157, 158, 159, 165, 167, 171, 173, 176, 191, 193, 200, 202, 226
Christianity, 35, 127, 232, 235-236, 237; *see also* Religion, state policy toward
Cissé, Ibrahima Ciré, 65
Citrus fruit, 27, 48, 141, 206
Civil service, 54, 55, 57, 58, 76, 78, 86, 96, 101-102, 122-123, 126, 129, 130, 132-133, 177, 196, 211, 216, 217, 221, 245
Climate, 25-28, 205, 208

Coffee, 28, 48, 49, 105, 109, 118, 141, 178, 198, 204, 205, 212, 214
Colas, 26, 28, 33, 49, 214
Collèges d'Enseignement Rural (CER; later, Centres d'Enseignement Révolutionnaire), 191, 199, 200, 202, 220, 227, 228, 231
Colonies Françaises d'Afrique (later, Caisse Franco-Africaine) franc (CFA franc), 25, 107
Colonization, European, 24, 38-51, 53
Combes, Antoine, 41
Comité d'Entente Guinéenne, 66-67
Comité d'Union de Basse Guinée, 63, 66, 69
Communist Party, French, 53, 64, 87, 150, 242
Compagnie de Financement du Commerce Extérieur (COFICOMEX), 180, 183, 197
Compagnie du Niger Français, 47, 86
Compagnie Française d'Afrique Occidentale (CFAO), 47
Comptoir Guinéen du Commerce Extérieur (CGCE), 105, 106, 110, 111
Comptoir Guinéen du Commerce Intérieur (CGCI), 107, 110, 122
Confédération Africaine des Travailleurs Croyants (CATC), 59, 74, 80
Confédération Française des Travailleurs Chrétiens (CFTC), 54n, 55
Confédération Générale des Travailleurs Africains (CGTA), 59, 87
Confédération Générale du Travail (CGT), 53, 54, 55, 58, 59, 68, 70, 86, 87, 242
Congrès National de la Révolution (CNR), 113, 114, 118, 226
Coniagui tribe, 24, 42, 216

Index

Constituent assembly, French, 62
Constitution, 94-96
Conté, Saidou, 131
Convention Africaine, 79, 80
Cooperative societies, 104, 105, 111, 112, 114-118, 173, 199-200, 202-203, 227, 228, 239, 243
Coopératives Agricoles de Production (CAP), 112, 117-118, 202; *see also* Cooperative societies
Coopératives de Production Agricole et de Consommation (COPAC), 202; *see also* Cooperative societies
Cornut-Gentille, Bernard, 87
Cotton, 112, 191, 198, 212, 231
Coulibali, Ouezzin, 65
Coumbassa, Firmin, 55
Coups d'état, attempted, *see* Plots
Courts, 96, 215; *see also* Trials
Crops: export and industrial, 26, 28, 46, 48, 111, 146, 160, 198, 202, 204-206, 207; subsistence, 26, 27, 28, 34, 35, 115, 146, 160, 198, 203-207, 221, 225, 241; *see also individual crops*
Cuba, relations with, 152, 153
Currency, 25, 46, 103-107, 119, 120, 129, 130, 145, 148, 149, 155, 156, 158, 176, 178, 208
Czechoslovakia, relations with, 156, 157, 185; *see also* Eastern European bloc, relations with

Daddah, Moktar Ould, 165; *see also* Mauritania, relations with
Dahomey, relations with, 49
Dara, Ibrahima Sory, 69
Debt, foreign, 119, 120, 143, 144, 147, 161, 164, 177-178, 208; *see also* Loans, foreign
Defferre, Gaston, 76
De Gaulle, Charles, 61, 81, 82, 84, 141, 149, 150

De Milleville, Mgr. Gérard, 235, 236
Démocratie Socialiste de Guinée (DSG), 69, 70, 73, 74, 75, 79, 80
De Sanderval, Olivier, 39, 40
Diakité, Moussa, 131
Diallo, Abdoulaye, 59, 74
Diallo, Abdouramane, 65
Diallo, Ibrahima, 127
Diallo, Saifoulaye, 75, 90, 113, 114, 165, 216
Diallo, Seydou, 59
Diallo, Yacine, 62, 64, 65, 67, 68, 69
Dialonké tribe, 36, 37
Diamonds, 49, 110, 141, 181-182, 212
Diawadou, Barry, 69, 74, 75, 79, 135
Dioula tribe, 33, 46-47, 48

Eastern European bloc, relations with, 84, 105, 119, 120, 141-144, 147, 150-154, 156-159, 163, 167, 169, 171, 183, 185, 187, 188, 242; *see also individual countries*
East Germany, relations with, 143-144, 185; *see also* Eastern European bloc, relations with
Economic policies, *see* Planning, economic
Education, 35, 44, 51, 83, 86, 92, 94, 101, 111n, 114, 122, 127, 128, 150, 151, 154, 160, 175, 196, 200, 207, 215, 220, 221, 225, 227-231, 235, 239
Egypt, relations with, 158, 170, 201; *see also* Nasser, Gamal Abdel
Eisenhower, Dwight D., 153, 156
Elections, 57, 62, 63, 64, 66-71, 74-78, 87, 94, 95, 100
Elite, evolution of, 124, 125-126, 129-130, 132-133, 134, 140, 230, 239-240, 243-244

Emigrés, 28n, 88, 122, 128, 135-140, 147, 149, 162, 168, 171, 177, 203, 204
Enterprises, state, 95, 96, 104, 109, 110, 112, 113-114, 118, 119, 126, 129-133, 146, 172, 176, 182, 188, 190-194, 221, 240, 243
Ethnic rivalry, *see* Tribalism
Europeans, status of, 56, 62, 84, 127, 195, 196, 197; *see also* Africanization
Exiles, *see* Emigrés
Exports, 105, 109, 110n, 185, 189, 204, 205, 206; *see also* Aluminum (alumina), Bauxite, Crops, export and industrial, *and* Trade, foreign

Fetishism, *see* Animism
Fofana, Karim, 131, 135
Fonds d'Investissements pour le Développement Economique et Social (FIDES), 82, 84, 155
Force Ouvrière (FO), 53n, 54n, 55, 59, 87
Forest peoples, 31-32, 34, 43, 44, 49, 192, 213-214
Forests, 27-28, 192, 207, 232
Fouta Djalon, 23, 25-29, 33, 36-41, 43, 45-48, 69, 72, 74, 116, 141, 213, 214, 215, 234
Foyer des Jeunes de Basse Guinée, 69
Frachon, Benoit, 86
France, relations with, 14, 63, 69, 79-84, 106-107, 127, 129, 135, 138-139, 140, 144, 146, 148, 149-150, 155-156, 158, 161, 164-168, 170, 171, 172; *see also* De Gaulle, Charles
Francheschi, Joseph, 65
Franco-African Community, 81, 82, 148, 150n, 156

French Union, 63, 71, 79
Fria Company, 50, 120, 166, 180, 182, 183, 185-186, 189, 196, 204
Front National de Libération de la Guinée (FNLG), 18
Fula tribe, *see* Peul (Fula) tribe

Gabon, relations with, 49
Gaétan, Adolphe, 61
Gambia, relations with, 149
Gendarmerie, see Police
Ghana, relations with, 49, 103, 148, 155, 158, 162-163, 166, 169; *see also* Nkrumah, Kwame
Giscard d'Estaing, Valéry, 150, 170
Gold, 33, 38, 48, 49, 110, 141, 181, 212; *see also* Mining
Gowon, Yakubu, 169
Great Britain, relations with, 139, 151, 157, 165, 166, 191; *see also* Western bloc, relations with
Groupe d'Etudes Communistes, 63
Guerzé tribe, 25, 31, 42, 212, 216, 232
Guèye, Bassirou, 59
Guèye, Doudou, 65
Guinea, Spanish, 14
Guinea-Bissau, 14, 24, 136, 138, 168

Haile Selassie, 163
Hausa tribe, 49
Health, public, 44-45, 111n, 114, 154, 175, 208, 220, 221, 227
History, pre-independence, 23, 24, 25, 32-33, 36-50, 61-82
Houphouët-Boigny, Félix, 66, 71, 79, 80-81, 87, 139, 144, 147, 160, 162, 169; *see also* Ivory Coast, relations with
Housing, 35, 111, 115, 116, 128, 175, 184, 186, 208
Humbert, Georges, 41
Hydroelectric power, 141, 151, 167, 173, 187-188, 189

Index

Imports, see Trade, foreign
Indépendants d'Outre-Mer (IOM), 66, 67, 74
Indigénat, 62
Industry, 51, 73, 74, 103, 111n, 146, 150-151, 154-155, 172, 193-198, 207, 208, 221, 240; *see also* Enterprises, state, Investment, foreign, *and* Mining
Inflation, 109, 119
Institut Français (later, Fondamental) d'Afrique Noire (IFAN), 45
International Monetary Fund, 154
Inter-State Committee of the Senegal River, *see* Organisation des Etats Riverains du Fleuve Sénégal (OERS)
Invasion attempts, 136, 138, 145, 168-169, 197, 236; *see also* Plots
Investment, foreign, 141, 146, 151, 154-155, 161, 166, 167, 172, 173, 176, 180, 181, 183-190, 193-198, 207-208, 239; *see also* Mining
Investment, public, pre-independence, 48
Iron, 28, 50, 56, 141, 170, 178, 181, 188, 204; *see also* Mining
Islam, 27, 33, 35, 36, 37, 39, 190, 214, 219, 232, 234-235, 237; *see also* Religion, state policy toward
Israel, relations with, 139
Italy, relations with, 151, 162, 192; *see also* Western bloc, relations with
Ivory Coast, relations with, 24, 29, 31, 135, 139, 143, 145, 147, 148, 160, 162-165, 167; *see also* Houphouët-Boigny, Félix

Japan, relations with, 188, 189
Jeunesse de la Révolution Démocratique Africaine (JRDA), 177, 224-225, 235

Kaba, El Hadj Lamine, 127
Kanku Mussa, 33
Kéita, Fodéba, 131, 135, 165, 226
Kéita, Koumandian, 69, 70, 127
Kéita, Madeira, 63, 66, 87, 90
Kéita, Modibo, 134, 145
Kéita, Moussa, 80
Kéita, Noumandian, 137
Kéita, Ouremba, 73
Kéita, Sundiata, *see* Sundiata
Kennedy, John F., 153
Kissi tribe, 25, 28, 31, 32, 212, 232
Konaté, Mamadou, 65
Konkouré dam, 167, 173
Kouranko tribe, 25, 31
Kouyaté, Diéli Bakar, 133

Labor: forced, 45, 62, 117; migrant, 48-50, 116, 212; organized, 50-61, 86, 99, 127, 128, 213, 240; unemployment, 102, 209, 226; *see also* Confédération Africaine des Travailleurs Croyants (CATC), Confédération Générale des Travailleurs Africains (CGTA), Confédération Générale du Travail (CGT), Strikes, Union des Syndicats Confédérés de Guinée (USCG), *and* Union Générale des Travailleurs d'Afrique Noire (UGTAN)
Labor Code, Overseas, *see* Overseas Labor Code, Dec. 15, 1952
Land regime, 30, 46, 115-117, 215
Landouman tribe, 26, 31, 232
Languages, 24, 31, 35, 37, 50, 70, 216, 231, 233
Lawrence, Antoine, 55
Lélé tribe, 31
Lerouge, Mgr. Raymond, 55
Levantine merchants, 47

Liberia, relations with, 24, 148, 163, 165, 169, 188, 205
Liberian American-Swedish Minerals Co. (LAMCO), 18, 188
Liurette, Albert, 67
Livestock, see Animal husbandry
Loans, foreign, 95, 103, 151, 158, 166, 169-170, 177, 183, 184, 186, 193; see also Debt, foreign
Loi-cadre, June 23, 1956, 44, 52, 60, 76-79, 100, 122, 142
Loi-cadre, Nov. 8, 1964, 109, 129, 133, 142, 161
Los Islands, 24, 26, 185
Lumumba, Patrice, 154

Magasin d'Alimentation en Gros (ALIMAG), 110n, 126, 132
Magassouba, Moriba, 132, 165
Mali, relations with, 24, 135, 148; see also Kéita, Modibo
Malinké tribe, 25, 27, 31, 32, 34, 37, 44, 49, 212, 214, 216, 217
Manding tribe, 25, 33, 36, 43, 45, 213, 241
Mauritania, relations with, 148, 165
Military service, 45, 50, 61, 149, 150, 170, 211; see also Army, role of
Militias, 124, 128, 168, 171, 177, 203, 224, 226-227, 245
Minerais de Fer de Guinée (MIFERGUI), 188
Mining, 15, 51, 146, 176, 183-190, 207, 208, 242; see also *individual minerals*
Mitterrand, François, 68, 150n
Mouvement de la Réforme Démocratique, 63
Mouvement Républicain Populaire, 66
Mouvement Socialiste Africain (MSA), 79, 80, 85

Nalou tribe, 26, 40, 232

Nasser, Gamal Abdel, 147, 163; see also Egypt, relations with
Nationalization, 104, 105, 122, 128, 130, 146, 158, 181, 182, 194, 195, 197, 198, 243
Navétanes, 49, 212
N'Dama, Thierno Ibrahima, 216
Négritude, 91
Neutralism, policy of, 84, 142-143, 152, 157, 159-160
Niane, Djibril, 127
Nigeria, relations with, 169, 188
Nkrumah, Kwame, 88, 89, 142, 145, 147, 148, 162, 169, 226; see also Ghana, relations with
Notables, role of, 43, 44, 72
Nyerere, Julius, 147

Office des Bauxites de Kindia (OBK), 186
Office du Commercialisation du Bétail (OBETAIL), 190
Oil palms, 26, 28, 46, 49, 105, 141, 160, 178, 192-193, 198, 214
Opposition, internal, 122-128, 131, 133-135, 138-139, 238-239, 244; see also Plots
Organisation de la Coopération Africaine et Malgache (OCAM), 148, 161
Organisation des Etats Riverains du Fleuve Sénégal (OERS), 18, 136, 148, 161, 163, 165, 167, 168
Organization for Economic Cooperation and Development (OECD), 18, 178n, 180
Organization of African Unity (OAU), 18, 148, 161, 162, 169
Overseas Labor Code, Dec. 15, 1952, 57, 58-59, 68

Pan Africanism, 7
Parti Africain de l'Indépendance (PAI), 18, 79, 128

Parti de l'Unité Nationale Guinéenne (PUNG), 18, 129
Parti Démocratique de Guinée (PDG), 25, 28n, 30, 52, 53, 57, 61, 64-69, 71, 73-76, 78, 79, 81, 82, 83, 85, 90, 92-101, 122, 124, 129, 130, 132, 133, 134, 140, 148, 149, 165, 172, 187, 202, 206, 210, 213-218, 221-225, 227, 230, 233, 234, 235, 242, 243
Parti du Regroupement Africain (PRA), 70, 80
Parti Progressiste Africain (PPA), 63
Partido Africano da Independencia da Guiné e Cabo Verde (PAIGC), 7, 18, 168
Peace Corps, 154, 163
Peanuts, 105, 193, 198, 206, 212
Peasantry, 57, 76, 112, 116-117, 122, 132, 133, 190, 191, 198-199, 200, 203, 204, 240, 241
Persian Gulf states, relations with, 170
Peul (Fula) tribe, 25, 27, 31, 32, 34, 36-39, 41, 49-50, 62, 69, 72, 73, 74, 213, 214, 216, 217, 234, 241
Pineapples, 26, 141, 178, 180, 183, 198, 204, 205
Planning, economic, 48, 89, 90, 92, 103-114, 128, 130, 151, 160, 172, 173, 177, 180, 182, 189, 190, 197, 202, 205-208
Plantations, 48, 49, 114, 115, 151, 173, 180, 191, 204, 205, 207; *see also* Bananas, Coffee, Colas, *and* Crops, export and industrial
Pleven, René, 68
Plots, 88, 120-140, 143, 145, 158, 161-162, 225, 226, 230, 231, 239; *see also* Invasion attempts
Police, 30, 72, 124, 125, 140, 145, 221, 233

Politburo, *see* Bureau Politique National (BPN)
Political system, 89-102; *see also* Parti Démocratique de Guinée (PDG)
Pompidou, Georges, 144, 150
Population, 28-32, 98, 204, 229
Ports and shipping, 47, 84, 108, 111, 113, 184, 186, 189
Portugal, relations with, 38, 137, 143, 147, 168; *see also* Guinea-Bissau
Pouvoir Révolutionnaire Local (PRL), 18, 97, 99, 199, 200, 207, 231
Pré, Roland, 64, 67
Press, 64, 67, 72, 94, 100, 126, 132, 133, 137, 139, 152, 165, 173n, 182, 199, 233
Price control, 96, 103, 104, 107, 109, 194, 197
Propaganda, communist, 152, 159

Radiobroadcasting, 111n, 165, 173n, 215, 233
Railroads, 44, 45, 47, 49, 54, 60, 111, 133, 184, 186, 188-189
Rainfall, 26, 27
Ramadier, Jean, 78n
Rassemblement Démocratique Africain (RDA), 52, 53, 54, 59, 63-72, 75, 76, 79-82, 86, 87, 147, 148, 160, 225, 242
Rassemblement du Peuple Français (RPF), 64
Referendum, Sept. 28, 1958, 60, 79-82, 141, 155, 156, 171
Regionalization, 30, 31
Religion, state policy toward, 127, 210, 232-236, 237; *see also* Animism, Christianity, *and* Islam
Repressive measures, 123-132, 134-140, 144-145, 169, 171, 226, 232-236, 242, 244, 245; *see also* Plots, Police, *and* Trials

Révolution Démocratique Africaine (RDA), *see* Rassemblement Démocratique Africain (RDA)
Rhodesia, relations with, 139
Rice, 26, 27, 28, 105, 109, 117, 154, 157, 160, 173, 178, 182, 198, 201, 203, 204, 212, 241; *see also* Crops, subsistence
Rioting, 72-73, 80
Rivers, 26-27, 32, 141, 201, 205, 212
Roads, 24, 47, 111, 114, 192, 207, 208, 227
Rubber, 46-48, 211
Rumania, relations with, 170, 187

Saillant, Louis, 86
Samori, 23, 40-41, 85, 117, 216, 231
Sano, Mamba, 64, 66, 67
Seck, Ibrahima, 127
Section Française de l'Internationale Ouvrière (SFIO), 64, 69, 70, 74
Senegal, relations with, 29, 49, 128, 135, 136, 145, 147, 160, 161, 163-169, 193, 201; *see also* Senghor, Léopold S.
Senghor, Léopold S., 79, 139, 147, 161, 169; *see also* Senegal, relations with
Senoufo tribe, 212
Shipping, *see* Ports and shipping
Shriver, R. Sargent, 154
Sierra Leone, relations with, 24, 38, 41, 49, 148, 149, 168-169, 185, 205
Slavery, 36, 38, 39, 41, 45
Smuggling, 48, 109, 137, 145, 181, 205, 239
Société Anonyme pour le Développement de l'Industrie de l'Aluminium de Tougué-Dabola (SADA), 187
Société Commerciale de l'Ouest Africain (SCOA), 47

Société de Bauxites de Dabola (SBD), 187
Société de Transports Maritimes (SOTRAMAR), 184
Société Guinéenne des Pétroles (SOGUIP), 189
Société Guinéenne d'Exploitation du Diamant (SOGUINEX), 181, 182
Société Guinéenne d'Exportation (GUINEXPORT), 110n, 126, 132, 133
Société Industrielle des Fruits Africains (SIFRA), 180
Société Minière Guinée-Alu-Suisse (SOMIGA), 187
Société Nationale d'Importation de Matériel pour le Batiment (BATIPORT), 110n, 126, 132
Société Nationale de Matériel Agricole (AGRIMA), 110n, 126, 132
Société Nationale des Textiles (SONATEX), 110n
Sociétés Indigènes de Prévoyance (SIP), 202, 214
Sociétés Mutuelles de Développement Rural (SMDR), 202
Songhai tribe, 36
Soumah, Amara, 67
Soumah, David, 55, 59, 80, 136
South Africa, relations with, 139, 143
Soviet Union, relations with, *see* U.S.S.R., relations with
Stevens, Siaka, 149
Strikes, 52, 56, 57, 68, 87, 124, 128
Students, African, in France, 76
Subsidies, foreign, *see* Aid, foreign
Sudan, relations with, 169
Sundiata, 33, 36
Susu tribe, 26, 31, 32, 34, 64, 70, 72, 73
Sylla, David, 72

Tall, El Hadj Omar, 39

Index

Tall, Habib, 75
Tanzania, relations with, 147, 148
Taxation, 41, 46, 48, 74, 95, 96, 103, 174, 177, 197
Tchidimbo, Mgr. Raymond-Marie, 232, 236
Third World, attitude toward, 147-149, 157
Tidjaniya brotherhood, 39
Togo, relations with, 49
Toma tribe, 25, 42, 44, 212, 216, 232
Topography, 23-28
Toucouleur tribe, 31, 36, 39
Tounkara, Jean Farégué, 131
Touré, Fodé Mamadou, 64, 69
Touré, Ismaël, 131, 165, 166, 185, 198
Touré, Mamadou ("Petit"), 129, 226
Touré, Mamouna, 131
Touré, Samori, *see* Samori
Trade: foreign, 46, 47, 103-111, 118, 122, 130, 146-149, 155, 160, 166, 170, 172, 177-183, 199, 201, 208, 209, 239; internal, 17, 34, 47-50, 103, 104, 107, 108, 110, 122, 126, 128-129, 130, 182-183, 193-199, 208, 214, 221, 239, 243
Traoré, Moussa, 148
Trials, 123, 125, 127, 136-137, 168, 169, 205, 231, 233
Tribalism, 24-25, 30, 31, 52, 62-63, 68, 71, 74, 80, 91, 92, 142, 210-218, 236
Tubman, William, 163, 165

Union Démocratique et Socialiste de la Résistance (UDSR), 68
Union des Métis, 63
Union des Syndicats Confédérés de Guinée (USCG), 19, 55
Union du Fouta, 69
Union du Mandé, 63, 65, 66, 69
Union Forestière Guinéenne, 63, 65, 66, 67, 69
Union Générale des Travailleurs d'Afrique Noire (UGTAN), 59, 60, 87
Unions, labor, *see* Confédération Africaine des Travailleurs Croyants (CATC), Cónfédération Générale des Travailleurs Africains (CGTA), Confédération Générale du Travail (CGT), Labor, organized, Union des Syndicats Confédérés de Guinée (USCG), *and* Union Générale des Travailleurs d'Afrique Noire (UGTAN)
United Nations, 94, 136, 137, 139, 164, 168, 173, 201
United States, relations with, 143, 146, 150, 151, 153-160, 162-166, 169, 171, 173, 183-184, 190; *see also* Agency for International Development (AID), Aid, foreign, *and* Western bloc, relations with
Upper Volta, relations with, 8
Urbanization, 29-30, 49, 208, 211, 212, 221
U.S.S.R., relations with, 128, 143, 146, 150, 152, 153, 157, 158, 159, 164, 165, 167, 171, 173, 186, 189, 192, 201; *see also* Eastern European bloc, relations with

Vietnam, relations with, 153, 202

Wages, 55-56, 67, 68, 123, 128, 177, 195, 214, 220
Western bloc, relations with, 141-144, 147, 156-157, 166, 183, 242; *see also* Belgium, relations with, France, relations with, Great Britain, relations with, Italy, relations with, United

Western bloc *(cont.)*
  States, relations with, *and* West Germany, relations with
West Germany, relations with, 143-144, 147, 151, 157, 159, 162, 163-166, 168, 190; *see also* Western bloc, relations with
Women, status of, 61, 72, 99, 100, 210, 218-223, 225, 231, 236
World Bank, 184

Yaméogo, Maurice, 161
Youla, Nabi, 164
Youth, 61, 69, 72, 99, 100, 126, 127, 151, 159, 177, 223-231, 235, 237-238, 243
Yugoslavia, relations with, 185, 188, 192; *see also* Eastern European bloc, relations with

Zaïre, relations with, 169, 187

GUINEA

Designed by R. E. Rosenbaum.
Composed by York Composition Company, Inc.,
in 11 point Intertype Baskerville, 2 points leaded,
with display lines in monotype Bulmer.
Printed letterpress from type by York Composition Company
on Warren's Number 66 text, 50 pound basis.
Bound by John H. Dekker & Sons, Inc.
in Joanna book cloth
and stamped in All Purpose foil.

Library of Congress Cataloging in Publication Data
(For library cataloging purposes only)

Rivière, Claude
 Guinea: the mobilization of a people.

 (Africa in the modern world)
 Bibliography: p.
 Includes index.
 1. Guinea—Politics and government—1958–
I. Title.
DT543.8.R5813   320.9′66′5205   76–50262
ISBN 0-8014-0904-7